Managing Risk: Technology
and Communications

by

Jonathan Armstrong, Mark Rhys-Jones and Daniel Dresner

LexisNexis™ UK

Members of the LexisNexis Group worldwide

United Kingdom	LexisNexis UK, a Division of Reed Elsevier (UK) Ltd, 2 Addiscombe Road, CROYDON CR9 5AF
Argentina	LexisNexis Argentina, BUENOS AIRES
Australia	LexisNexis Butterworths, CHATSWOOD, New South Wales
Austria	LexisNexis Verlag ARD Orac GmbH & Co KG, VIENNA
Canada	LexisNexis Butterworths, MARKHAM, Ontario
Chile	LexisNexis Chile Ltda, SANTIAGO DE CHILE
Czech Republic	Nakladatelství Orac sro, PRAGUE
France	Editions du Juris-Classeur SA, PARIS
Germany	LexisNexis Deutschland GmbH, FRANKFURT and MUNSTER
Hong Kong	LexisNexis Butterworths, HONG KONG
Hungary	HVG-Orac, BUDAPEST
India	LexisNexis Butterworths, NEW DELHI
Ireland	LexisNexis DUBLIN
Italy	Giuffrè Editore, MILAN
Malaysia	Malayan Law Journal Sdn Bhd, KUALA LUMPUR
New Zealand	LexisNexis Butterworths, WELLINGTON
Poland	Wydawnictwo Prawnicze LexisNexis, WARSAW
Singapore	LexisNexis Butterworths, SINGAPORE
South Africa	LexisNexis Butterworths, DURBAN
Switzerland	Stämpfli Verlag AG, BERNE
USA	LexisNexis, DAYTON, Ohio

© Reed Elsevier (UK) Ltd 2004

Published by LexisNexis UK

A CIP Catalogue record for this book is available from the British Library.

Disclaimer: Every legal problem is different and legal questions must be addressed on a case-by-case basis and in accordance with each specific factual situation. This book is solely a source of general information and not a source for legal advice.

While every care has been taken to ensure the accuracy of this work, no responsibility for loss or damage occasioned to any person acting or refraining from action as a result of any statement in it can be accepted by the authors, editors or publishers.

ISBN 0 7545 2468 X

Typeset by Columns Design Ltd, Reading, UK
Printed and bound in Great Britain by The Cromwell Press Limited, Trowbridge, Wiltshire

Visit LexisNexis UK at www.lexisnexis.co.uk

Managing Risk series

The Managing Risk series is designed to help business people work efficiently and manage risks in an effective way. Every organisation must assess and control the risks they face on a regular basis: ignoring them and failing to frequently review internal control systems can affect productivity in many ways, from harming staff morale to complete business failure.

Books in the Managing Risk series help you address such challenges in the most commercially sustainable way. By highlighting the hazards and explaining the practical steps that you can take each book in this series is an indispensable tool for staying on top of the risks to your organisation. The Managing Risk series helps you:

- prevent accidents;

- avoid expensive litigation;

- limit exposure to fines;

- avoid compensation claims or even imprisonment;

- maximise shareholder value;

- inspire customer confidence; and

- maintain competitive advantage.

Books in the series include:

Business Risk Management (due August 2004) – 075452163X

Managing Risk: Technology and Communications (due September 2004) – 075452468X

Managing Risk: The HR Contribution (due November 2004) – 0406971455

Managing Risk: The Health and Safety Contribution (due December 2004) – 0754524310

Visit our website: www.lexisnexis.co.uk

For further information please contact Customer Services on 020 8662 2000 (or by fax on 020 8662 2012).

Preface

The e-commerce guru Colin Slatter said at the height of the dotcom revolution that:

> 'An ill thought out e-commerce strategy is a bit like strapping a beagle to a rocket and entering it in a greyhound race. You get a brilliant head start, but things will get really messy when you hit the first corner.'

Looking at the risk involved in any application of technology has to be part of that planning process. We face risks in our lives each day – most of the time we do a quick risk assessment, largely subconsciously. When we cross the street we assess the risk of cars hitting us, when we take a bus or an airplane we assess the minor risks of its timetabling compared to the major risks of it crashing. More so than ever, we have to balance the low probability, high impact risk of war and terrorism with the more frequent exposure to fraud and general computer misuse. This book gives a solid basis for balancing the people, process and technology risks keeping within regulatory, legal and ethical frameworks.

What we have found in our time in practice is that people are not so good at understanding, assessing and mitigating risk when dealing with technology applications. In some of the cases, we have seen people being cavalier as to the risks they face or not truly understanding the dangers. In other cases, businesses have spent too long looking at possible problems – they have tried to develop a risk-free business but have found that by the time they were ready to launch the market had moved against them. We have tried in this book to help develop an understanding of the risks involved in using technology in business. And the message is there for us all to take responsibility for information assurance from central and local government, corporate and small business, charities and education through to the home user. Any one of us can be the weakest link. We have tried to use real life examples. This book does not pretend to analyse every risk involved but highlights what we think are the ones likely to cause the most difficulty for most of us. It concludes with a pragmatic approach to risk assessment and mitigation which you can apply to your own organisation's business continuity.

Over the years all three of us have had help from people too numerous to mention here. We would particularly like to thank all of the clients and members who have allowed us to work with them and our colleagues at Eversheds LLP and The National Computing Centre who have given freely of their time. Particular mention must be made of and thanks passed to Richard Allan, Neil Barrett, Keith Blacker, Lucy Bolton, Bruce Cairns, Richard Charman, Donald A. Cohn, Brian Corduff, Philip Cracknell, Lisa Frood, Richard Hackworth, Phillip Harris, Richard Levick, Robert Marcus, Graham Pettit, Joanne Radford, Jeffrey Ritter, Matthew Seymour, Gillian Watkins and Professor Bob Wood. We would also like to thank our families for allowing the three of us to lock ourselves away and 'just finish off a section'. We must also thank Cara Annett and Helen Bolton at LexisNexis UK for convincing us the book would be a good idea and for mitigating the risks that may have prevented our first book making it to the shelves.

Any research of this kind can only aspire to be a snapshot of the world around us. The early days of risk awareness were (and still are) blighted by the understandable reticence to share the risks encountered. E-crime rides on a tsunami of secrecy. Finally, we would like to hear from you too about your experiences so that future editions can keep track of those elusive, emergent risks. If you have an incident you would like to share with us please email us at risk@lexisnexis.co.uk. We would love to hear from you so that we can warn others. Anonymously of course.

Jonathan Armstrong and Mark Rhys-Jones
Eversheds LLP

Daniel Dresner
The National Computing Centre

About the Authors

Jonathan Armstrong
Eversheds LLP

Jonathan Armstrong is one of the UK's leading experts in technology law. A regular broadcaster on TV and radio, Jonathan's practice includes counselling multinational companies on a range of technology issues. As well as being a solicitor, he is a member of The Chartered Institute of Marketing and the Georgetown University Advanced Institute on Electronic Commerce, Washington DC. He has also been involved in developing a number of technology applications, including one of the first ten law firm sites in the UK.

Mark Rhys-Jones
Eversheds LLP

Mark Rhys-Jones is Chair of the Eversheds Technology Dispute Resolution practice. Mark is accustomed to acting for both suppliers and users in complex IT disputes and focuses on the identification and reduction of risk. He is also an accredited mediator and is identified in several legal directories as a leading individual in his field. He is Secretary of the Wales Commercial Law Association and a member of the Directors' Information Assurance Network.

Daniel Dresner
The National Computing Centre

Daniel Dresner delivers the NCC's information systems risk management research programme. One of the UK's leading experts on standards implementation, Daniel contributes to IT standards nationally (including TickIT), across Europe (source code escrow) and through the International Standards Organisation (user documentation). He brought the NCC/DTI Towards Software Excellence scheme online and manages NCC's Security Knowledge Network. He is the technical authority for the NCC's assessment service for the e-Government Interoperability Framework (e-GIF).

Contents

ix

x

Table of Cases

Table of Statutes

Table of Statutory Instruments

Chapter I
Security – Why Bother?

Foreword

by Richard Hackworth

Computer and communication systems are now central to the success of most, if not all, significant organisations. For the majority of large businesses dependence on information technology (IT) has become critical. If the technology falters then the business is at risk – inability to process transactions, reduced customer service and, potentially most seriously, loss of management control.

Businesses trust IT to protect their business information – information integrity and confidentiality for example. If computer systems fail to provide this protection, the core business benefits of IT are at risk. Effective management control of computer systems is therefore essential. If you doubt this, consider what damage might be caused to the organisation by decisions based on misleading and unquestioned business information (and perhaps ask when the accuracy of the information delivered by the computer systems was last checked).

Rapid increases in use of the Internet, whether for publishing information or for delivering direct transactional services, means that IT mediates the complete relationship between the business and its Internet customers. To an extent, the technology *is* the customer experience and directly represents the organisation's brand, its values and its integrity.

Computer and communication systems are, therefore, a core business asset and management has a fundamental responsibility to protect assets. Company and criminal law and (where relevant) industry regulators have recognised this and have placed direct responsibilities on boards of directors and senior management to safeguard information systems. These include responsibilities to protect the privacy of personal information about staff, customers and possibly others. Failure to fulfil these obligations might risk breaking the law as well as risking the success of the enterprise.

IT is, therefore, no longer a backroom activity taking place out of site of customers and competitors (if it ever was). It is in the front line and must be managed accordingly. This chapter presents a concise guide to the main issues and the kinds of practical action that the board should take to address them.

(Richard Hackworth, Group Head IT Security HSBC Holdings)

Introduction

Only five years ago, any company director, when asked to identify the core assets of his or her business, would almost certainly have answered that it was its products or its workforce. Today, more and more businesses are recognising that one of their most valuable assets is the information they hold. Whether that information is customer databases, know-how or accounting records, the ability to securely store, retrieve and manipulate that information is key to an organisation's success. Information technology (IT) plays a pivotal role in the utilisation of information assets.

The events of the last few years, with damage caused to large organisations on a scale seen before only in disaster movies, have lead corporate responsibility for an organisation's assets to assume paramount importance. This was clearly demonstrated by the US Congress' approval in November 2002 of a $903 million measure to improve cybersecurity in the US. As a result, information technology is no longer the exclusive preserve of programmers, technicians and associated specialists, but has moved out of the basement and into the boardroom.

During this period, events at Worldcom, Enron, Arthur Andersen and, most recently, Parmalat have seized the attention of financial regulators, the general public and the press with the result that the actions of companies and their directors are being scrutinised as never before.

This scrutiny is not simply aimed at ensuring proper accounts are kept, but also at ensuring that directors act appropriately in all aspects of their roles, including looking after the assets of the company. In the UK and elsewhere, directors and boardrooms should be looking to ensure that they are fulfilling their duties and obligations to their companies and shareholders.

In broad terms, the list of directors' duties is well established and can be found in the relevant legislation or case law. However, this list is growing and the number of factors that directors must consider when making decisions is increasing as the environment in which companies operate becomes more complex.

This chapter considers the general scope of a director's duty, the changes that are imminent and their duties specifically in the area of IT. This will provide the context for the remainder of the book which will look at how to protect a business from specific threats posed in the arenas of IT and communications and offer practical advice on managing these risks in a way that does not have a negative impact on a company's business imperative. It should be remembered that over-management of these risks, ie overly complex and expensive systems, can be as detrimental to reaching business goals as under-management. The aim is to ensure that risk management is efficient and effective.

Directors' existing duties 1.2

A director is obliged to comply with all of the duties which an employee must comply with. However, directors are elevated to a greater level of authority and responsibility. A director represents the company both internally and externally and must therefore act properly at all times. The law relating to a director's duties has been developed through case law and statute.

A director has three primary duties which apply to all areas of his or her work.

1. A fiduciary duty to act and exercise all his or her powers in good faith and in the best interests of the company 1.3

This is a broad duty and includes many aspects, although not all, at first sight, are of the most relevance to IT and communications. First, a director must act in good faith in the best interests of the company. Second, directors have a duty not to put themselves in a position where there is an actual or potential conflict between their personal interests and those of the company. Third, they must exercise their powers for a proper purpose. This means exercising their powers over the company's assets (including, for example, IT infrastructure) only for the purpose for which those powers are intended or for the benefit of the company. The final aspect is that a director must not make a personal profit from any opportunities that may result from his or her position without the consent of the company, even if he or she is acting honestly and for the good of the company.

2. To exercise such skill and care as may reasonably be expected of the role 1.4

The duty of skill is judged on a subjective basis and a director is expected to display a level of competence that it would be reasonable to expect from a director with his or her knowledge and experience. In other words, a director with a particular skill in IT will be required to pay closer attention to IT issues than perhaps a fellow director whose experience lies in manufacturing.

The standard of care that is expected of a director is judged objectively. He or she must display a standard of care which would be expected of a reasonable person.

3. To carry out the duties imposed by statute 1.5

A wide range of statutory provisions impose a number of duties on companies and their directors. The most obvious is the *Companies Act 1985* and all directors should be fully aware of the requirements imposed on them by the Act. These largely relate to matters of internal management.

There are many other important pieces of legislation which directors need to be aware of in their daily work. Failure to comply can frequently lead to a director being personally liable. For example, the *Health and Safety at Work Act 1974* states under *section 37* that:

> 'where an offence under any of the relevant statutory provisions committed by a body corporate is proved to have been committed with the consent or connivance of, or to have been attributable to any neglect on the part of any director, manager, secretary or other similar officer of the body corporate or person who was purporting to act in any such capacity, he as well as the body corporate shall be guilty of that offence.'

Proposed reform   1.6

The duties outlined in **1.3** and **1.4** above were set to be codified as part of the Companies Bill which was published by the Government in 2002. In the White Paper, the Government made clear its intention to codify directors' duties in order to clarify the often complex rules, which are currently laid down by inaccessible case law. However, the Government's intentions are taking some time to come to fruition and the Bill is yet to be enacted.

Nonetheless, the Companies Bill certainly reflects the view shared by many, including the Government, that directors must be made more aware of their duties. Deciding on an appropriate method of promoting such awareness has brought its own controversies. The steering committee appointed to review current company law recommended that directors should be required to sign a statement confirming that they had read and understood their statutory duties, in much the same way as under the US rules on financial probity. Instead, the White Paper expressed the Government's view that this kind of statement would 'give a false impression that it was a comprehensive statement of directors' responsibilities'. This would not be the case because, for example, the statement would not include directors' obligations to make returns to Companies House. The Government also believed that there would be a technical problem if directors were made to sign this statement as the obligation to comply with their duties would be binding whether or not they signed the statement; signing would have no legal effect. The Government decided instead to build on the existing procedure of Companies House of sending all new directors a leaflet setting out the procedural information directors must file at Companies House.

A schedule to the Companies Bill sets out the general principles by which all directors (whether executive or non-executive) are bound and a brief summary of these principles can be found at **APPENDIX ONE**. The Bill signifies a continuing trend towards holding boards of directors to greater account for their actions and for those of their company. It is easy to see how some of these principles have a clear relevance to IT. For example, the implementation of suitable IT systems can have a huge positive impact on the promotion of a company's objectives. Conversely, an improper use of technology can have seriously detrimental consequences to both the company and its directors. As with the current law, the

Bill lays down the principle that an IT director must pay greater attention to issues involving IT than his or her fellow directors and may be held to account for a failure to do so. For example, an action could be brought against an IT director by fellow directors and/or shareholders for any loss suffered by the company as a result of his or her failure to exercise the skill expected from a director with knowledge of IT. These civil remedies are laid down by case law and there are no plans to codify them.

Attention is particularly, and intensely, focused on the way large companies conduct themselves at the moment following the major corporate failures at Enron, Worldcom and Parmalat. A Private Member's Bill (Performance of Companies and Government Departments (Reporting)) is currently before the House of Commons. Amongst other changes, it seeks to make social, financial and environmental reporting mandatory as well as establishing a regulatory body to oversee environmental and social standards. It also seeks to place specific duties and liabilities on directors and companies with respect to social, financial and environmental issues. At the time of writing, the Bill has not been timetabled to proceed to committee, however, the Bill is indicative of a move towards codification of the duties imposed on companies and their directors in order to improve the transparency and accountability of corporate governance. This is also true of the Companies (Audit, Investigations and Community Enterprise) Bill, which has been before committee and is currently progressing through the House of Lords. This strives to restore investor confidence in companies following the financial scandals of the past few years. It will implement the recommendations put forward in a number of reports following Enron and Worldcom, principally on the strengthening of audit regulation and creating improved answerability in corporate governance.

IT   1.7

As mentioned above, the correct use of IT can enable a business to fully exploit its informational assets thereby increasing efficiency, customer service and, ultimately, its profits. However, IT poses specific problems to a company and a company's involvement with IT can have a significant detrimental impact on its business in a myriad of ways if it is not managed properly. These include the following.

System crashes   1.8

Sudden computer failure can cause chaos resulting in business interruption and significant loss. Many of us who work in offices will be all too familiar with the effects the failure of a computer system can have. Those effects are even greater where a system crash results in an interruption in the supply of goods and services to customers, often leading very quickly to severe damage to reputation and to a loss of business. The Chartered Management Institute (CMI), in association with the Business Continuity Institute, Colt Telecom and Nortel, has recently undertaken research into how well prepared UK companies are for events that may cause disruption to their business. The results were rather worrying; only 47 per cent of organisations have any kind of business continuity plan, meaning that more than half of the businesses in this country would be totally unprepared for a disaster, large or small. The business continuity plans that are in place were found to concentrate heavily on disruption caused to business from a loss of IT or telecommunications services. Although this is a vital area to cover in any continuity plan (nearly half of the incidents of disruption to business were found to be caused by an interruption or failure of these services), it must be borne in mind that there are a number of other disruptive events that should be given consideration when orchestrating a business continuity plan, everything from damage to a company's reputation to a terrorist attack.

It is also vital that, once in place, these continuity plans are rehearsed by businesses in order to test their efficacy. In its study, the CMI found that of the businesses which do rehearse their contingency plans, 83 per cent found that such rehearsals revealed weaknesses in the plans. Rather shockingly, one in ten business which found inadequacies in their plan did nothing to improve them. CHAPTER TWO – RISKS TO THE NETWORK looks at ways to minimise the risk of network failure and the damage caused, should the worst happen.

Viruses   1.9

Viruses can cripple a company's IT systems and result in a loss of confidence in its ability to provide a fast, efficient and reliable service. One particular incident of a successful virus attack led to around five days' lost global production. It is, therefore, important that appropriate and effective security is in place and anti-virus software is used and updated. CHAPTER TWO and CHAPTER THREE – EMPLOYEE-RELATED RISK will discuss Internet and email policies that should be implemented in order to reduce the risk of a virus being introduced into the company's network.

Internet and email abuse   1.10

A company needs to control and often monitor its employees' access to the Internet and the emails they send from the company's computers whilst at work. This may seem to be an onerous and time consuming task but it may in fact improve on productive working hours and prevent potential damage to the company's reputation. For example, a company may be responsible for 'flame-mails' which are aggressive, inflammatory, abusive or deliberately anti-social emails.

Internet and email abuse can adversely affect a company's general prosperity as well as specific assets, such as its IT resources or its brand. It follows that a failure by the board to protect against these events may well be a breach of a director's duties. A recent, well publicised case from the US illustrates the point. An Internet start-up credit card processor, ZixIt, commenced a claim against Visa over 437 message board postings made by one of Visa's Vice Presidents on a

Yahoo! message board relating to ZixIt's stock. A court in Texas was told how the individual concerned posted the messages seeking to undermine ZixIt by challenging its own information and urging those who had already bought stock to sell 'before it's too late'. ZixIt alleged that Visa used the executive as its agent in its online campaign and then started an offline campaign against it using other employees.

Visa argued that the employee had not acted as its agent. The trial lasted for three weeks and the jury spent two and a half days deliberating before it reached its verdict. The jury found that the employee was not acting within the scope of his employment and dismissed the case against Visa. Despite this apparent victory to Visa, it must be remembered that both companies suffered damage to their reputation from harmful allegations made against them in court and both will have incurred irrecoverable legal costs. All things considered, it is hard to see how either party could come out of such a situation well.

In another US case in 2001, two ex-employees caused over half a million pounds worth of damage to their former employer by posting 14,000 messages on 100 stock-related message boards. When Enron collapsed, its fall was accelerated by employees' postings on message boards, including over 1200 items being made available for sale on one online auction site alone. These cases show the need for companies to protect their online reputation by monitoring what is being said about them and to take care about what their employees might be saying about rival companies. **CHAPTER THREE** discusses ways of minimising the risks associated with employees' use of the Internet and email at work, and **CHAPTER FIVE – REPUTATION RELATED RISK** looks specifically at how the directors of a company can protect its online reputation from such things as cybersmearing.

Security 1.11

The Information Security Breaches Survey 2004 produced by the Department of Trade and Industry (DTI) found that 87 per cent of businesses believe their business is highly dependent on sensitive or critical information, and 75 per cent of businesses believe information security is a high priority to senior management. The risk to business of a security attack is significant, having risen to 68 per cent of UK businesses suffering at least one malicious security breach in the last year compared to 44 per cent in the 2002 survey.

The cost of a security breach to a business can be significant. The DTI survey found that the average cost of a serious security incident was £30,000 and several businesses had incidents that cost in excess of £500,000. Despite these potentially significant costs, the DTI found that 49 per cent of businesses are either not covered by insurance, or do not know whether they are covered or not. Security issues extend across the whole of a company's IT activities. Security breaches not only affect a company's operations, but also do little to enhance the public's confidence in conducting business electronically, a factor that has hampered the growth of e-commerce in recent years.

Improving a company's information security may even come down to something as simple as enabling a standard security measure. In December 2001, the Institute of Information Security (Instis) conducted a vulnerability survey into the use of wireless local area networks (LANs) in the City of London. Wireless LANs are essentially a group of computers which are linked to each other without cables. Earlier investigations by the BBC had already found that even empty Pringles crisp tins can be used as an antenna to help hackers break into a wireless LAN system. Most wireless LANs come with encryption capabilities in order to combat the risk posed by hackers, but the majority of businesses appeared not to have switched this on. In its December 2001 survey, Instis found that 65 per cent of LANs detected were not encrypted. Despite significant press reporting on this topic, Instis found that the problem had surprisingly got worse by April 2002 with 71 per cent of the wireless LANs detected not encrypted. The failure to turn on the encryption system is such an obvious failure on the part of an organisation that it is likely to mean the organisation is in breach of the seventh Data Protection Principle (see **1.12**), leaving its directors and managers liable to prosecution. **CHAPTER TWO** looks more closely at the issues surrounding wireless LANs technology.

It must be remembered, however, that security does not only take place inside the four walls of the company. Directors also need to practice due diligence on suppliers, particularly of IT services, and to put proper legal agreements in place to regulate what will be done to protect the company. An example of what can go wrong is provided by the collapse of the UK ISP Cloud Nine in 2002. The Internet service provider (ISP) folded after two security breaches of its system left around a thousand other companies who used Cloud Nine without service and with no compensation. In the UK alone, simple server downtime is estimated to have cost £565 million. With the current uncertain economic climate, more IT services companies are likely to fail – directors must make sure that their supply of critical services does not disappear with them.

Ways in which directors can specifically guard against these problems are discussed in **1.14**.

Data Protection Act 1998   1.12

One of the best examples of the need for directors to have an appropriate level of involvement in IT is the *Data Protection Act 1998 (DPA 1998)*, a statute which specifically adds to the responsibilities of a board member. The Act came into force on 31 March 2000 and encompasses a number of principles of good practice. Relevant extracts of the Act are reproduced in **APPENDIX THREE**. Of particular relevance is the seventh Data Protection Principle which states:

> 'Appropriate technical and organisational measures shall be taken against unauthorised and unlawful processing of personal data and against accidental loss or destruction of, or damage to, personal data.'

The definition of processing is a wide one and is defined by *section 1*:

'"Processing" in relation to information or data, means obtaining, recording or holding the information or data or carrying out any operation or set of operations on the information or data, including:

(a) organisation, adaptation or alteration of information or data,
(b) retrieval, consultation or use of the information or data,
(c) disclosure of the information or data by transmission, dissemination or otherwise making available, or
(d) alignment, combination, blocking, erasure or destruction of the information or data.'

Section 4 makes it a duty of the data controller to comply with the Data Protection principles in relation to all personal data with respect to which he or she is the data controller.

Accordingly, in every company directors must have regard to up-to-date technology and consider on a regular basis whether, given the nature of the data held by the company, additional security measures should be put into place. The directors, in doing so, must also take reasonable steps to ensure the reliability and compliance of colleagues who have access to personal data and, as a result, an employee policy which is properly policed should be put into place. If data is processed on an organisation's behalf by a third party, or is transmitted outside the European Economic Area, then additional measures must also be put in place.

Somewhat surprisingly, a recent survey commissioned by Compuware (which was carried out by Vanson Bourne) showed that data protection is not currently being given the attention it requires within IT departments themselves. Forty-two per cent of IT directors said that they use customer data for testing an IT system. This is despite the fact that the *DPA 1998* prohibits the use of personal data for any purpose other than that for which it is collected. Ignorance of the *DPA 1998* was widespread with about 13 per cent of IT directors questioned saying that they viewed the Act as 'outside their area of responsibility'. Another 47 per cent said they were only vaguely familiar with it.

The consequences of being held personally liable were well illustrated when two directors, Andrew Cole and Paul Slocombe, were successfully prosecuted at Chichester Crown Court for acts committed by a company of which they were both directors, Academy Credit Limited ('Academy'). Academy had attempted to procure information in breach of the *DPA 1998* (Academy went into liquidation 6 April 2000). The investigation came about after the Inland Revenue had told the Information Commissioner that Academy had been contacting the Inland Revenue in attempts to get information about individuals. The two directors were prosecuted personally and were given a conditional discharge but ordered to pay £1000 each in costs.

In addition to the ultimate penalty of potential criminal liability under the *DPA 1998*, inadequate website security can also lead to civil liability. There have been many instances in the press of cases where financial institutions have experienced problems with their online security. A civil claim may be launched against an institution if a customer can prove that he or she has suffered some loss. Even the frantic alteration of online banking terms which some banks have been engaged in may not stand up to judicial scrutiny. In one incident, a company reportedly offered £50 per customer to compensate for a breach of security relating to that customer's account. Whilst this amount may not appear significant, consider the discussion in the boardroom when it was discovered that one breach had resulted in 5,000 customers' details being accessed.

As well as the problems posed by outsiders gaining access to information held, there have been cases in the US which show that this data must be kept secure from purchasers of the company's assets. The most high profile case concerned the collapse of online retailer Toysmart.com. Toysmart had published a privacy policy on its site stating that any customer information (for example, name, address, shopping preferences) which was voluntarily submitted by visitors to the site would not be shared with third parties. In the UK, a policy like this was made mandatory by the *DPA 1998*. Toysmart subsequently went out of business and offered its database for sale in the Wall Street Journal. Toymsart was sued by the US Federal Trade Commission for attempting to sell personal information in breach of its privacy policy, clearly demonstrating the ongoing nature of privacy obligations.

This area of law is fast moving and 4 September 2002 saw the publication of Part II of the Data Protection Code of Practice, which deals with employment records. Amongst other things this gives useful guidance on the release of information to third parties. The recurring theme of the Code is the need to keep employees aware of the information being held and to use that information only for those purposes of which the workers are aware.

European perspective   1.13

As well as having regard to the duties outlined above there is also a significant amount of European legislation that directors must consider. For example, the *Electronic Commerce (EC Directive) Regulations 2002 (SI 2002/2013)* ('the regulations') implement the main requirements of the E-Commerce Directive 2000 (00/31/EC) into UK law. The aim of the regulations is to encourage greater use of e-commerce and give consumers greater confidence. The regulations set out what information end users must be provided with. This information includes full contact details of the business and VAT number. Any communications with details of a company's goods (such as special offers) must be clear. For electronic contracting there are also requirements, such as the need for a clear description to be given to the end users of the different technical steps that must be taken in order to conclude a contract online.

The penalties for breaching the regulations can be severe. A customer could cancel his or her order, seek a court order against the company concerned and/or sue the company for damages for breach of statutory duty (providing they can prove that he or she has suffered a loss). Perhaps more importantly, the consumer protection aspects of the regulations will also be subject to the *Stop Now Orders*

(EC Directive) Regulations 2001 (SI 2001/1422). This means that the Director General of Fair Trading and Trading Standards Departments can apply to court for a Stop Now Order if the failure of a company to comply with the regulations 'harms the collective interests of consumers'. Failure to comply with a Stop Now Order may lead to contempt of court proceedings with the result that those involved could face a fine and/or imprisonment.

Action directors can take to protect themselves
1.14

There are a number of steps directors can take to protect themselves:

- Work closely with the IT team – this obligation exists even if IT is outsourced.

- Take e-strategy to the top level.

- Act prudently and keep up to date with technology and developments in the company's business.

- Put information assurance as a standing item on the board meeting agenda.

- Understand the interests of the company.

- Understand the duties involved and do not accept duties that cannot be discharged.

- Attend board meetings, ensure they are accurately minuted and ask questions – do not be afraid to disagree.

- Make notes of meetings and ensure the regular flow of information as well as ensuring that there is a sound system of internal control.

- If in doubt, take legal advice.

It is important that directors implement an integrated risk management process. Following on from the Cadbury and Turnbull reports in the 1990s, directors need to make sure proper processes are in place. This principle does not just apply to the aspects of corporate governance which Cadbury and Turnbull considered, but to IT as well. One specific option directors may wish to consider in relation to IT is implementing ISO 17799, which is the International Standard of Information Security Management (the standard is considered in detail in CHAPTER SEVEN – MANAGING OPERATIONAL ICT RISK WITH STANDARDS AND BEST PRACTICE). A recent DTI report showed that British companies have been somewhat slow to implement this standard. Indeed, many companies are unaware of it. The DTI found that only 42 per cent of large companies (with 250 or more employees) were aware of the standard and this percentage decreased significantly for smaller businesses.

The ISO 17799 originated in the UK (BS 7799) and has been transformed from a national to an international standard. It provides a framework to initiate, implement, maintain and document information security. It is a business-led approach to best practice and is claimed by the Government to be an effective corporate response to the challenge of information security. ISO 17799 allows a company to create a management framework for information, assess security risks and give guidance in the selection of controls that those risks which have been identified are guarded against.

The Government has also announced new guidelines at the first International 17799 Users Conference. These guidelines overhauled the original guidelines published by the Organisation for Economic Co-operation and Development more than ten years ago. In announcing the new guidelines, the Government's then e-commerce minister, Stephen Timms, also praised the updated British Standard for Information Security Management (BS 7799) which was published 5 September 2002, stressing the value of the standard and the fact that it will bring information security into the mainstream of good business practice.

ISO 17799 does, however, need to be complemented by management and audit mechanisms that give boards the assurance they currently lack. This was, therefore, one of three initiatives launched by the Information Assurance Advisory Council (IAAC) in 2002. IAAC are working with professional bodies, such as auditors and accountants, as well as cross-sector groups to develop corporate governance guidelines for information risk management and to encourage the use of best practices.

There are many other non-technical steps directors should take. For example, a company should have a written policy on how a company's online reputation is to be protected, coupled with monitoring and enforcement action. Directors should also ensure that their staff are aware of security issues and should also have in place business continuity plans to ensure major IT problems do not cripple the business.

In addition, there are the perhaps more obvious technical precautions a company can and should take. Whilst directors will clearly not be required personally to implement these provisions, they should be ensuring that they are dealt with in the company. A short summary of some of the technical precautions that can be taken can be found at **APPENDIX TWO**.

Conclusion   1.15

With all eyes focused on the boardroom, directors who believe that IT issues are the exclusive preserve of the IT department and do not take note of their obligations and duties may face severe consequences. Those consequences can include fines and possibly prison for those involved. There is a delicate balance – whilst directors must have regard to their responsibilities in IT they must equally ensure that their company embraces new technology. New technology can have great benefits. For example, it can improve the efficiency of the service offered to a company's customers and also reduce the costs of products and services thereby improving a company's competitiveness in the market. Failure to embrace new technology can quickly result in a business falling behind its rivals with the inevitable fall in revenue which will follow. IT is not an issue that can be ignored.

Chapter 2
Risks to the Network

Foreword

By Donald A. Cohn

After 9/11, the greatest threat to the modern multinational corporation is cyber terrorism. Governments and corporations have spent billions of dollars strengthening the physical security of buildings, plant sites, airports and power plants but relatively little money to improve their electronic security. Compounding this misallocation of resources is the growth of the global economy and the creation of a so called information super highway which has become a backbone of global trade, but which was never designed or built for this purpose.

A breach of the physical security of a plant or office can cause significant damage, but the penetration of a company's intranet by a terrorist from half way around the world can bring an entire business to a grinding halt or cause massive physical damage on an unprecedented scale.

Ironically, much of the blame for these electronic faults can be laid at the feet of the major software vendors and developers. Companies can pour significant time and effort into making their systems less vulnerable but be defeated by actions of vendors over which the companies have no control. The current vendor business model requires a vendor to rush its products to market with inadequate testing to gain market share and then 'fix' resulting security problems with a cascade of patches and upgrades. At the same time, the more sophisticated vendors use their bargaining power to contractually shift the risks of failure for these security gaps to their licensees, even if the loss or damage arose because of the vendor's own negligence. It is time that legislatures and courts adopt a principle that the risk of loss or damage to networks caused by flawed software cannot be shifted to licensees as a matter of public policy.

Most supply contracts contain force majeure clauses that suspend performance of a contract if the performing party is unable to act because of events beyond its control (often 'beyond its commercially reasonable efforts'). Many suppliers are adding terrorism as a force majeure event. We do not know whether this terrorism exemption will work or what degree of effort the supplier must undertake to be able to sustain an argument that the terrorist act was beyond

(cont'd)

its control. The standard of care necessary to protect an IT infrastructure is going to be a moving target as systems become more complex, global outsourcing continues to spread and more people gain access to the Internet and become computer literate.

Companies are also being forced by the global marketplace to integrate their supply chain partners into their infrastructures to eliminate costs. Integrating suppliers, distributors, warehousing, customers and other supply chain members creates added cyber vulnerability. A company's electronic security is often only as strong as the weakest member of its supply chain. The problem is compounded because individual companies are adopting their own due diligence methodology to screen potential supply chain partners. We are all about to be bombarded by multiple, inconsistent questionnaires or audits from our key, strategic customers asking for confidential information about our company electronic security systems and demanding the implementation of inconsistent security fixes. There is, currently, no recognised, broadly adopted certification program upon which companies can depend.

This chapter shows why corporations must increase their electronic security investment to better protect their global IT infrastructures. The ideas and recommendations in this chapter are critical to a company's business success and, more importantly, to its survival. For companies to be truly electronically secure, they must expend more resources and they must challenge their vendors and supply chain partners to share responsibility for the integrity of company infrastructures and the viability of the commercial Internet as a whole.

(Donald A. Cohn, lead technology lawyer EI DuPont de Nemours & Co, Inc, Co-chair Georgetown University Advanced Institute on Electronic Commerce, Washington DC)

Introduction   2.1

For some companies, such as Internet Service Providers (ISP), the network is the means by which they earn money. Without their network, they literally have no service to offer. Even for those companies whose business lies in other areas the corporate network is the backbone of the business. If the network 'goes down', then emails cannot be sent or received, letters cannot be written, communication with other offices is made more difficult and documents and electronically stored 'know-how' cannot be accessed. If a company uses a network-based diary, then employees may even miss vital appointments.

Access to the network can also enable a hacker with criminal intent to access data about a business' staff, its customers and its future plans and to exploit these for criminal gain leading to potential financial losses for the business, exposure to adverse publicity and potential loss of customers and future business.

Any business' network and IT systems are vulnerable to attack from numerous sources – from criminals seeking to take financial advantage; vindictive or mischievous hackers; untargeted viruses through to careless members of staff who unwittingly allow others to penetrate security systems.

Therefore, it is a matter of vital importance that the network is protected. This protection takes many forms and does not necessarily need to involve highly technical and sophisticated solutions. Sometimes, the simple steps can significantly cut down risk, such as enabling password protection and physically barring access to certain computers and systems.

This chapter looks at the vulnerabilities of networks and some of the methods of protection available.

Paperless office   2.2

The risks to which a business is exposed as a result of vulnerabilities in its network naturally grow with the extent to which that business is dependant on its network for its smooth running. This dependency increases as many businesses move to a paperless office and this is a good time to look at the legal implications for a paperless office.

The benefits of a paperless office are clear – space and cost can be saved by not having to store hardcopy documents and a fast and accurate method of locating documents can be established. Recent developments in both EU and UK legislation support the use of electronic data with the *Electronic Commerce (EC Directive) Regulations 2002 (SI 2002/2013)* and the *Electronic Signatures Regulations 2002 (SI 2002/318)* being good examples.

At a basic level, English law allows for the production of electronic documents (including electronic copies) in civil proceedings and the courts are gradually becoming more used to dealing with documents in an electronic form. However, there are issues (which may be avoided in advance when the documents are actually stored) as to what weight and importance should be attached to such documents. For example, a court might be concerned at the risk that a document may have been edited or tampered with in the course of it being stored electronically. There are also areas of the law, particularly certain statutes, which require hard copies of documents to be retained – for example tax legislation.

As one would expect, the introduction of any paperless office system needs to be accompanied by a detailed policy document identifying the criteria for electronic storage of documentation, retrieval processes and deletion policies.

Basic protection   2.3

Basic steps that need to be taken by directors include thinking about what makes the network operate and then posing a series of 'what if' questions. For example:

15

- Computer networks need power. What happens if there is a power cut? Does the company have backup generators that kick in so workers can carry on as normal? Or is there at least an uninterruptible power supply system that can supply power to the network for long enough for workers to save what they are doing and shut down machines safely?

- Where are the network hard drives? What if there is a fire in the room or the building where they are kept? Is there a backup system off site? How long will it take to transfer to these servers? Is the time measured in minutes, days or weeks? Remember the saying 'time is money'.

- Is there adequate insurance cover in place? The UK-based ISP Cloud Nine was subjected to a denial of service attack in January 2002. This caused the company to close because it could not afford the cost of restoring its system and it did not have insurance cover.

One would hope that these basic issues would be considered and addressed by a business whilst it was establishing its crisis management plan to ensure continuity of service following any business interruption. It is surprising and worrying, however, how many businesses fail to consider such issues despite the very real threat to business continuity in today's society. But drawing up such a plan is not sufficient in itself. Such plans need to be constantly reviewed to ensure that they remain relevant and capable of implementation in an emergency.

Physical protection   2.4

Protecting a network from unauthorised access is as much about physical barriers, such as locked doors, as it is about technological barriers, such as firewalls. It is also important to recognise that 'unauthorised' does not only mean 'outsiders'; it means anyone who is not immediately connected with the running of the network (essentially IT staff). Any amount of technical wizardry and complex access systems can be undone by a cleaner unplugging something vital so he or she can plug in a vacuum cleaner. The risks can range from a temporary loss of access to the network (if the plug is pulled out) to permanent damage from a malicious attacker – who could, by way of example, physically attack the machines, or introduce damaging code into the system, or access confidential data.

The physical protection surrounding important parts of the network needs to be sufficient to keep out both the malicious attacker and the 'innocent and ignorant' who may wander into room because they are lost. Therefore, as a minimum, the door to the room needs to be kept locked. Other measures may also be considered, but directors need not throw money at security wantonly – for example in the film Mission Impossible the CIA computer is protected by a vast array of devices, such as pressure sensors, retinal scans and the like but they fail to keep out intruders, whereas a simple closed circuit television (CCTV) camera pointed at the computer may have been much more effective.

CCTV and Data Protection Act 1998   2.5

CCTV is a concept which is familiar to everyone and it seems difficult to move in today's society without finding that a person is being filmed by one camera or another. Whether he or she is walking down the street, shopping in the local supermarket, visiting the bank or travelling through an airport it is likely that a camera will be recording his or her movements. However, such proliferation does not mean that the use of CCTV is without control. The law is ever conscious of the demands of society for privacy and the right to have information held about them to be held only for legitimate purposes and for as long as required.

The area of CCTV is potentially covered by the *Data Protection Act 1998 (DPA 1998)*, though in the case of *Durrant v Financial Services Authority [2003] EWCA Civ 1746* the court recently considered the extent to which the Act applied. Whether a CCTV system is covered by the Act will depend on how the system is used and whether it affects the privacy of an individual. The court decided that two matters were important: is a person the focus of the information and does that information tell you something significant about them. A basic CCTV system may no longer be covered by the Act.

It is necessary for a business to consider what it is trying to achieve by using CCTV. Is it there to learn about individuals' activities for its own business purposes (such as monitoring a member of staff giving cause for concern). If so then it will still be covered. However, if the business can answer no to the following questions, it will not be covered:

- Are the cameras ever operated remotely in order to zoom in/out or point in different directions to pick up what particular people are doing?

- Are the images ever used to try to observe someone's behaviour for the business' own purposes, such as monitoring staff members?

- Are the recorded images ever given to anyone other than a law enforcement body, such as the police?

Some of the issues arising from the *DPA 1998* have already been looked at in CHAPTER ONE – SECURITY – WHY BOTHER? and relevant sections of the Act are reproduced in APPENDIX THREE. The same legally enforceable information handling standards as are applied to those processing personal data on computer also cover CCTV and the collection and processing of images of individuals.

The *DPA 1998* requires compliance with eight Data Protection Principles (contained in *Schedule 1* of the Act) which say that data must be:

- fairly and lawfully processed;
- obtained only for one or more specified and lawful purposes;
- adequate, relevant and not excessive;
- accurate;
- not kept for longer than is necessary;

- processed in accordance with the individual's rights;

- protected against accidental loss, destruction of or damage to, or unauthorised or unlawful processing; and

- not transferred to countries without adequate protection.

The Information Commissioner has produced a Code of Practice relating to CCTV. This Code deals with surveillance in areas to which the public have largely free and unrestricted access (for example, town centres), but its provisions will be relevant to other users of CCTV. In addition, further guidance is available through the CCTV Small User Checklist. Even where the CCTV system is not covered by the *DPA 1998*, the Code of Practice and Checklist gives good practice advice.

Signs should be installed to notify that CCTV is being used. The signs should be clearly visible and legible. A sign on entering a building/office need only be to A4 size because it is at eye level when entering the premises. Signs which are at the entrances to town centres or car parks will need to be large enough to be observed as they will be viewed from further away. The signs need to contain the following information:

- identification of the person/organisation responsible for the scheme (the 'data controller');

- the purpose of scheme – legitimate reason to process images; and

- details of whom to contact regarding the scheme.

For example, where a picture/image of a CCTV camera is *not* used on a sign, wording similar to the following ought to be used: *Images are being monitored for the purposes of crime prevention and public safety. This scheme is controlled by [Company]. For further information contact XXXX XXXXX.*

Where a picture/image of a CCTV camera *is* used on a sign, wording similar to the following ought to be used: *This scheme is controlled by [Company]. For further information contact XXXX XXXXX.*

Portable computers   2.6

Remember that portable computers, eg laptops and PDAs, may also contain information that is held on the network and they are probably most at risk from a security perspective. They are attractive targets to thieves both as items, because they are high value and small, and for the information that they contain – an unscrupulous rival company may decide that the easiest way to gain access to the network is to snatch a laptop from someone leaving the office rather than any other way.

A laptop may also contain documents that are currently being worked on and have not been backed up. Then the information is not only gained by someone else but also lost from the company. US Senator John Kerry (the Presidential candidate) was a high profile victim of such a problem when a laptop was stolen from a member of his campaign team. It was believed to be a routine theft rather than anything more sinister, but even so his campaign spokesman was quoted as saying: 'The information in the computer far exceeds the value of the computer'.

There are three separate risks that attach to portable computers and each requires a different approach:

- Risk of theft. This is very much down to common sense and encompasses the obvious, such as not leaving the laptop unattended, and the not so obvious, such as not advertising the fact that you are carrying a laptop. Look at the carrying cases that are provided to staff – are they supplied by the laptop manufacturer? If so, do they have the name of the manufacturer emblazoned on them? This makes it obvious to a potential thief that you are carrying a laptop. The same also applies to third party laptop cases – a thief will know what sort of case usually contains a laptop so try and use less obvious substitutes.

- Risk of confidential information falling into the wrong hands. This can be minimised by limiting the information that can be carried on the laptop at any one time. If employees are using a laptop to work from home, then perhaps the laptop itself need not have any information on it and the employee can instead dial in to the server to access documents. This obviously limits where the laptop can be used and will not always be suitable so also consider a 'one project at a time' policy where only one set of information can be carried at once.

- Risk of documents being lost as the laptop contains the only copy. The only solution to this is to backup and backup regularly. Ensure that laptops automatically backup/transfer documents to the network whenever they connect to the network, and require travelling employees to dial in to the network to allow the laptop to backup files at least once a day.

Companies need to ensure that they impress upon their staff the importance of following all the procedures that are laid down. Keep this under review so that the rules are not honoured more in the breach than in the observance.

The next section looks at network protection but it is worth mentioning here that laptops and PDAs can represent a significant risk to the security of a network. If employees are connecting these to other systems outside the office or to their home computers then there is a risk of cross contamination of viruses from that other system into the company's network. Protection must be provided against this and a company may wish to implement a policy preventing staff from connecting business equipment into other systems or from connecting personal PDAs into the company's network.

Personal storage media 2.7

Differing forms of virus and malicious code which can cause damage to any network are dealt with later, but one of the easiest routes for these to enter a network is through infected storage media, such as floppy disks or CD ROMs.

If a business' staff are bringing into the office their own storage media and introducing this to the network without adequate security checks, they could be introducing the cause of untold damage 'through the back door' and thereby avoiding the firewalls which might have been installed to protect the 'front door'. Such acts will by no means be malicious. Indeed, they could be borne out of an employee's dedication to the business such that he or she has been working out of office hours on his or her own personal computer and has stored work on a floppy disk to download into the office the following day.

A policy should be introduced and strictly enforced requiring staff to have any external storage media checked for viruses by the IT department prior to it being introduced to the network.

Network protection   2.8

Network protection means protecting the network as an entity, ie ensuring that information can flow freely around the network and that nothing gets in (or indeed out) without approval. The public image of network protection is preventing hackers from gaining access to the system. There is some truth to this but it is important to also remember that hackers come in many forms, from those who want to break into a system for the thrill or just to see if it can be done (this has happened to many companies, including the New York Times in February 2002), to those who want to cause damage to the system (possibly those with a grudge against the company) or those who are hacking into the system on the instruction of a competitor whose aim could be to steal as many secrets as possible or damage the system as much as possible. The case of Cloud Nine (see **2.3**) serves as an example of what a network attack, when combined with other factors, can do to a company. Although this is very much a worst case, it does demonstrate how catastrophic a failure to understand IT risk can be.

Hackers can even use a company server to store their own files and this brings its own problems, for example the hacker would be using network resources so the network would run more slowly than it would otherwise do thereby wasting valuable employee time, or the files stored may have illegal content (eg child pornography or copied music). The US Education Department was attacked in this way in 2001 and for several months hackers used its servers to store films and music.

Passwords   2.9

The first step in protecting the network is to use passwords. Each user should have a unique user ID and password that he or she will need to enter when he or she logs on to the system. This will protect the network from unauthorised users attempting to log on from a computer in the office. Passwords and IDs can also be used to restrict what rights an individual has when connected to the network (eg only IT staff can delete files or save to certain areas of the hard drives, only human resources staff can access employee information etc). Directors should also consider using tracking software to show who accessed the network and what information they accessed. Monitoring of employees' actions in this way has to be considered carefully (this is discussed in more detail in CHAPTER THREE – EMPLOYEE-RELATED RISK).

Passwords are only effective when used properly. Employees need to avoid using obvious passwords such as birthdays, spouse's name or the word 'password'. Many companies set limits on what passwords are acceptable, eg many Internet banking services require passwords of at least six characters and they have to contain both letters and numbers. Software can be configured to reject dates and other choices, thereby forcing the user to conform to the password policy. It is important, however, that passwords are not overly controlled as this would have the effect of limiting the pool of available passwords. Passwords can also be set to automatically expire so employees have to change their passwords regularly. Many companies set the expiry date at 30 days. When employees leave the company their accounts need to be deleted as soon as possible so that they do not still have access to the network.

It goes without saying that staff should be advised not to disclose their passwords to others and not to record the passwords in obvious places. It is amazing how many people will store their password on a piece of paper in their desk drawer or even worse on a post-it sticker on the computer screen. This may be considered to be human nature when one reflects on how many different passwords individuals are required to remember for everyday life at both home and the office, but this will be little comfort to the business which finds its security compromised as a result. In a survey conducted for the Infosecurity Europe trade show in 2004, a staggering 70 per cent of people surveyed were prepared to reveal their computer passwords for a bar of chocolate. Staff need to be continually educated to the risks involved.

Whilst the use of passwords prevents unauthorised users from logging into the system, an unattended logged on PC will still be an open door into the network. To combat this, consider requiring employees to log off whenever they leave their desks or install password protected screen savers that require employees to re-enter their password when returning to their computers after a period of inactivity. If staff know that they are to be away from their desk for a period of time, encourage them to log out of the system without waiting for any password protected screen saver to kick in, particularly out of office hours when there may be fewer colleagues around to spot suspicious individuals hanging around unattended computer screens.

External threats 2.10

Once steps are taken to prevent unauthorised access from the company's own machines, attention needs to turn to access attempts from other machines. If the company network is connected to the Internet, as it will be if employees can access the Internet from their desks, then other users of the Internet will potentially be able to access the company network. This risk can be reduced in these ways:

- By using a firewall. A firewall 'sits' between the computers on the network and the Internet where it checks information that passes through it. This reduces the risk that a hacker can access information contained on the network. The sophistication of firewalls vary significantly from the basic level, which can be downloaded free of charge over the Internet, to expensive, high security systems. Each business need to assess the level of risk it faces and choose a system accordingly.

- Keeping software updated. Software companies are frequently the target of hacker attacks. The hackers try and discover security flaws in software that the companies develop. When a flaw is discovered, the software company will usually issue a patch or upgrade to solve the problem in the software. Therefore, if programme X has a flaw, users need to ensure that the patch is installed because otherwise they will be running software that has a flaw that is common knowledge in the hacker community. Companies need to have policies that ensure that software is kept up to date. Perhaps the most commonly used software is checked daily or weekly with other applications checked fortnightly or monthly, and a member of staff then needs to ensure that the patch is installed on all the computers running the software.

Viruses and malicious software   2.11

The risk to computers caused by viruses is probably the area that receives the most media attention. News reports of viruses sweeping the globe are occurring with ever more frequency.

Viruses are programs that are designed to attach themselves to other programs or files. They are capable of copying themselves and this is how they spread from computer to computer. This behaviour is similar to the way that biological viruses spread, hence the name virus. Other types of malicious software do not spread themselves but nonetheless harm computers when they are installed.

Trojan Horses, for example, are similar to a virus in that they can be transmitted through email, by downloading infected software from the Internet or by using an infected storage media. The code may often appear to be a legitimate program. A Trojan Horse cannot replicate itself but once installed on a computer it can cause damage or hackers can utilise it to gain access to the computer and operate the computer as if they were sat at the keyboard. In this way, the hacker can use the infected computer to target an attack on a third computer and it will appear as if the infected computer is the source. Another sinister use of Trojan Horses came to light in 2003 when companies reported that cyberextortionists had been threatening to plant child pornography on their computers through use of a Trojan Horse if a fee was not paid.

Worms are not capable of transmitting themselves from one network to another but instead replicate themselves within a network potentially causing damage, but in any event tying up the network and causing the legitimate processing of the network to be slowed considerably.

As well as damage to the firm's systems, there is also the danger that a virus may be passed on via emails or documents. It goes without saying that a firm's reputation will suffer if viruses are passed to customers or suppliers or if the business' own computers are used as a source of attack on that customer or supplier.

The damage created by viruses varies. They may be written purely as a nuisance (eg by turning the cursor into a carrot on 1 April) or to delete information (eg by deleting files). Some viruses, such as Chernobyl, attempt to overwrite the BIOS of a computer with the result that the computer will not boot and the motherboard may need to be replaced.

The main protection against viruses comes in the form of anti-virus software. It is imperative that the software is regularly updated as manufacturers react to new viruses by updating the virus database within the software.

Procedures need to be in place to prevent, as much as possible, employees from introducing virus infected software into the network. This could be done by requiring all incoming floppy discs and CDs to be virus checked by IT staff before they are used in computers and by putting strict instructions that only certain types of email attachments can be opened without recourse to IT, and even those must be scanned before they can be opened. To require all attachments to be checked by IT would probably have the effect of stifling the business, especially if documents are commonly passed to customers and suppliers. Anti-virus software can be configured to automatically scan both incoming and outgoing emails and so can reduce this risk.

A risk that runs parallel with viruses is the hoax virus message. These are usually emails that urge the recipient to forward the message to as many people as possible and/or delete files on their hard drives. Whilst not being viruses per se, these hoaxes still have the effect of viruses in that they cause vast numbers of emails to be sent and vital system files to be deleted. The solution to this is to ensure that all employees are aware that only IT staff should delete files on hard drives. Indeed, rules of this sort should be in place in any event so as to prevent employees meddling with their computers.

Denial of service attacks   2.12

Denial of service attacks have attracted substantial publicity in recent months due to a number of high profile attacks. Already mentioned is the attack on the ISP Cloud Nine, which resulted in the company going out of business in January 2002, but some of the better known Internet giants such as eBay and Yahoo have themselves also been attacked.

Denial of service attacks are caused when an attacker uses one or more other computers to overload the target system with useless traffic causing it to overload. Essentially, the network is gridlocked and a business' server is rendered useless for extended periods of time.

The risk of denial of service attacks is something which a business should take into consideration when considering the appointment of an ISP. The business should satisfy itself that the security is addressed and enquire as to what steps would be taken in the event of an attack to ensure continuity of service. It would also be worthwhile, in light of the Cloud Nine experience, to establish what insurance cover is held. Finally, many denial of service attacks are launched against service providers which have upset the Internet community. So it would be worth reviewing the service provider's attitude toward spam being sent through its system. If it is not seen to be working hard enough to prevent spam, some might consider this makes it a legitimate target.

Wireless LANs   2.13

A wireless LAN (Local Area Network) is a network that operates without cables. Wireless LANs have a number of uses:

- they can be used to link neighbouring buildings without the expense and difficulty of running cables;

- they can be used within one office, again removing the expense and difficulty in maintaining cables; or

- they can be used to support mobile working – where a user is free to access the network from anywhere within range of the LAN (typically 200 metres or so although specialist aerials can extend this five kilometres or more).

This is becoming more popular in the home as well as advertisers place great emphasis on wireless LANs allowing users to access the Internet from their gardens. It is also becoming more prevalent for wireless LANs to be installed in public places where they can be accessed by those with the appropriate hardware. This offers a potential source of income as wireless access can be offered on a pay as you go basis.

Wireless LANs share many of the risks of traditional fixed networks, eg vulnerability to viruses and hackers. However, they also have other risks that stem from the nature of the wireless network. For simplicity, consider a network in an office with no connection to the outside world. When this is a wired network it is easy to see if a computer is connected to the network because there is a cable coming out of the back of the computer physically connecting it. If this is a wireless network then this visual check is futile. A visitor in reception may be accessing the network as may a board member using his laptop in the restaurant. The signal may even be picked up by someone using their laptop in the pub across the street. Wireless LANs are designed to be easy to access and, therefore, it is important for companies to ensure that unauthorised access is prevented.

Wireless LANs are dealt with in more detail in CHAPTER SIX – OTHER COMMUNICATIONS RISKS, but for the time being it is important to be aware of the risk they pose to security.

Personal digital assistant 2.14

The personal digital assistant (PDA) is a current must-have item amongst the technology literate. As well the risks that have been documented above, the PDA also brings other risks, especially when the PDA is the personal property of the employee rather than one provided by the company. A PDA is basically a pocket computer. A large number of models use a specially written version of Microsoft Windows and models have diary/organisers and word processing programmes installed. PDAs can be connected to desktop computers and information can be transferred between them. Therefore, the PDA can be carried and information entered onto it that can then be updated onto another computer on return to the home/office. This can mean that employee personal data can be accidentally uploaded onto the office network, or company data may be uploaded onto the home PC (that may or may not be accessible by others and may or may not have a firewall and other protection). Instances where secret meetings have accidentally been uploaded onto the network are not unknown (imagine everyone being able to see that the managing director is having a meeting to discuss redundancies). There is also the potential for viruses to be brought into the network in this way.

Employees will need to be educated about the safe use of PDAs in a similar way to the other employee-related risks to networks, but there is one difference in that PDAs could easily be personal property rather than company property.

Radio Frequency Identification Technologies 2.15

Radio Frequency Identification Technologies (RFID) are not new, indeed, it was used by British forces in World War II to identify friendly aircraft. Improvements in manufacturing and the subsequent reductions in price and size have meant that the possible uses for RFID tags are now much more widespread.

RFID is an automatic identification system. An RFID system consists of a portable device (a 'tag') which transmits data which can be read by an RFID reader and then processed by a computer. A wide range of data can be transmitted, including identification or location information – for example in the case of products, specific information such as price, colour or size. A use of RFID technology is to place a tag in packaging, which would then be read by a reader as a trolley full of goods is pushed through the checkout. This would then eliminate the need to scan a barcode on every item, which would speed up transactions in supermarkets. RFID is frequently touted as a replacement for barcodes and numerous stores, including Wal-Mart, are starting to use RFID tags to track supplies, such as pallets of stock.

Privacy groups have voiced concerns over RFID because the tags in products could be read at any time without the customer knowing. It would be possible to place readers at the entrance of a store so as to read RFID tags carried by a customer to give the store a better idea of their clientele. RFID tags can be placed in anything and so a scanner could conceivably learn more about a customer than a loyalty card ever could. This is obviously attractive to companies but a number of issues need to be borne in mind. The *Data Protection Act 1998* regulates the manner in which personal data may be collected, processed, used and disclosed in the UK and, in most cases, the consent of the individual is required before information about them can be obtained. It is likely that the Information Commissioner will take a dim view of any surreptitious use of RFID technology. There would also undoubtedly be issues of public relations to consider and a large amount of negative publicity could ensue. Benetton had planned to incorporate RFID tags into clothes but was forced to back down after a backlash lead by privacy campaigners and rumours abound that Central Banks is looking at ways to put RFID tags into banknotes.

RFID may appear an attractive technology for any business seeking to keep track of items within the business, whether that might be stock, laptops loaned to staff for business purposes or even pass cards which are given to visitors or staff. The ability to track an individual's movements is something which might be attractive to an employer but needs to be approached very cautiously and with specialist advice in view of the potential ramifications.

Piracy and licensing   2.16

Risks to the network not only lie with events which impact on how the network operates, but might also arise from the way that the network is run. Each business will have a suite of programs which are run over the network, whether they be Microsoft Word processing packages, email packages or accounting packages.

When purchased, the user does not acquire the title to the program itself (unless it has been written on a bespoke basis with an assignment of intellectual property rights), instead what is purchased is a licence to use the software. Such a licence will have conditions attached to it and the breach of these conditions may well invalidate the licence and cause the business to face a claim for breach of intellectual property rights.

The most common form of infringement of a licence is allowing too many users to access the software. Nearly all licences will include a limit on the number of users, whether this be a single user for a single application or a multi user licence of several hundred. Either way, it is important for a business to be aware of this limitation and to repeatedly check that it satisfies the criteria. Frequently, a multi user licence will be purchased by a business where the number of licensed users substantially exceeds the businesses requirements. Because the limit of users appears unattainable, it might be forgotten. Following a period of growth, however, the business might be in the fortunate position of finding that the number of users of the software has grown rapidly, but without a review of the licence terms and the purchase of additional user capacity to the licence the business will quickly find itself in breach of the licence.

Another problem occurs where a licence is limited to a single site and the business subsequently expands to additional premises and moves the software with it without updating the licence.

Despite these risks, many businesses might take the view that the risk is worth taking because the problem is virtually undetectable. How would the owner of the software be realistically able to police and monitor its rights? Unfortunately, many businesses which have taken this approach have found out to their cost that the software owners have a number of tools up their sleeve to help them. They are also keen to use legal remedies to reinforce their rights in an area which is becoming increasingly high profile.

The Business Software Alliance (BSA) is a private organisation funded by its membership which includes many of the major software houses. The BSA has many functions but one of its key ones is to fight software piracy. Piracy in this regard is not limited to acquiring illegal copies of software 'off the back of a lorry'. All businesses would likely deny any involvement in such activity, though this in itself is questionable. Many small businesses may have been tempted to acquire a software package at a reduced price from a regular supplier without asking too many questions or asking why it is such a bargain. The fact is though that any business which is operating software without the appropriate licence in place is participating in software piracy.

The BSA gains its knowledge about piracy from many sources, not least of which might be a business' own staff. Dismissed or disillusioned staff might relish the prospect of extracting a piece of revenge from a business and with the BSA offering a whistle blowing service, numerous businesses have found their piracy exposed by a former member of staff.

Where an act of software piracy has occurred, the owner can instigate legal proceedings resulting in search orders being executed, injunctions restraining further infringement being obtained and damages being awarded. Additionally, any original licence may be forfeited and a substantial amount of adverse publicity be achieved.

To avoid these risks, there are a number of steps which can be taken:

- Introduce a policy, requiring staff not to introduce their own software onto the business' system.

- Ensure that software is acquired from legitimate suppliers and that genuine licence paperwork is supplied.

- Undertake regular audits of the network to monitor what software is being run.

- Check the licence details to hand and regularly ensure that the businesses remains compliant in the number of users, sites etc.

- If any infringement issues are identified, take steps to remedy them quickly.

Chapter 3
Employee-Related Risk

Foreword

By Lucy Bolton

Human Resources is not about policing the net, checking Internet usage or monitoring use of technology, but it is about providing guidance to managers about what is or is not acceptable.

The Internet and technology in general has brought changes to many jobs – more self service, less paperwork, quicker response times and a wider database to pull ideas from. But as with all new things, there is a downside.

The challenge is to take the vast, creative opportunity that technology represents, ensure everyone is aware of the dangers, give people choices and, above all, trust that people will do the right thing. Some guidelines about what a business expects (and also what is unacceptable) should be contained in the company handbook, but care must be taken not to stifle individuality or curb any business advantage.

If trust is breached, or rules are broken, any investigation must be conducted in an unbiased manner. For example, if a business discourages Internet use and an employee has spent an afternoon surfing the web looking for an NHS dentist for his or her child, should this be judged in the same way as an employee who has spent the afternoon in a chatroom? Both employees are guilty of cyberskiving and HR must take care not to judge only with regard to what was accessed.

Many companies I know have Internet policies which are hard to justify, difficult to explain and are interpreted differently depending on how senior you are. If this is the case, HR can help by going back to the basics and asking what the company's philosophy is and by educating people to work within that environment, safely and with regard for others. This chapter is an excellent starting point and contains many discussion topics that HR can raise with IT and management boards to ensure that technology remains an asset to a business rather than a liability.

(Lucy Bolton, EMEA HR Director, RSA Security)

Introduction   3.1

A huge expansion in the use of IT and technology in the work place has clearly brought great advances to business with access to almost limitless sources of information and instant communication across the world at the touch of a button. But this expansion has also resulted in employers being exposed to new and greater risks through the use their staff make of the technology. This has led to new concerns for Human Resource (HR) departments in how to guide, restrict and monitor employees. CHAPTER TWO – RISKS TO THE NETWORK touched upon the subject of how increased access to a business' IT systems increases the exposure to risk from both malicious and careless acts of staff. Appropriate measures need to be implemented to protect against such risks.

A responsible employer also needs to consider how technology might expose its staff to new avenues of risk in relation to sexual harassment, for example.

With many businesses allowing their staff to access the Internet for the purpose of undertaking their work, the necessity to control and monitor what material is accessed and the extent to which personal interest takes precedence over the business interest needs to be monitored and controlled. The cautious employer might seek to impose rigid policies preventing non-business use of technology and monitoring the activity of all staff to police this policy. However, in an age when employers demand more from their staff in terms of time commitment, many consider it is fairer to allow staff occasional access to the Internet. In any event, an employer needs to be aware of an employee's right to privacy and to ensure that its staff's rights are protected in the extent to which it monitors what they do.

All of these issues mean that policies should be written to give staff guidance on what is and what is not acceptable and management decisions must be made as to the extent to which these policies will be policed and implemented.

This chapter will seek to identify some of the specific concerns and possible solutions.

Internet access   3.2

Every business needs to decide at the outset whether, and the extent to which, staff are to be given access to the Internet. For many, it might be an integral part of their job, whereas others may require only occasional access or none at all. Even if access is not a necessity, an employer may decide to allow access in any event but such access needs to be controlled.

Staff may find the worldwide web a substantial distraction from their work resulting in reduced productivity. Anybody who has accessed the Internet will be familiar with how easy it is to be distracted by interesting, but realistically irrelevant information, when attempting to research a specific point. This phenomena even has a name – cyberskiving. Time spent on irrelevant personal surfing is time that is not being committed to the employer's business.

Franxhi v Focus Management Consultants [2001] All ER (D) 119 concerns web browsing at work. Widely regarded as the first case in which an employee was dismissed for using the Internet improperly (although it is unlikely that it is the very first case), the issues raised highlight some important points for employers. Ms Franxhi was dismissed for using the Internet for personal reasons during working hours. She brought a claim alleging sex discrimination and unfair dismissal. The employment tribunal rejected both claims. The employer argued that the employee had not told the truth when questioned about her Internet usage. Although the dismissal was upheld as fair, the employee was entitled to receive pay in lieu of notice. It is clear, therefore, that the tribunal did not regard her Internet use as gross misconduct but rather ordinary misconduct which justified the dismissal because it followed a written warning that she had already received for not observing company procedures.

Consideration needs to be given to the risk of staff accessing illegal or inappropriate material. Reports of individuals accessing child pornography are prevalent but if such material is accessed through a company's equipment, the images will be downloaded into the network. Even if the company can avoid prosecution itself, the discovery of such material on a network can be highly embarrassing and damaging to the reputation of any business.

Even if the material accessed is not illegal, it may still be indecent or offensive. No business is likely to want to have pornography, for example, being downloaded onto its system. But the risk is far more tangible than potential damage to its reputation and might result in direct claims against the company.

Sexual harassment has been defined in *British Telecommunications Plc v Williams [1979] IRLR 668* as unwanted conduct of a sexual nature or other conduct based on sex affecting the dignity of women and men at work. It is clear, therefore, that conduct of any type could be considered to be harassment, which could include fellow employees accessing pornographic websites or sending lewd emails around the office. Just such a situation occurred in *Morse v Future Reality Ltd (London (North) Employment Tribunal (22 October 1996, Case No. 54571/95))* where a female employee resigned after male colleagues had upset her by downloading pornographic material from the Internet.

Similarly, employees accessing racist or hate group sites could lead to claims of racial discrimination from staff. Even if information is not circulated, there is the issue of who else might view the materials. Open plan working arrangements make it more and more likely that work colleagues could oversee material that has been accessed.

CHAPTER TWO looked at the issues surrounding viruses and noted the protection that businesses should have in place. Employees downloading material from the Internet is an easy route for viruses to be introduced to a network.

Access to chat rooms and bulletin boards by employees are another area of risk. Apart from the distraction of time, they could also result in defamatory or offensive material being posted. Defamation is an area which is considered in **3.3** below.

Pirated software and music files are another area of particular concern at the moment as the owners of copyright seek to enforce their rights against those who download their materials illegally and without licence. Staff might download material for business or personal use but, either way, the employer is potentially exposed to copyright infringement claims if the material is discovered on the company's network. Organisations such as the Business Software Alliance (a private organisation whose members include many of the major software houses) work hard to enforce the rights of its membership. Piracy is also covered in CHAPTER TWO (**2.16**).

The issue of downloaded material can also have a significant impact on the efficiency of a network. Graphics and image files, such as jokes and cartoons, video files and sound files which are frequently circulated amongst staff take an enormous amount of capacity and can significantly erode storage space. The next time the IT director requests a budget to upgrade server capacity consider whether this is simply to accommodate unauthorised use of the Internet or email within the business.

Email   3.3

The huge growth in the use of email as a method of communication in both business and private life presents additional risks to businesses.

Whilst email is undoubtedly an effective method of communication in appropriate circumstances, its use in place of face to face conversations can be detrimental to internal relations.

The ease and speed at which a piece of information can be distributed to a large circulation list has led to information overload with most people in business finding themselves copied into emails without any real understanding of their relevance. Additionally, an exchange of emails over a period of hours or days might eventually resolve a problem but with the recipients often wondering whether it could have been dealt with in a simple and fast telephone call. Email has also led to the 'off my desk' culture – if I have sent an email to a colleague on a matter it is off my desk until he or she has time to reply.

The perceived informality of email is another problem. They may be written without the same care and attention which would be paid to a letter or memorandum which might be rewritten or pondered over before being sent. This lack of care is compounded by the fact that an email has no emotion and cannot convey tone leading to numerous and obvious cases of misinterpretation.

Whilst for internal email this may cause problems for management to deal with, when email is used in communication with third parties, such as customers or suppliers, then it can present a more serious issue with the potential for upsetting relationships.

There can be no doubt that email is a formal and recorded method of communication. It is an effective method of creating or varying contracts and it is important to ensure that all staff are aware of this. Also, in any disputes, the courts will expect parties to disclose email records in the same way as any other written document during the process of disclosure in a case. Staff should be warned not to commit anything to email that they would not be prepared to commit to a paper form.

Whilst the legitimate use of email can present difficulties, the unauthorised use is also of serious concern. The speed with which email traffic can be passed around a network and the ease with which it can be transmitted to numerous recipients at once mean that it is easy for harmful and damaging emails to become common knowledge and to lead a company into major problems.

In the case of *Western Provident Association Limited v The Norwich Union Life Insurance Company Limited (1987, unreported),* Norwich Union agreed to pay a reported £450,000 in compensation for certain unguarded remarks about Western Provident's financial position, which had been circulated extensively within Norwich Union by one of its managers.

In 2001, the city law firm, Charles Russell, found itself in the headlines when a departing black secretary saw an exchange of emails between two of its solicitors. They suggested that she should be replaced by a 'busty blonde' who '...can't be any more trouble and at least...would provide some entertainment'. The secretary's sex and race discrimination claim was settled out of court.

Excessive use of email can itself quickly clog a business' system, reducing the speed with which important client focused emails can be transmitted.

In light of these risk, the role of HR is to design and implement policies and procedures which facilitate the use of email to the advantage of the business and ensure that the use is appropriate whilst guarding against the risks of unauthorised use.

Bulletin boards and blogging   3.4

Electronic bulletin boards can also expose a company to risk if its employees post messages to them.

One example of this is the ZixIt case discussed in **CHAPTER ONE – SECURITY – WHY BOTHER?** (**1.10**). Although Visa escaped liability in that case, other companies may not be so fortunate.

A bulletin board operated or hosted by a business on its own website will attract even greater risk as it may well be held responsible for entries submitted by employees or others.

In addition to messages on bulletin boards, the practice of blogging is a relatively recent development. Blogging is a technique to enable newsfeeds to be updated on a site from different locations quickly and easily. The basic technology effectively allows access to a website via a back door and allows people to add content. Some sites that want to be dynamic and continually changing allow anyone to blog the whole site or specific areas of it.

This not only exposes the site owner to potential litigation if the content of blogs are defamatory, but if employers allow employees to blog sites from work the employer may find itself identified as the source by a trace on its IP address.

Telephones and mobile telephones   3.5

Nearly all of us have ready access to a telephone either as part of our work or at work. For many employers, completely outlawing the use of work telephones for all personal calls is unworkable or unenforceable. With tracking equipment increasingly being more easily available, however, such an approach is by no means impossible. The key will be to have a clear policy statement setting out what is the acceptable use of the telephone for private calls (if any) and to make sure that the policy is well communicated and applied (see policy considerations in **3.6**). Many employers, as with email or Internet use, adopt a more relaxed approach allowing 'reasonable access' provided it does not interfere with workload.

A far more contentious issue associated with telephone use at work is the use of mobile telephones. A clear policy decision should be taken upon whether personal mobile telephones must be switched off at work and the extent of their use during working hours. Annoying and disruptive ring tones are a familiar part of life these days but in a work setting can be highly distracting.

Use of mobile telephones on the move has recently become a particular area of contention following new road traffic regulations which were introduced from 1 December 2003. A well publicised road traffic offence has been created in respect of mobile phone use. The offence will apply not only to drivers speaking or listening to a phone call, but also using any device interactively for accessing any sort of data, sending or receiving text messages or other images provided the device is *held in the driver's hand* at least during part of the period of its operation. Employers can potentially be held liable for 'causing or permitting' an employee to use a handheld mobile phone or similar device while driving. The current penalty for contravention will be a fixed fine of £30 or a fine on conviction of up to £1,000 (£2,500 for drivers of goods vehicles or buses/coaches).

The Department for Transport has indicated that it does not consider employers would be liable simply because they supplied a phone or because they happened to phone an employee who was driving. Employers would probably be liable, however, if they required their employees to use a handheld phone while driving and possibly if they failed to warn employees that they should not use such phones when driving on company business.

Employers with 'mobile' employees would be advised to issue guidance on the new offence to their employees making it clear that they should not use a handheld phone while driving. Where necessary, employers may wish to consider supplying fully hands-free equipment to their employees. In doing so, however, it is necessary to bear in mind that a large percentage of road accidents occur as a result of mobile phone use in a vehicle even on a hands-free system and it is estimated drivers are four times as likely to be involved in an accident. There may be potential health and safety issues involved therefore in promoting mobile phone use in such circumstances. Prohibiting phone use whilst driving is a preferable approach. Additional matters relating to video-phones are discussed in CHAPTER SIX – OTHER COMMUNICATIONS RISKS (**6.15**)).

Policies and procedures

Content of an email, Internet and telephone policy   3.6

The preceding sections have made clear the need for detailed policies to be drawn up by employers to give guidance to their staff as to the appropriate use of technology and to form the basis for disciplinary action if this is found necessary.

It is advantageous if HR and IT departments work together to build policies which are workable, user friendly and deliver guidance and control. Generally, the component parts will include:

- safeguards to protect confidentiality, eg passwords and the need for encryption;

- restricting access to sensitive parts of the system to authorised staff;

- monitoring provisions for Internet and email (see **3.10**);

- the use of appropriate disclaimers in emails;

- restrictions on access to inappropriate sites and a prohibition on accessing or downloading inappropriate materials, such as pornography, and the procedures to be adopted if such material is inadvertently received;

- guidelines on personal use of the PC, email, Internet and telephones (including company provided mobiles) – consider a prohibition or limitation on personal use. Generally restricted to 'reasonable' and only in own time, for example lunch hour or after work;

- guidance on the use of mobile phones while driving (preferably prohibiting such activity);

- a prohibition on creating or forwarding inappropriate material, internally or externally;

- the importance of appropriate use of language and etiquette when using the telephone or sending emails; and

- awareness of the potential for harassment and discrimination through emails.

Implementing the policy 3.7

Policies need to be living documents which require the information contained within them to be updated and cascaded to all employees in order to ensure a clear understanding of the boundaries. Training sessions should be given to staff and a copy of the policy should be given to all new employees on induction. Consideration should also be given to having the policy accessible through the business' intranet site in order that any updated versions are always accessible.

Commitment from the most senior level is vital if employees are to learn by example. Organisations must decide how the policy is to be supported by disciplinary action in an event that a breach occurs. Care should be taken, however, to ensure that sanctions are not disproportionate for telephone or cyber offences and fit with the general disciplinary rules.

Managing misuse 3.8

Inappropriate behaviour, which may constitute harassment, bullying or victimisation, should be dealt with quickly and competently. The clear message of a good policy is to avoid anything which may be deemed unacceptable by another. For example, employees sending messages which are sexually explicit or racially offensive should be subject to the company's harassment procedure and may result in disciplinary action including possible dismissal.

An employer has a legal duty to protect its employees from harassment and may be vicariously liable for any discrimination. In defending claims the employer will need to show that it took all reasonable steps to prevent its employees from undertaking discriminatory acts. The absence of a policy to supervise the use of email and the Internet will make it far more difficult, if not impossible, for an employer to mount a successful defence.

The absence of express terms relating to email, harassment and disciplinary policies which set out the penalties for misuse and the fact that misuse might constitute gross misconduct may render a dismissal unfair.

Liability for defamation applies to e-communication in the same way as it does to the publication of defamatory material in any other form. The author of a libellous message will be legally responsible for it and that includes employees. Equally, the 'publisher' of a message can be liable in damages to the defamed person. Liability can, therefore, extend to the employer under the normal principles of vicarious liability or as publisher through the provision of the facilities, ie the computer system. An employer's principal concern should be to avoid liability for publishing defamatory material by prevention rather than cure. Care should be taken with the management of bulletin boards or other computer based facilities that allow (or encourage) the informal exchange of views or sale of goods between colleagues.

Sanctions   3.9

There is a requirement to cross reference computer misuse or inappropriate use of the electronic communications systems between the disciplinary policy, equal opportunities and harassment policies, the PC usage policy and the personal conduct policy.

Employers should assert their right to:

*   prohibit access to all or certain Internet resources;

*   remove or substitute hardware or software;

*   withdraw the employee's access to any computer, software, network or communication service;

*   dismiss employees, summarily in cases of substantiated gross misconduct, for abuse of the Internet and email;

*   instigate a police investigation where appropriate; and

*   possibly resort to criminal proceedings, where appropriate.

In certain circumstances, an employer may wish to include in the policy a right to recover from any employee found guilty of misuse of email or Internet facilities any costs incurred by the company as a result of that misuse.

Monitoring and surveillance   3.10

Having established a clear policy, the ability to monitor what employees do may be critical to establish breaches, however, this is an area fraught with difficulty.

Of greatest importance is for employers to make employees aware of their monitoring intentions (once these are decided) so that there can be no doubt in the employee's mind of his or her entitlement or otherwise to privacy or ownership of information on their employer's systems, for whatever business or private purpose they created it. In many cases it will be wise to consult with employees or their representatives before introducing monitoring and in some jurisdictions outside the UK consultation with representative bodies, such as a Works Council, will be mandatory.

Whilst a simple 'business system – business use only' policy has the appeal of clarity, it is neither truly sustainable nor, in the modern business environment, is it likely to be considered reasonable. Occasional personal use of the telephone, email and, within limits, the Internet, which does not interfere with the employee's work, should be considered and included in a policy if appropriate. In the case of email or Internet use, an explanation should also be provided of which types of material may not be transmitted, downloaded, viewed or stored. Care should be taken to ensure that implementation of the policy and the application of sanctions are handled reasonably and consistently.

The *Regulation of Investigatory Powers Act 2000 (RIPA 2000)*, the *Telecommunications (Lawful Business Practice) (Interception of Communications) Regulations 2000 (SI 2000/2699)* ('the Lawful Business Practice Regulations') and the *Human Rights Act 1998 (HRA 1998)* all impact upon the rights of employers to monitor personal emails or to track Internet sites visited by their staff. In an employment context it is also vital that employers bear in mind the implications of the *Data Protection Act 1998 (DPA 1998)*. The information which is collated from any monitoring will be data for the purposes of the 1998 Act and can only be obtained, stored or used for one of its legitimate purposes.

The Regulation of Investigatory Powers Act 2000   3.11

The *RIPA 2000* came into force on 24 October 2000 and extends the powers of the security services by permitting the interception, surveillance and investigation of electronic data in specified circumstances, such as preventing and detecting crime and protecting public health and safety.

It has been widely criticised. Internet Service Providers (ISPs) are now under a duty to surrender details of encryption codes (ie a code used to get access to a particular computer file or system).

On the face of it, the Act may not seem relevant to most commercial organisations because its purpose is to regulate the powers of the investigative authorities, such as the police and intelligence services, by establishing the basic principle that communications may not be intercepted without consent except in specified circumstances. Businesses are concerned because, save for specified exceptions, consent will be required to intercept/monitor communications and they consider this impractical and limiting in enabling them to monitor staff. However, the Act enables the Secretary of State to make regulations which will allow 'businesses' to intercept communications in the course of lawful business practice without the consent of the sender and recipient in certain circumstances.

The Act sets out the rules regarding the recording, monitoring or diverting of communications in the course of their transmission over a public or private telecommunications system. In brief, *section 1* provides that it is unlawful for a person, without lawful authority, intentionally to intercept a communication in the course of its transmission by way of a public or private telecommunications system.

The *RIPA 2000* creates offences of unlawful interception of a public telecommunication system as well as a separate tort of unlawful interception of a private telecommunications network. There are both criminal penalties and civil liabilities for breach. In practice, an employer that unlawfully intercepts an email or telephone call on its own system risks being sued by the maker of the communication, the sender, the recipient or the intended recipient. The civil remedy will be damages if the claimant can show that he or she suffered loss as a result of the interception or, where appropriate, injunctions may be granted.

Section 3 of the Act provides a defence for employers: it will not be unlawful to intercept a communication if the interceptor reasonably believes that both parties to the communication consented to the interception. The effect of *section 3* is that it provides for monitoring with consent. In practice, the majority of employers will not encounter difficulties in determining whether their employees have consented to monitoring. Inclusion of appropriate wording in policies is accordingly essential. It will be more difficult for employers to communicate effectively with third parties who may be party to the communication in question to confirm their consent. As a minimum, employers would need to give third parties a clear opportunity to refuse consent and be able to continue with the communication without being monitored.

A further practical defence is offered by *section 4(2)*. This provision gives the Secretary of State power to issue regulations to authorise:

> 'any such conduct described in the Regulations as appears to him to constitute a legitimate practice reasonably required for the purpose, in connection with the carrying on of any business, of monitoring or keeping a record of: (a) communications by means of which transactions are entered into in the course of that business; or (b) other communications relating to that business or taking place in the course of its being carried on.'

It is under this power that the Secretary of State has issued the Lawful Business Practice Regulations which set out the circumstances in which businesses may lawfully intercept communications without consent.

The Lawful Business Practice Regulations 3.12

The purpose of the Lawful Business Practice Regulations is to provide for circumstances in which businesses may lawfully intercept communications without consent. For employers, these regulations are clearly of great importance in allowing them to monitor the activities of staff. The effect of any interception falling within the scope of the regulations is that the interception will be regarded as lawful for the purposes of the *RIPA 2000*, regardless of whether the parties to the communication have consented to the interception. The regulations expressly allow businesses to intercept emails and telephone calls and to monitor Internet use in order to detect crime or the unauthorised use of a business' own telecommunications system.

Authorised interceptions 3.13

Regulation 3(1) of the Lawful Business Practice Regulations authorises businesses to monitor or record communications on their telecommunications systems without consent for the following purposes:

- To establish the existence of facts relevant to the business. This might be to record the terms of a transaction concluded through emails or over the telephone.

- To ascertain compliance with regulatory or self-regulatory practices or procedures relevant to the business, for example in the financial services industry. It would also cover interceptions to ensure that the business is complying with its own internal policies (for example, an email and Internet policy).

- To ascertain or demonstrate standards which are or ought to be achieved by persons using the telecommunications system. This could include monitoring for the purposes of staff training or quality control.

- To prevent or detect crime. This could include the monitoring of staff emails to detect fraud or corruption. Alternatively, it could enable employers to detect and prevent the downloading and potential publication of offensive material from the Internet.

- To investigate or detect the unauthorised use of the telecommunications system. This could include monitoring to ensure that employees do not breach company policies.

- To ensure the effective operation of the system. This could include monitoring for viruses or hackers infiltrating the system.

The regulations also authorise businesses to monitor, but not record, without consent for the purposes of determining whether or not the communications are relevant to the business. This could include monitoring employees when they are off sick or on holiday.

The requirement to inform staff 3.14

Although the Lawful Business Practice Regulations permit employers to carry out monitoring and recording activities without consent in the circumstances set out above, they still require employers to make all reasonable efforts to inform their staff that monitoring may be carried out. It should be relatively straightforward for employers to inform staff that monitoring may be carried out. For example, a statement could be included in the company email and Internet policy or elsewhere in the employee handbook. In some cases, monitoring will be authorised even where notice of interception has not been given by the employer, for example an illegal act such as the downloading of child pornography from the Internet.

It would be more difficult for employers to satisfy the notification requirements in relation to external users who may use the system by, for example, initiating email correspondence. How can employers inform these users that their communications will be monitored by the recipient before they have sent the email? In practice, it is anticipated that employers will not be required to take steps which are impractical or impossible to undertake as the extent of their obligation is only to make 'all reasonable efforts to inform'. It is now common place for employers to issue pre-recorded telephone announcements, for example, or to send email alerts warning of this possibility.

Human Rights Act 1998   3.15

The *HRA 1998* does not impose direct obligations on employers outside the public sector. Nevertheless, employment tribunals are required to interpret UK employment law in accordance with the European Convention on Human Rights and its associated case law. Consequently, private sector employers should take account of the provisions of the Act when formulating policy on employee monitoring.

Criticism has been made of the *RIPA 2000* and the Lawful Business Practice Regulations on the basis that they are inconsistent with Article 8 of the *HRA 1998*. Article 8 gives individuals the right to respect for private and family life, home and correspondence. This right clearly extends to the workplace. In *Halford v United Kingdom (1997) 24 E.H.R.R. 523*, a senior police officer alleged that her private work telephone was being tapped by her employer. The European Court of Human Rights ('ECHR') held that she would have had a reasonable expectation of privacy as she did not have any prior warning that her employer was liable to intercept her telephone calls. The ECHR stated that the telephone calls made on that line were covered by Article 8 and that the interception of the calls was an unlawful breach of that Article.

The corollary of this decision is that it can probably be assumed that if an employee does not have a reasonable expectation of privacy, an employer is free to monitor calls. The monitoring must, however, be for a defined purpose and must be proportionate to the objective it seeks to achieve.

It is probably the case, therefore, that the *RIPA 2000* and the Lawful Business Practice Regulations are not inconsistent with the *HRA 1998* as employees may not expect privacy if they have been made aware that their employers reserve the right to carry out monitoring. In practice, this means that employers who comply with the Lawful Business Practice Regulations are unlikely to breach employees' privacy rights under the *HRA 1998*. However, the fact that these regulations are satisfied does not alleviate the employer from the need to comply with the *DPA 1998* (see **3.16**). Employers should, as a matter of best practice, always seek to ensure that they only undertake such monitoring as is necessary in the circumstances.

This approach will in itself reduce any risk of breaching employees' privacy rights. For example, in relation to telephone calls, implementing an itemised call recording system which identifies the number of the caller, rather than recording the call itself, may be sufficient for many employers' purposes.

Care must also be taken with telephone calls where one of the parties to the call is outside the UK as some countries have taken a firmer stance with regard to their obligations under human rights legislation and have specific and strict provisions in place dealing with the monitoring by an employer of an employee's calls.

Data Protection Act 1998   3.16

Data Protection is considered in CHAPTER ONE and CHAPTER TWO and a copy of the relevant extracts of the *DPA 1998* are reproduced in APPENDIX THREE. Under the Act, any information which an employer records electronically or manually and which identifies an individual will be subject to the Act. This includes, therefore, the recording of telephone calls, emails or CCTV footage. The Act explains when it is lawful to gather any such data, how it should be stored and the way in which it can be used.

As seen above, the Lawful Business Practice Regulations give an employer the authority to monitor, or record in certain circumstances, a variety of communications. It is the information gained once it has been recorded however that is caught by the *DPA 1998*.

To consider monitoring in a data protection context it is essential to revisit the eight date protection principles set out in *Schedule 1* of the Act (see APPENDIX THREE). The first principle is that monitoring must be fair. This is likely to turn on the extent to which an individual has a reasonable expectation of privacy. The second and third principles are also important here, the former making clear that an employer must have good reason for monitoring and the latter that monitoring should be minimal and specific.

A Code of Practice has been issued by the Information Commissioner to provide guidance upon the Act. The general tenor of the Code as far as it relates to surveillance of employees is that employers should only monitor after first establishing that there is a problem that calls for monitoring. The Code promotes the use of 'impact assessments' so that employers should ask themselves three questions: 'What are the likely benefits? What is the likely adverse impact?' and 'Can the same end be achieved through alternative, less intrusive means?' Only if monitoring is still found to be appropriate should it proceed.

Some guidelines on monitoring can be identified as follows:

• establish a policy on the use of electronic communications which sets out clearly to employees the circumstances in which they may or may not use the employer's telephone systems, email system and Internet access for private communications;

• be aware that if the stated policy is not enforced, it is the practice rather than the stated policy that will be used in assessing whether monitoring is proportionate. So turning a blind eye to infringements of the policy may result in problems in later attempts to enforce for breach;

• account should be taken of:

 – the impact of monitoring on the privacy of people making calls/sending emails to the organisation as well as employees;

 – the impact of the monitoring on the privacy of people referred to in a conversation/email;

- the impact of the monitoring on the autonomy of staff as well as on their privacy;

- the fact that privacy concerns are not confined to personal calls;

• take care to identify the risks to the organisation that need to be controlled;

• limit monitoring to what is necessary for the organisation in particular:

- monitor traffic data (eg frequency) rather than the contents of communications;

- undertake spot checks or audit rather than continuous monitoring;

- automate the monitoring to prevent information being shown unnecessarily to third parties;

- target monitoring on areas of highest risk;

• ensure those making calls to/receiving calls from the organisation are aware of any monitoring and the purposes behind it;

• provide some lines at work (for example, payphones) which employees can use for private calls which will not be monitored;

• if it is necessary to check the email boxes of absent employees make sure they are aware this will happen; and

• provide a means by which employees can effectively expunge from the system emails they receive or send.

Covert monitoring (ie monitoring of which employees are entirely unaware) is something employers should generally avoid and is particularly restricted under the *DPA 1998* and the Code. As such an intrusive step into areas where an employee might reasonably expect privacy, this form of monitoring should only be considered for the detection of serious crime. The Code suggests that employers should not embark on covert monitoring unless the matter they are seeking to investigate is one that the police would be interested in. Petty theft in the workplace, for example, is unlikely to warrant covert monitoring. Reasonable suspicion of more serious crime may justify it but only if a full impact assessment has been carried out and all reasonable alternatives considered.

Interestingly, with the introduction of all of the above legislation, the courts too seem to struggle to balance the need to hear all of the evidence, whilst not wanting to condone intrusions into employees' private lives. One of the first cases to emerge on this subject arose in 2003 in the case of *Jones v University of Warwick [2003] EWCA Civ 151 CA*.

The employee, Jones, was claiming continuing disability as part of her personal injury claim against the university. The subsequent use by the university's insurers of covert filming presented the court with just such a dilemma. Whilst clearly uncomfortable with the insurer's conduct, the court nonetheless decided the video evidence should be admissible in the case. As a reflection of its clearly expressed disapproval, however, the court also made an order for costs against the university.

Criminal sanctions   3.17

Employers are finding themselves more and more at risk from disgruntled or aggrieved former or existing employees who are intent on causing difficulties for their employer as a form of revenge.

The options are almost limitless from existing employees using their position to interfere with the employer's network, corrupting data or information and stealing databases of customer details, for example, to former employees using their knowledge to hack into the network and cause disruption and havoc.

Of course the best safeguard against such action is efficient security measures as detailed elsewhere but it may be of some comfort to employers and some deterrent to the employees in question to know that many such activities are illegal under the *Computer Misuse Act 1990 (CMA 1990)*.

Section 1 provides:

'1(1) A person is guilty of an offence if (a) he causes a computer to perform any function with intent to secure access to any program or data held in any computer; (b) the access he intends to secure is unauthorised; and (c) he knows at the time when he causes the computer to perform the function that that is the case. (2) The intent a person has to have to commit an offence under this section need not be directed at (a) any particular program or data; (b) a program or data of any particular kind; or (c) a program or data held in any particular computer.'

Accordingly, the mere act of seeking access to a system or network on an unauthorised basis is a criminal offence. The Act goes on to create an offence if the wrongdoer accesses a system and causes an unauthorised modification of the contents of any computer. Such modification includes the alteration or erasure of any program or data held in the computer concerned or addition to the contents of any program or data.

The authorities are keen to utilise the powers of the Act and numerous high profile cases have appeared before the courts. These cases serve as a worrying reminder of the vulnerability of business. In *R v Vallor (2004) 1 Cr App R (S) 54*, the defendant was sentenced to two years imprisonment for releasing computer viruses onto the Internet. It was revealed in the case that the virus was detected in 42 countries and infected 27,000 computer systems. In *R v Lindesay [2001] EWCA Crim 1720*, a computer consultant with a grievance who had been on a short-term contract was found guilty of tampering with the systems of his employer by using passwords he had obtained whilst working there. This attack caused much inconvenience to the company and its clients. From this case it is possible to see that whilst the access was not an 'attack' as such – because the defendant had the right passwords as far as the computer was concerned he was authorised – in fact this was an unauthorised access that carried with it criminal sanctions. This is an example of a risk that could and perhaps should have been mitigated by the company – if the passwords had been changed after he had left then he would not have found it so easy to attack the systems. Another example, the case of *R v Scott Reid (1999, unreported)*, is discussed in **CHAPTER SIX** (**6.12**).

The UK Government has, however, recognised that the Act was drafted before the Internet had become a widely used public network and so may not deal with all current concerns. The All Party Parliamentary Internet Group (APIG) has recently held an inquiry into updating the Act and has concluded that the UK does need to update its laws and introduce more effective legislation to prosecute those who maliciously attack computer networks. The report produced by the inquiry called for hacking to carry a maximum two year prison term, an increase from the current maximum sentence of six months, which will also now make the offence extraditable under the International Treaty of Cybercrime, closing a previous loophole. Also, it recommends that denial of service attacks are explicitly criminalised with the creation of a new offence of 'impairing access to data' because the current *CMA 1990* position might not stretch to all denial of service activity. The report further recommends that the Director of Public Prosecutions should set out a permissive policy for private prosecutions under the CMA, saving his extensive powers to discontinue cases only where they are inappropriate or vexatious. In launching that inquiry, Richard Allan MP, the joint Vice Chairman of the APIG, said:

> 'The motivation for this inquiry was a recognition that the current legislation, the *Computer Misuse Act 1990*, was drafted before the Internet had become a widely used public network and so may not deal with the situations that are of concern today…We are also interested to hear about how not to do it as there are often valid concerns about Government legislating for the Internet in ways that will be overly burdensome and/or may not anyway achieve the desired result. Legislation in this area will require an understanding of the technology as well as of legal process, especially as it relates to rules of evidence, if it is to be of any use to prosecuting authorities.'

It seems clear that further legislation can be expected in this area.

Chapter 4
Transaction-Related Risk

Foreword

By Richard Allan MP

The general thrust of public policy in the UK, as in many other countries, is to encourage businesses and individuals to use the Internet for an increasing range of functions. This is done in the belief that this will bring economic and social benefits as private businesses and public services use IT and networks to increase their productivity and offer innovative services. The benefits that are being sought are not those that come from mere 'brochureware', the use of websites as a form of advertising, but from the shift to conducting transactions over the Internet.

In its capacity as a provider of masses of information to the reader, the Internet is a relatively uncomplicated medium. There may be legal complexities in the status and use of the material that we download from the net, though the surfer is often oblivious to these. But when it comes to transactions across the net, especially those involving money, we are entering a different realm of risks and the consequent need for knowledge to deal with these.

In setting out the principal issues that are relevant to online transactions this chapter aims to answer that need. As well as having concerns about financial security, people are becoming increasingly interested in issues of privacy and data protection. Personal data is gaining a value of its own as companies develop their marketing techniques and the need to balance the privacy of the individual against the interests of business is recognised in a growing body of EU and national law. The need for protections for consumers trading across national borders is also a spur for new regulations.

If we sat down and thought about all the potential complexity of doing business across the net in a wholly secure way then it would probably never happen. Technologists, businesses and the public have not waited for everything to be sorted out but started to work this way in a very pragmatic fashion. This could now be derailed if public confidence is damaged by problems that cannot be resolved either pragmatically or legally.

(cont'd)

47

The hope is that a growing awareness of how business can be conducted in a proper manner within the regulatory framework will lead to the anticipated benefits of transactions across the net being realised. If this chapter can make a contribution to that aim then it will have performed a valuable public service.

(Richard Allan MP, Co-chair All Party Internet Group, former Chairman on House of Commons IT select sub-committee)

Introduction 4.1

There are an almost limitless number of types of transaction that can be concluded online and most fall into one or more of the following categories:

• transactions involving the transfer of funds;

• transactions where the parties commit to actions or contracts that may give rise to financial or legal obligations;

• transactions involving information protected under data protection and privacy legislation imposing a requirement that access to that information is restricted; and

• transactions where the subject matter itself is controlled or regulated.

The differing types of transaction each involve distinct areas of risk and require the employment of various measures to control and minimise that risk. The growth in online shopping, banking and bill payments in the UK has been explosive. Government statistics from October 2003 showed that almost 31 per cent of all adults in Great Britain have ordered tickets, goods or services over the Internet. Figures from the Association for Payment Clearing Services show that £9.12 billion of card (credit/debit) transactions were made online in 2003. However, this rapid growth has resulted in a commensurate increase in fraud, theft and identity crimes of various types. In the bricks and mortar world there are checks that can readily be made to determine that an individual is who he or she claims to be, yet in the online world these checks are not straightforward and, at the most basic level, it is not easy to determine whether an individual attempting to make a purchase of alcohol or place a bet online is even legally old enough to do so.

Online contract formation 4.2

The standard requirements for a legally enforceable agreement are an offer, acceptance, the intention to create legal relations and consideration (price). These requirements are equally applicable to online contracts. In addition, the standard legislative provisions relating to the sale of goods and services, such as the *Sale of Goods Act 1979* (as amended by the *Supply and Sale of Goods Act 1994*), the *Consumer Protection Act 1987* and the *Unfair Contract Terms Act 1977*, affect online sales. Legislation and regulations have also been written which are specifically directed at further regulating or are particularly relevant to online activity, including the *Electronic Commerce (EC Directive) Regulations 2002 (SI 2002/2013)* ('the EC Regulations'), the *Consumer Protection (Distance Selling) Regulations 2000 (SI 2000/2334)* ('the DS Regulations'), the *Data Protection Act 1998 (DPA 1998)* and the *Privacy and Electronic Communications (EC Directive) Regulations 2003 (SI 2003/2426)*. The impact of these is discussed below.

Offer and acceptance   4.3

The determination in any particular transaction of when an offer and acceptance have been made is something which has occupied many courts over the years. It is, however, generally accepted that a display of price-marked goods in a supermarket or other self service store is not an offer to sell by the retailer, which is capable of acceptance. The display is instead an invitation to the customer to make an offer to purchase the goods (an invitation to treat) which can be accepted by the retailer to form a binding contract at the checkout.

The display of price-marked goods on a website is analogous to the supermarket scenario and is generally thought to be treated in the same way, such that a contract could only result if the business operating the website subsequently accepted an offer to purchase made by a customer.

The area is currently lacking legal precedent and in certain situations, where the information concerning goods or services available on the website is in sufficiently definite terms, the advertisement could be interpreted as an offer which, if accepted by a visitor to the website, would form a binding contract. Additionally, the terms and conditions of the vendor could themselves suggest that a contract is formed at that point. It is not difficult to anticipate the problems which might result. Once a contract has been formed, if the retailer cannot honour the agreement it will be in breach. Consider for a moment a small business with a presence on the web which finds its products of greater appeal than it anticipated. Contracts could be formed for in excess of the production capacity resulting in disappointed customers and potential claims for compensation.

Pricing errors also cause problems for businesses in this area in often a very public manner. In 2003, Amazon.co.uk made the headlines when it mistakenly advertised Hewlett Packard Pocket PCs on its website for a mere £7.32 each. Amazon claimed that this was an invitation to treat pursuant to its conditions of use and no contract was formed until the customer received an email from Amazon stating that the item purchased had been shipped. Certain customers, however, interpreted this as an offer capable of acceptance and a number of customers who had ordered the PDA even received an email confirming that the item had been ordered giving an anticipated delivery date and providing information on how to cancel 'the contract'.

PC World Business ran into similar difficulties recently when it advertised the price of a box of 100 CD-Rs on its website at 89 pence instead of 89 pence per

CD. PC World subsequently offered reimbursements to customers that attempted to take advantage of the generous offer, but despite the acknowledgement of order email from PC World stating that the email did not constitute acceptance of the order it failed to make clear when a binding contract would actually be formed and the terms and conditions also failed to clarify this.

Even if binding contracts do not arise as a result of pricing errors, the resultant embarrassment and adverse publicity for the seller should be sufficient to encourage vigilance in pricing and for the website to make it clear when a contract will be formed.

Electronic Commerce (EC Directive) Regulations 2002
4.4

Arguably the two situations above arose in part because the two companies concerned failed to adequately explain to customers in unambiguous terms the steps necessary to form a contract. This in itself is a breach of the EC Regulations, regardless of any risks to the companies concerned arising from the resulting contractual uncertainty and the associated negative publicity.

The regulations were implemented in the UK pursuant to the European Commission's E-Commerce Directive 2000 (00/31/EC) which was introduced to ensure that 'information society' services could be freely provided across the European Union (EU).

One of the objectives of the E-Commerce Directive is to clarify where the responsibility lies for enforcement of e-commerce obligations within the European Economic Area (EEA). UK enforcement authorities regulate information society services provided from the UK wherever in the EEA they are delivered. In the same way, services provided from elsewhere in the EEA are regulated by the appropriate authorities in those member states. This means that UK companies which offer, or intend to offer, services throughout the EEA only have to concern themselves with the UK authorities, which makes for easier administration when expanding into new markets.

The EC Regulations distinguish between business-to-business transactions and business-to-consumer transactions, and business customers can agree with the online service provider to opt out of the provisions relating to the conclusion of contracts online.

Several of the regulations warrant particular comment here. *Regulation 9(1)* requires that prior to an order being placed online, the site operator/service provider must provide the customer in a clear and comprehensible manner with the following information:

- the technical steps necessary to conclude a contract on the website and an explanation as to when the customer will be committed to the transaction;

- language options for the customer to use in forming the contract; and

- the means by which any errors in the customer's order can be identified and rectified.

Additionally, the service provider must make available any terms and conditions applicable to the contract in a form that allows the customer to store and reproduce them.

After an order has been placed online, and subject to the opt out available to business customers, *regulation 11* provides that the service provider must acknowledge receipt of the order and provide an effective and accessible method to identify and correct input errors to the order.

Businesses should remember, however, that a number of the provisions in the regulations (including the two referred to above) do not apply to contracts concluded exclusively by email or by equivalent individual communication. So a business which is approached on an isolated occasion through email by a customer where all communications leading to the formation of the contract are by email will not be caught by *regulations 9* or *11*.

Unsolicited commercial communications   4.5

Businesses which use email as a method of marketing their products or services need to be familiar with the restrictions in this area. The problems and frustration caused by unsolicited emails or spam are well publicised and known to all with an email account. *Regulation 8* of the EC Regulations provides that any unsolicited electronic mail has to be clearly and unambiguously identified as such, thereby allowing users and Internet Service Providers (ISP) to identify and block or delete the mail without opening it. Further provisions were included in the *Privacy and Electronic Communications (EC Directive) Regulations 2003* which came into force on 11 December 2003. These regulations introduced two new rules for email marketing:

- In all marketing messages sent by electronic mail, regardless of who the recipient is, the sender:

  - must not conceal his or her identity; and

  - must provide a valid address for opt-out requests.

- In relation to *unsolicited* marketing messages sent by electronic mail to *individual subscribers*, senders cannot send such messages unless they have the recipient's prior consent to do so.

This rule on unsolicited messages is known as an opt-in rule as it requires the recipient to choose to receive the message. Therefore, on an online or paper page where a user is entering information, he or she has to tick a box to indicate that he or she wishes to receive unsolicited mail. This must not be confused with opt-out systems where the box is already ticked and the user must untick it on screen or tick a box on paper to indicate that he or she does not wish to receive mail. Opt-out systems are ONLY permitted where the following criteria are met:

- the recipient's email address was collected in the course of a sale or negotiation for sale (the sale does not need to have been completed);

- the recipient's details may be used only by the same entity to whom they were originally given. This has implications for transfer of customer lists between the group companies and trading parties;

- the sender only sends promotional messages relating to 'similar products and services' (note: the courts have not yet ruled what is and is not classed as similar); and

- when the address was collected, the recipient was told about the possible use of his or her details for future marketing and given the opportunity to opt out (free of charge except for the cost of transmission) which he or she did not take. The opportunity to opt out must be given with every subsequent message.

Consumer Protection (Distance Selling) Regulations 2000   4.6

As suggested by the name, the DS Regulations apply to business-to-consumer transactions and place requirements on companies selling over the phone, by fax, mail order, through interactive digital television and over the Internet. The purpose of the regulations is to increase consumer confidence in distance selling. Key features include:

- the consumer must be given clear information about the goods or services offered;

- the consumer must be sent confirmation of the purchase; and

- the consumer must be given a seven-day cooling off period.

The aim of the cooling off period is to give consumers an opportunity to examine the goods being offered as they would have had if making a purchase in person from a shop. The regulations require that the consumer takes care of the goods prior to returning them but the cost of repackaging/restocking, disputes with consumers over the condition of returned goods, when such goods were delivered/returned and the problems the business will face if reselling the goods as new are all issues of major concern.

E-payment   4.7

Payment is one of the main areas of concern for companies that do business online. Obviously a method is needed of ensuring that payments are made and received safely. The risks of carrying out transactions on the Internet are frequently the subject of news stories, but with a little preparation these risks are easily reduced or eliminated. This section will first consider the various methods of payment, then look at some of the legal issues that surround e-payments.

Methods of payment

Credit and debit cards   4.8

For the consumer credit and debit cards are the main method of payment over the Internet. Cards are attractive both for customer and company because of their familiarity if nothing else. In 2002, payments to a total value of £9 billion were made using credit and debit cards by 11.8 million people according to the Association for Payment Clearing Services.

Despite this level of online business, the frequent news stories about Internet fraud mean that consumers are becoming alert to the need to only transact business with companies which can show that their websites and payment mechanisms are secure. Essentially, this means that the part of the site where credit card and other personal details are entered needs to be encrypted and identified as such with the familiar padlock symbol. Further details about encryption are given in **4.11**. Smaller businesses may also suffer from the possibility that customers will only trust their card details to companies that are perceived as reputable (eg those companies with strong brands) and will be more wary when buying from companies that they have not used before. This may make it difficult for new entrants into the market if the only method of payment they accept is cards.

A key area of concern for businesses accepting payment online by credit or debit cards is that of fraud. Without a signature to verify, or even sight of the card, how can businesses reassure themselves that the transaction is genuine? Internet payments are categorised by the clearing banks that process credit cards as 'Cardholder Not Present' transactions. As the name suggests, these transactions are ones where the merchant, cardholder and card are not all in the same place at the same time. So physical checks, such as examining the signature, are not possible. When the clearing bank authorises the payment, all that authorisation signifies is that the card has not been *reported* lost or stolen and that there are sufficient funds in the account.

Authorisation from the card issuer, therefore, is not a guarantee of payment nor does it confirm that the person placing the order is the genuine cardholder. If the genuine cardholder disputes the transaction at a later date or any discrepancies arise, the card issuer may recover the funds from the merchant, even if the transaction has been authorised.

There are some steps that can be taken to minimise the risk of being a victim of this type of fraud:

- Check the email address against the customer's name and look for names within the email address that have no apparent connection to the customer.

Did the customer simply spell the email address incorrectly, or is it perhaps that it does not exist?

- Check for bounced emails, for example if a purchase receipt email is returned before it gets to the customer the reason should be investigated and suspicions aroused.

- Check the billing address given by the customer against the card company's records.

- Check the Card Security Code (the numbers on the signature strip on the back of the card) against the credit card company records.

- Ask the customer to provide a contact telephone number. Check the STD code of the contact telephone number against the address given by the cardholder.

- Does the card have a valid expiry date?

- If the card is a Switch or Solo, does it have a valid issue number or start date?

- What is being bought? Some products are more desirable than others – the most desirable products are those that have a high resale value. If multiple copies of the same item are being purchased, would a customer really need that many?

- If the delivery address is outside the UK and the usual customer base or product is UK based, exercise care. If in doubt, do not send the goods out. Try contacting the customer to establish that the transaction is genuine.

- Arrange delivery through recorded or registered post or a reputable carrier. Where possible obtain signed proof of delivery. Instruct the delivery agent to obtain a signature as this information may be asked for if the transaction is charged back to the business.

- Do not allow the carrier to receive instructions to change the delivery address.

Electronic Data Interchange   4.9

Electronic Data Interchange, or EDI, is a method of transmitting information, such as purchase orders and invoices, to another party. The system is used for business-to-business communications, such as supplier to retailer. Payments can also be sent using this route. EDI has the advantage of being secure and the quantity of paperwork generated is reduced. It is also possible to operate a business with smaller quantities of stock since orders can be processed instantaneously. However, the main drawback is the limited scope of the system in that both parties need to use EDI and it is purely a B2B system.

Electronic money   4.10

Electronic money is data representing money. The data can be transferred by means of a computer network and can be traded as a token exchangeable for real money. Essentially, the aim of electronic money is to mimic currency, but instead of existing as notes and coins it exists as computer data. The security of the system can be extended by the use of biometrics to verify the identity of the holder of the money.

Electronic money has key advantages on two fronts. First, as a method of payment for low value products over the Internet (where credit cards may be prohibitively expensive). Second, as a safer alternative to cash in face-to-face transactions. For example, in high value transactions, such as the purchase of a car, electronic money could be used as an alternative to the Banker's Draft or cash or to avoid delays historically experienced whilst waiting for cheques to clear.

Electronic money systems work by an electronic money provider exchanging currency for digital tokens (which can be in many forms). These 'tokens' can then be spent with the person holding the token being able to return them to the electronic money provider for currency. Typically, a fee will be charged to convert money in and out of the electronic money format and the electronic money provider will also be able to invest the currency it holds ('the float') and thereby provide itself with a further revenue stream. There are a number of alternative providers of electronic money systems, including Mondex (owned by Mastercard) and PayPal (owned by the auction website ebay), and the number of providers is likely to grow over coming years.

Electronic money systems are still mainly in their infancy, but businesses need to consider whether to offer electronic money payment facilities on their websites. This is not an easy decision, particularly in an embryonic development. Failure to offer these payment mechanisms may place the business at a competitive disadvantage, whilst having a system that is later shown to be flawed in some way may prove to be expensive in terms of cost revenue and negative publicity.

Since electronic money ultimately needs to be exchanged back into currency with the provider, it is important to ensure that the provider remains solvent. A business would be left in a difficult position where it holds a large quantity of electronic money but is not able to redeem it.

Understandably, electronic money providers are closely regulated across the world. In Europe, the EU has introduced several directives in this area which are implemented in the UK by the *Financial Services and Markets Act 2000 (Regulated Activities) (Amendment) Order 2002 (SI 2002/682)*. Providers of electronic money are also subject to regulation by the Financial Services Authority (FSA) and are required to hold capital of one million Euros at the point of receiving authorisation. Thereafter, its capital must be equivalent to two per cent of the higher of:

- its *e-money outstandings* at that time; and

- the average of its *daily e-money outstanding amount* for the six-month period ending at that time.

There are also detailed rules on how the float is to be managed.

As ever, fraudulent transactions remain a risk. There are two types of fraudulent transaction that can affect electronic money. The first is that the buyer of goods is not the owner of the electronic money account that he or she is using. This is the same problem that affects stolen credit cards and, to a large extent, the steps to minimise risk detailed above are equally applicable. Alternatively, some electronic money companies are guaranteeing payments and bearing the risk of fraud themselves. The second risk is one that affects 'real' cash – counterfeiting the cash itself where a computer expert finds a way to replicate the digital form of the electronic money just as counterfeiters now print bank notes. Defences against counterfeiting are under constant review in the world of cryptography. There may be little that most businesses can do to protect themselves other than vigilance, but as electronic money is based on a contractual relationship with the provider, it might be appropriate to negotiate with the provider of the service for it to bear the risk of counterfeit transactions.

Encryption   4.11

Any business which is engaged in transacting over the net will want to ensure security for the communication, whether it is to protect payment, customer details or other confidential or private information. Additionally, it may be important to be able to verify the identity of the other party to the transaction. In any scenario, security of one form or another is key.

The use of encryption, digital signatures and public key infrastructure (PKI) (see **CHAPTER SEVEN – MANAGING OPERATIONAL ICT RISK WITH STANDARDS AND BEST PRACTICE (7.46)**) is the solution for many businesses.

Digital signatures in a PKI environment work on the basis of two keys: the 'private' key, kept secret and used by the sender to sign what is being sent, and a corresponding 'public' key, accessible by anyone and used to prove that the sender actually sent the message with its private key. If a public key 'unlocks' the message, the recipient knows that what it is looking at was sent by the person in control of the relevant private key.

The process involves encryption of at least some part of the sender's original message. Using this method, the recipient should:

● be fairly certain of the identity of the person who signed the document;

● know that the person in control of the private key was personally involved;

● know that the person intended to sign the whole document, not just the signature page; and

● be confident that it will be hard for the private key holder to deny involvement in the transaction.

Most digital signatures are issued by digital certificate authorities, which confirm that the signature on what is received belongs to a particular entity or person. The authority issues a digital certificate containing the holder's identity, the public key and the identity of the issuing authority. The certificate is signed with the authority's own digital signature so it can be confirmed that the certificate is not a forgery. The certificate can also specify limitations, for example that it should not be relied upon for transactions valued at more than a certain amount.

Companies should ensure that digital certificates are kept up to date and also need to keep abreast of technological developments. The current industry standard relies upon 128-bit encryption and while this provides robust encryption against similarly equipped hackers, 512-bit technology is capable of breaking 128-bit encryption. 512-bit encryption will shortly become industry standard and organisations reliant on the secure transmission of data over the Internet will need to update their technology.

Data protection   4.12

The issue of personal privacy has assumed considerable significance in the digital era and it is therefore interesting that data protection legislation was actually introduced prior to the massive growth in the processing of personal information through the exploitation of new technologies. Some of the *DPA 1998* has already been looked at in **CHAPTER ONE –SECURITY – WHY BOTHER?** and **CHAPTER THREE – EMPLOYEE-RELATED RISK**, however, the following seeks to identify the key issues arising in the context of online transactions.

Two principal concerns have been identified as impediments to the universal take up of the Internet as a medium over which to purchase goods and services. First, the threat of identity theft and second the fear that everything an individual does online is tracked and recorded by operators of databases who then sell on these aggregated consumer profiles to direct marketing companies. Data protection legislation attempts to minimise these risks and compliance with the *DPA 1998* certainly goes some way to addressing the legitimate concerns of online consumers.

Businesses selling goods and services online need to obtain certain information from their customers to enable them to provide these goods and services. However, the more information it is possible to obtain about a particular individual, the more valuable the information becomes as it allows the company to develop a profile of the customer for either its own purposes or to sell on to other organisations. Companies are, therefore, understandably reluctant to limit data collection when they are presented with an opportunity, such as an online registration form that customers are required to complete to obtain goods or services.

Much of the information sought by online registration forms typically includes 'personal data', defined by the *DPA 1998* as:

● data which relate to a living individual who can be identified:

— from that data; or

— from that data and other information which is in the possession of, or is likely to come into the possession of, the data controller.

The data controller is whoever obtains the personal data in the first place and does anything with it subsequent to collection, such as putting the data into a database, combining the data with other data, disclosing the data to a third party or destroying the data. In many situations this will be the same business that is offering the goods and services online, but businesses are increasingly outsourcing the 'fulfilment' element of online transactions, such as the delivery of the goods or services, receiving payment, after sales services etc, and there may be several data controllers with responsibility for ensuring compliance with the *DPA 1998* in respect of a single customer's personal data.

Personal data which has been collated needs to be dealt with in compliance with the eight key principles as set out in CHAPTER THREE (**3.16**). Of particular relevance is the seventh Data Protection Principle, which is reproduced in CHAPTER ONE (**1.12**) and APPENDIX THREE.

Businesses need to observe this closely as they will be held responsible for anything that happens to personal data under their control. The Act makes it a duty of a data controller to comply with the Data Protection Principles in relation to all personal data with respect to which he or she is the data controller (*DPA 1998, s 4*).

Businesses should also post a privacy statement prominently on their websites which sets out its *DPA 1998* compliant policy on how personal data is used.

Data transfer overseas 4.13

To ensure compliance with the requirement to keep personal data secure under the *DPA 1998* and the underlying EU Data Protection Directive 1995 (95/46/EC), businesses need to be cautious about transferring personal data held by them overseas.

The transfer of data among countries within the EEA is permitted, but personal data should not be transferred to a country or territory outside the EEA unless that country or territory ensures an adequate level of protection for the rights and freedoms of data subjects in relation to the processing of personal data. However, to date, the European Commission has only recognised Switzerland, Hungary, Canada and Argentina as countries which do offer sufficient protection with respect to personal data to allow transfers within the Directive. As protection of personal data is mainly self-regulatory in the US, it does not qualify for such recognition. This could potentially cause businesses considerable problems as large amounts of data may be transferred between the EEA and the US.

As a result of these problems the Commission agreed the so-called 'safe harbor' proposals with the US government. Under this system US companies may voluntarily sign up to a set of data protection principles, called the safe harbor principles, which adequately protect the transfer of personal data in accordance with the Data Protection Directive. Companies transferring personal data from the EU to the US will be able to rely on the safe harbor principles as ensuring compliance with that aspect of the Directive. If a US company which has signed up to those principles breaches them, this will constitute an offence under US law.

If data is being transferred to a non-EEA country or to a US company which has not signed up to the safe harbor principles, then a transferring company will have to enter into an approved individual contract with the recipient to ensure compliance. The Information Commissioner has neither produced a model contract nor is approving contracts. The Commission has, however, produced model clauses which, if used, must be accepted by the member states as complying with the eighth Data Protection Principle. These are available on the website operated by the UK Government's Information Commissioner.

Gaming and promotions 4.14

As e-commerce rapidly grows, offering a mixed variety of opportunities and threats to commercial sectors, so does the phenomenon of 'Internet gambling'. Due to the nature of Internet gambling, estimates for the size of the market vary widely but it is thought that there are many thousands of gambling sites online at present, contributing billions of pounds to global gambling. This market is inevitably set to grow as access to the Internet becomes more widely available. Accordingly, it is an area worthy of specific mention.

There are numerous different categories of websites available, however, they generally fall into two categories: sites which offer access to terrestrial gambling (betting), eg bookmakers take bets via email as they would by telephone, and sites where gambling takes place exclusively on the Internet (gaming).

At present, betting on the Internet is permitted in the UK provided it is offered by licensed operators based in the UK as this is merely seen as an extension of placing a bet over the telephone. The operation of gaming sites within the UK, however, is not permitted although it is not illegal for a person resident in the UK to gamble online at a site which is situated somewhere else in the world.

This anomaly arises as a result of the fact that the legislation relating to gambling dates back to the 1960s. Measures have been taken by the Government to modernise the law and a draft Gambling Bill was published in July 2003 in response to a report produced by the Gambling Review Body. The report highlighted the primary concerns surrounding Internet gambling, such as crime and disorder, unauthorised access by children and vulnerable persons and addiction to gambling (informality of use suggests that people with a problem may be more receptive to this approach).

The Bill also makes provision for a Gambling Commission that would be responsible for the regulation of Internet sites and monitoring of licensed operators within the UK.

Calls have been made by the Gaming Board, the industry itself, MPs and Peers etc to license Internet gambling in the UK and create a safe environment in which UK consumers can gamble. The change in law will not only benefit the consumers but it is thought that operators which are based overseas are likely to move their business to the UK for the perceived improved legitimate status.

Though it is clear that in the near future the law will permit operators offering online services to be based in the UK, it is not apparent when the changes will be implemented.

Illegal trading 4.15

In addition to regulatory offences that can be committed by failing to comply with prescribed means of conducting business over the Internet, businesses also need to ensure that the goods or services themselves can be legally provided in the jurisdiction in which the company is doing business and offering its services. An online auction site run by Yahoo! fell foul of French legislation prohibiting the advertising and sale of Nazi memorabilia when it permitted the listing of Nazi era items. In many countries the sale of certain books, films and types of software (including console game cartridges) is prohibited. Additionally, the sale of medicines and prescription drugs will be regulated to varying degrees in most countries.

In most instances, businesses can avoid liability by ensuring their website access agreement specifically states which country or countries the website is directed to and refusing to ship goods or provide services in jurisdictions where their legality is questionable or unknown.

Website access arrangements 4.16

The access agreement, or the terms and conditions of use of a website, is what governs the relationship between the website user and the visitor. This important document may have wide ranging repercussions should a dispute over the website ever arise and any business operating a website therefore needs to ensure that it has protected itself.

The following is a list of the basic areas that the agreement should cover.

The access agreement should make clear the ownership of the website. This is important as the identity of service providers is required under the DS Regulations. It is also useful from a commercial perspective as it allows visitors to the site to contact the owner.

The access agreement should cover acceptable use of the website. Intellectual property laws, such as copyright, may protect the website and so the business should identify what the user can do with the information on the site. Is the user permitted to print information from the website? Is this for personal use only? Can information be passed on to others? The business may consider that if information from the website is circulated this may improve the business profile and reputation. If so, then the access agreement needs to state that information can be copied and distributed, but only if the source is acknowledged. Many access agreements make a distinction between commercial and personal use, with personal use being treated more leniently than commercial. It is important to note that this would not stop any minded person from printing or copying the website but if the company then chose to take action against an offender, it would be clear to the court exactly on what terms access to the website was allowed.

Where the website links to other sites, the access agreement should make clear that any links to external websites do not imply any recommendation on the part of the company. It is also a good idea to only link to site home pages to make it clear that the visitor is entering a new site.

Most website terms and conditions devote a large section to disclaimers. Generally, these need to cover what the company does and does not take responsibility for on the website, particularly with regard to any viruses etc which might be inadvertently passed to users through access onto the website.

Outsourcing 4.17

So far this chapter has looked at the risks associated with transacting through the medium of technology. In addition, the issue of outsourcing where businesses contract with third parties to provide some or all of their IT needs also needs to be considered.

The high cost of ownership of complex IT systems, including the salaries of the engineers, programmers and analysts required to support them, makes outsourcing an attractive option, increasingly so as competition within the industry and rapid technological developments have together rendered the process cheaper and virtually seamless.

Whether a business is a large scale data-driven IT user, such as financial institutions, energy suppliers or telephone companies, or a smaller business looking to have its network managed, outsourcing is undoubtedly an option which most businesses will consider at some point or other.

The key issues organisations contemplating outsourcing need to examine at the outset can broadly be grouped under five headings: the tendering process; provisions in the outsourcing agreement; the issue of employees; exit management and managing disputes.

Tendering 4.18

- Choose the operations and processes to outsource carefully with clearly defined and measurable objectives – after firstly putting your own house in order.

- Ask the right questions.

- Work hard to produce a good Invitation To Tender, with requirements that bids accommodate future service changes. Consultants can be extremely useful at this stage, however, use them with care in clearly defined roles.

- Do not place bidders at arms length – spend time getting to know them as the organisation will need to work extremely closely with the company eventually selected, and clashes between dramatically different corporate cultures should be identified at this stage.

The outsourcing agreement   4.19

Considerable care should be taken with the negotiation and drafting of this agreement as the organisation will have to work with the terms agreed, possibly for some considerable time.

- Work out well in advance any contracts to be assigned, for example software licences and real estate leases, and ensure that this can be achieved without impacting on the financial viability of the outsourcing.

- Describe the services being contracted for as fully as possible without becoming diverted by over elaborate service credit schemes.

- Monitor the degree to which the organisation will be completely reliant on a particular service provider and resist giving exclusivity for unrelated services.

- Even if outsourcing the bulk of IT services, do not get rid of the entire in-house IT team and at the very least keep an IT director.

- Negotiate with two bidders simultaneously, if possible, and insist on interviewing proposed key personnel with whom the organisation will have considerable dealings, such as transition and project managers.

- Set out clearly the circumstances in which termination can occur. Failings on the part of the service provider that it might consider to be inconsequential could have significant impacts on mission critical elements of the operations, and the option to terminate in such instances is important – do not just leave termination to 'material breach'.

- From the extensive due diligence carried out on the short-listed service providers, the organisation should have a clear idea about whether a parent company guarantee or performance bond is necessary and, if determined that it is, insist on it.

Employee considerations   4.20

This can be a very complex area requiring advice from employment law experts, particularly with respect to the operation of the *Transfer of Undertakings (Protection of Employment) Regulations 1981 (SI 1981/1794)* (TUPE) questions that need to be contemplated (listed below). However, all outsourcing situations are different and the consequences of mistakes when dealing with employees can be disastrous.

- Are the employees currently doing the proposed outsource activity to be retained or will they be assigned to the provider. Whatever the case, start consultations early and advise employees of their options.

- What are the potential costs of employee transfers and has it been agreed with the service provider whether TUPE applies and what will happen to employees. Do not forget the transferring employees may come back to the original employer.

- Any dismissal in connection with a TUPE transfer is automatically unfair, therefore, a compromise agreement for any dismissed employees must be obtained prior to the transfer.

Exit management and transition plans   4.21

It is a simple fact that all outsourcing agreements come to an end at some point. This issue and the termination options are directly linked to the outsourcing agreement, and the extent to which this process can be smoothly facilitated is a function of the care with which the agreement was negotiated and drafted. Termination/exit costs can be very high and an organisation should not underestimate these costs when considering its options.

- Is the decision to terminate a knee jerk reaction to an isolated, albeit serious, failing on the part of the service provider, or is it the latest in a series of minor but resolvable problems? Alternatively, are there new commercial considerations unrelated to the performance of the service provider that render the original outsourcing deal no longer financially viable?

- If the service provider has defaulted, is there provision for compensating for any losses suffered, or involving the prior calculation of liquidated damages?

- If possible negotiate a flexible approach to determining the method of exit with a fluid transition period through which an organisation can manage an orderly transfer.

- It is very important to secure post termination rights so there is no business interruption on exit, and identify essential intellectual property rights, contracts, systems and assets to the operation. Get the service provider to update business process and operational manuals so the information is at an organisation's fingertips.

What if it goes wrong?   4.22

The nature of outsourcing arrangements is such that it is highly likely that disputes will arise relating to one or more of the issues identified above. Typically, these can be worked through by the parties and very few disputes escalate to the commencement of court proceedings. Frequently it is a matter of proactively managing the service provider, ensuring clear communications at all times and at an appropriate level and raising any material or contractual issues at regular meetings. However, it should be borne in mind that litigation is always a possibility and a business should prepare accordingly. This will involve creating and maintaining from the outset a contract file incorporating the original agreement, all amendments and all correspondence between the parties. Minutes from meetings, details of telephone calls and, most importantly, emails should all be archived in an accessible way and a senior employee or officer of the company should be given responsibility for this task. Disputes that arise should be escalated internally in both organisations in an orderly and amicable manner and it is advisable to work with solicitors at an early stage when it becomes apparent that there is the potential for a dispute to arise.

Chapter 5
Online Reputational Risk

Foreword

by Richard S. Levick

To appreciate the critical importance of the material covered in this chapter, imagine that an unscrupulous competitor has just posted a defamatory 'revelation' about your company, which is full of unsubstantiated allegations that are close enough to certain fact patterns as to seem superficially credible. The enemy does not identify themselves but instead posted the charges under the rubric of a fictitious public service group.

Eventually, you trace the source. Your efforts to debar further scurrilities are successful. You are planning a law suit. But your enemy accepts litigation as a cost of doing business. They are satisfied. Why? Because dozens of newspapers and legitimate online outlets have already picked up the false story and published it with caveats like 'reportedly' and 'allegedly'.

About half those media outlets called you for comment. You denied the allegations. You stated for the record that it was a nefarious scheme by a dishonest competitor. Your comments were duly noted in the coverage. But damage has been done.

If traditional media presents a minefield to corporations and the lawyers who defend them, the Internet has ratcheted up the threat to a level that few defence barristers are prepared. Every precedent, courtroom misstep, rumour or small town newspaper article is now racing around the Internet at the speed of thought. Major media reporters are tapping those sources, adding a weight of alleged fact to the appearance of truth.

Power once reserved for only the great barons of the news media is only a click away for anybody to access. The prosecution, its clients and their public relations counsel will use technology to their immense advantage unless the defence is prepared to make it otherwise.

Readers should therefore think on two levels as they read this chapter. One, what are the legal issues and legal solutions? Two, how can you, apprehend the business damage that may result from Internet malfeasance?

(cont'd)

Perhaps the ultimate strategic consideration suggested by the examples in this chapter is: How can victims of online defamation use the Internet to their own benefit, mounting a response even more aggressive and far reaching in effect than the original attack?

(Richard S. Levick, President, Levick Strategic Communications, Washington, DC)

Introduction 5.1

Technology has been like manna from heaven for many people who want to damage the reputation of big business. Since (almost) the dawn of time aggrieved employees, business rivals and others have tried to spread rumours about organisations to try and do them harm. The problem for them has been that whispering campaigns by their very nature are quiet. The mainstream media which have had the power to spread rumour and innuendo have been cautious to do so, particularly in the UK where a combination of responsibility, regulation and the threat of litigation has proved to be a brake on these rumours being taken up.

Technology has changed all of that. Now anyone who wants to do harm can set up his or her own website, send an email or join in a message board. His or her story goes from urban myth to truth in less than 24 hours. People tend not to question what they see on the Internet. As a result unfounded rumours are treated as fact and businesses and individuals suffer as a result. For several years the emerging trend of cybersmearing and the harm which has been done to reputation in Europe and the US have been highlighted. It has had some pretty dramatic consequences for a number of companies and their officers. Individuals have been affected too – from David Beckham having to say that his marriage is still intact to Britney Spears reassuring the world that hers is not. This section will look first at 'traditional' defamation actions which have featured technology and then the new world of cybersmearing – wholly new ways to damage a company's reputation online. Further, how the Internet can be used to damage reputation more generally and the action that can be taken to make sure that this does not happen to a business will be looked at.

Defamation – the two best known cases 5.2

The two best known cases on Internet defamation in the UK – *Western Provident Association v Norwich Union (1997, unreported)* and *Godfrey v Demon Internet Ltd [1999] EMLR 542* – both give their names to two different types of liability

Western Provident liability 5.3

Western Provident liability is so called after the case of *Western Provident Association v Norwich Union*. The case concerns defamation on a company's intranet. It settled before reaching court and full details of the case never emerged but it arose from certain unguarded remarks about Western Provident which a Norwich Union manager circulated to a number of colleagues. Western Provident and Norwich Union were rivals and it seems the desire of the particular manager was to spread rumours of Western Provident's alleged financial difficulties – presumably for his sales force to then pass on to potential customers choosing between the two for a policy. Norwich Union agreed to pay a reported £450,000 damages to Western Provident in compensation.

The principles illustrated by *Western Provident* are also shown by another case, *Exoteric Gas Solutions and Andrew Duffieldv British Gas (1999, unreported)*, where British Gas agreed to pay the claimants £101,000. The case involved an email sent by a British Gas area manager about a former employee, Andrew Duffield, who had left to set up EGS. The email instructed British Gas staff not to have dealings with Duffield or EGS. The claimants argued that this had the effect of stifling Exoteric's entry into the market. British Gas made a payment into court to settle the action which probably brought with it a costs payment to the claimants of around £125,000.

Given the likelihood of extremely high damages awards in this type of case, companies must keep their employment terms and the guidance it gives employees under review (see **CHAPTER THREE – EMPLOYEE-RELATED RISK (3.6)**).

Godfrey v Demon liability 5.4

Another defamation case emerged in *Godfrey v Demon Internet Ltd* which concerned an Internet Service Provider's (ISP) liability for defamatory material in newsgroups. The case concerned defamatory statements made in a newsgroup about a university lecturer. Dr Godfrey complained to Demon about an anonymous message about him (which pretended to come from him) posted on an online news group on the Demon network in January 1997. Dr Godfrey complained that the message was defamatory but Demon ignored his request to have it wiped from its server. At a preliminary hearing Morland J ruled that it was an ISP's responsibility to control the information transmitted through its servers. The defence of innocent dissemination, under *section 1* of the *Defamation Act 1996*, used by bookshops and printers was not available to ISPs if they were aware that the messages they were transmitting were libellous. The case was settled in Dr Godfrey's favour shortly before it came to court for a full trial, but with the publicity surrounding the case another Demon case came to light – *Demon Internet Ltd and Clifford Martin Stanford v Neil McRae [1996, unreported]*. In this case, Demon successfully sued a newsgroup user for a defamatory posting about the company in its UK legal newsgroup. McRae was a former Demon employee and he posted an apology for his comments the day after they appeared. Demon still pursued him and issued proceedings against him, according to the BBC Online report of the case, four days later. McRae did not contest the proceedings and Demon obtained judgment in default and an injunction preventing McRae from repeating his comments.

Whilst cases like this will be decided differently after new Europe-wide legislation aimed at protecting ISPs, *Godfrey v Demon* still highlights the issues involved.

Defamation actions on the increase   5.5

Since these two cases there has been a rise in defamation cases in Europe and an increasing trend for consumers to bring actions themselves. Cases like the Friends Reunited case in the UK and the David Trimble action against Amazon provide ample evidence. The Trimble case *(Rt Hon David Trimble MP v amazon.co.uk Ltd (2002, unreported)* was the second libel action brought by David Trimble against online bookseller Amazon over Amazon's offering for sale of a book on political assassination in Northern Ireland by Sean McPhilemy. Trimble first sued Amazon in 1999 following sales to UK customers from the amazon.com site. amazon.co.uk had already delisted the book. Trimble then successfully sued Amazon for libel for a second time. According to the evidence Trimble put before the court the book, which was published in the US, contained allegations against Trimble which McPhilemy subsequently withdrew. Amazon's website carried reviews of the book, written by UK customers, some of which repeated the libellous suggestions. In November 2000, Trimble's first libel action was settled on payment of undisclosed damages. However, it was said that before the settlement could be announced in court Trimble discovered that Amazon was again selling the book on its site and publishing customer reviews which repeated the allegations. Amazon undertook in court not to sell the book again and to pay additional damages. Amazon said that it had not been aware of the contents of the book or the defamatory nature of the customer comments before Mr Trimble's first complaint. It said it was impossible for Amazon to be aware of the content of each of the 1.5 million books it distributed. It assured Trimble that 'this was not deliberate and was the result of an administrative error'.

In the Friends Reunited case (unreported), a posting on a school reminiscences site which proved to be inaccurate led to judgements against the person who posted it. The posting related to a former teacher who, the posting said, had had to leave the teaching profession after sexual impropriety. The teacher sued and won in the County Court. Ironically, however, the poster was himself a teacher and as well as a damages award came an investigation by his professional body into his conduct.

The question of international Internet defamation also came before the House of Lords in the UK in 2000 with the cases of *Boris Berezovsky* and *Nikolai Glouchkov – Berezovsky v Forbes Inc (No.1)*; *Glouchkov v Forbes Inc* (also known as *Berezovsky v Michaels* and *Glouchkov v Michaels [2000] 1 W.L.R. 1004)*. In these cases both of the claimants were Russian and complained of the publication of defamatory material in a US publication which circulated in England. The Lords decided that the claimants' right to sue did not arise solely in the country where the libel originated, but could arise in any jurisdiction where the claimants had a connection and reputation to uphold. Accordingly, the English courts could entertain the action. One of the factors relied upon by *Berezovsky* and *Glouchkov* was the publication of the magazine in question on the Internet which could be accessed in the UK. Whilst the Lords did not specifically rule on this point the case is likely to bring with it what lawyers call 'forum shopping' – that is international litigants choosing the most favourable court to sue in, wherever that is in the world.

Despite the legislative changes the initial *Godfrey v Demon Internet Ltd* ruling and the Lords ruling in this case will make England and Wales the courts of choice for many. Defamation actions and other 'intellectual' litigation is probably more likely in the UK than in many other jurisdictions because of the greater white-collar profile of Internet users.

What is Cybersmearing?   5.6

Cybersmearing does what it says on the tin. It is the smearing of an individual or company online. Cybersmearing can take a number of different forms, including websites, message boards, email and auctions. Each of these will be looked at in turn, but first a case that is a little more light hearted than most might illustrate the issues.

Back in May 2001, the Irish courts heard their first cybersmearing case when an Irish businessman, Frances Kenny, was convicted for malicious publication of a defamatory libel under the *Irish Defamation Act 1961*. Kenny ran a sandwich business in Castlerea, Co Mayo, as did his business rival Maureen Walker.

Kenny posted Walker's details on a website which advertised for escorts and prostitutes as he believed that she was taking his business. The advert placed was headed 'Exclusive Maureen' and included details of the services that Walker would provide, including something described as 'water games'. In evidence, Walker said that she had received over 100 phone calls in the first two days alone – positive proof perhaps that Internet advertising can work. The explanation for the calls came to light when one of the callers had not withheld his number. Walker called him back and persuaded him to tell her how he came by her. At this stage the police became involved and Kenny admitted his actions. His offer of 10,000 Irish pounds in compensation was rejected by the judge as 'totally inadequate'.

There have been a number of cases on both sides of the Atlantic which show that this type of practice is not uncommon and we have also seen the catastrophic effect cybersmearing a company can have on its share price. Cybersmearing takes many forms but amongst them are the following.

Cybersmearing by website   5.7

The oldest form of cybersmearing was to set up a website pretending to be that of the company that a person wanted to defame. The trend started around eight years ago but as businesses have become better at protecting their own trading and brand names as domain names, cybersmearing by site has become more sophisticated. The issues around domain names are discussed in **5.24**.

There are a whole host of motives for cybersmearing but many of the dedicated cybersmearing sites are set up to advance a particular political cause, such as attacking a company for the way in which it allegedly exploits child labour overseas, is providing tools used for war or the way in which it has handled a particular industrial dispute. This type of cybersmearing is not just confined to the technically able, for example a site was set up by two truck drivers who were effectively trying to encourage their fellow drivers to work to rule or walk out and the 'evidence' relating to the unofficial industrial dispute was shown on the site. This illustrates another point. It is not just companies that have an Internet presence that are vulnerable, in fact, the reverse is often true. Because the company in the example above did not have a meaningful Internet presence, it was easy for the drivers' site to get significant prominence on the Internet to the extent that in some search engines the site about the dispute ranked more highly than the company's official Internet presence.

Cybersmearing by site can take a sinister form as in the case of *Marks & Spencer Plc v Craig Cottrell (2001) 24(7) I.P.D. 24046*. In this case, the High Court heard that Cottrell registered nine common mistypes of the Marks & Spencer domain name including Marks&Spencers.com. He copied the legitimate Marks & Spencer site onto his server but instead of the payment mechanism he told people that there was a software problem with the site and he told them to email their credit card details. When Cottrell's computer was seized there was evidence that over 80 people had done this. After prolonged court proceedings Marks & Spencer was successful in getting a court order to transfer the domain names back to it and in having a prison sentence for contempt of court passed against Cottrell.

Cybersmearing by email   5.8

Perhaps the most well known case – *Intel v Hamidi*, is still rumbling through the US courts more than two years after being issued. The case involved an ex-employee of Intel sending six separate emails to up to 35,000 Intel employees after he left.

In August 2001, there was an extreme case of cybersmearing by email in the education sector when a former student with a grudge spread false information that the director of a local education authority was a member of the Ku Klux Klan, that another director was openly homophobic and that the institution's General Counsel and his team were neo-Nazis. The complaints resulted in an investigation lasting almost a year at the end of which all three were cleared. A detailed programme of harassment against some of the institution's officials started soon after. This included:

- A former employee who changed job was accused of being a member of the Ku Klux Klan and hate letters signed with his name were sent to the newspapers and churches in his new home town.

- A bill was sent to the office of one of the lawyers demanding payment for a number of unpleasant medical procedures.

- Email messages were sent to a Jewish group to antagonise them, supposedly signed by one of the lawyers and concluding with his home phone number.

The tools for this type of attack are readily available. In some of the cases, the attacks have only needed one member of staff to leave his or her office with the computer still logged on for the cybersmearer to send emails as if from that person. Clearly this requires no technical knowledge and less than two minutes at the keyboard thus making it difficult to trace the culprit.

Cybersmearing by a message board   5.9

Another US case – the *Varian Associates v Delfino and Day* case – involving around 14,000 postings on a hundred different message boards is also still continuing. In these messages, Delfino and Day falsely accused various members of Varian management of being homophobic, discriminating against the pregnant, having sexual liaisons and secretly video taping employees whilst in the bathrooms. Varian estimated that the loss through Delfino and Day's activities was just over £530,000.

August 2002 saw another case – the $699 million claim case in Texas concerned an allegation by a rival credit card processor, ZixIt, against Visa over 437 message board postings made by one of Visa's Vice Presidents on a Yahoo! message board relating to ZixIt's stock (there is more detail on the ZixIt case in CHAPTER ONE – SECURITY – WHY BOTHER? (1.9)).

Both cases remind us all that executives in an organisation need to be told, via a company's acceptable use policy, that disparaging rivals, or indeed commenting on the organisation's own performance, however well intentioned, will not be tolerated (see CHAPTER THREE).

The latter point was reinforced by another case in February 2003 with another large action against former employees, this time brought by US-based credit card company Metris against two former employees, Bryan Williams and Ken Corbin. Metris alleged that Williams and Corbin posted defamatory and misleading messages about it and its former CEO, Ronald Zebeck, on Internet message boards. The case alleged that the employees used anonymous user names to obscure their identities and give the impression that they were privy to inside information.

Metris claimed that as the result of the postings it lost revenue, income, investors, customers and relationships with business prospects. Unspecified damages were sought. It also stated that the messages were posted to bring Zebeck and Metris into 'disrepute with the domestic and international business and investment communities'. Metris parted company with Zebeck after the postings. Interestingly, Williams is also accused of being a skilled polyglot having supposedly posted messages in English, French, German, Norwegian, Italian and Portuguese. The case continues.

The cases are not just limited to the US. In February 2004, the Canadian courts looked at the case of *Vaquero Energy and Waldner v Nick Weir*. The case concerned a financial message board known as Stockgroup and Vaquero, an oil and gas company in Calgary. Waldner was Vaquero's CEO hired to consolidate the business. In 2002, Waldner became aware of a number of messages on Stockgroup's site from two anonymous posters which accused Waldner of being 'insane, retarded, managing the company for his own benefit' and compared him to Osama bin Laden, Hitler and Saddam Hussein. Forty-eight messages were discovered which had been sent over a four-month period.

The messages were eventually traced back to Weir who had spoken to Waldner a couple of times and had written to ask for a place on Vaquero's board. Proceedings were served on Weir and the postings stopped the day they were served. Weir then started a class action lawsuit against the company. Weir said the messages were not his but the court heard detailed evidence against him, including evidence related to IP addresses and the use by both of the anonymous posters of 123456 as their password.

The judge found Weir liable for defamation. She said that there was no evidence of financial damage to Vaquero and ordered Weir to pay it 10,000 Canadian dollars. The messages directed at Waldner had caused him real concern and he was awarded 40,000 Canadian dollars in damages. Punitive damages were also awarded of 25,000 Canadian dollars.

Closer to home, the Court of Appeal heard details in December 2001 of a case involving message board postings in the UK. In that case, *Totalise plc v The Motley Fool Ltd and Interactive Investor Ltd [2002] 1 WLR 1233*. Totalise complained about anonymous postings left on message boards operated by Motley Fool and Interactive Investor. Both provided forums where users could anonymously exchange information about companies and their stocks and shares. One of the users, registered under the name Zeddust, posted defamatory comments about Totalise. Totalise said it wanted to sue Zeddust but could not until it knew his true identity. Motley Fool and Interactive Investor refused to provide these details but the Court of Appeal ordered them to saying that the comments could cause extensive damage to Totalise.

Incidents of cybersmearing by message board are happening every day. Large message board hosts which take their legal liabilities seriously are now often asking specialised moderators to monitor message boards or chatrooms (where the same issues can occur). To give an idea of the scale of the problem perhaps the best known specialist moderator in the UK, Chat Moderators, uses human moderators to read about 30,000 comments every day working in seven different languages across Europe. Many providers of chatrooms and message boards are clearly taking their potential liability seriously and brand owners should be equally assiduous in looking at what is being said on message boards about them.

Cybersmearing via other means   5.10

One of the great features of the Enron debacle has been the role that the Internet has played. Message boards were full of Enron-related information both before and after its collapse. It is undoubtedly the case that part of Enron's climb to the dizzy heights of its share price was due to small investors on message boards significantly over valuing the company and its prospects. It is also true that its fall has been accelerated by message board postings, but one of the more interesting aspects of the cybersmearing of Enron has been the role that auction sites like eBay have played in its collapse. Traditionally, the disaffected have used message boards and, perhaps, dedicated websites to hasten a company's demise or simply just to hit its share price so that their former bosses who generally have significant stock options and whose pay is linked to share price will suffer.

In Enron, however, some employees saw that as well as having their former bosses suffer, they could profit by selling what they knew and what they had accumulated with a news hungry audience online. One auction site alone at the time of the Enron collapse had over 1200 Enron-related items for sale, including confidential memos, letters, internal Enron procedures and more mundane items such as golf balls with the Enron logo and words like 'integrity counts' stamped on them. In particular, one of the memos that seemed to hasten recategorisation of Enron from a collapse to a scandal seems to have been purchased by a newspaper from one such auction site – some of the material was going for as little as $150, a small price to pay for a worldwide scoop.

In January 2003, this trend continued in a case brought by Robert Grace, the publisher of a Los Angeles legal newspaper, against the auction site eBay and an eBay user, Tim Neeley. Grace claimed that Neeley used the buyer feedback function of eBay to smear him and that Neeley and eBay refused to remove the comments when asked. According to Grace, Neeley's reply was simply 'get a life, dude'. Grace's action, which is still ongoing, seeks damages of $2.5 million from eBay and $100,000 from Neeley for the harm done to him.

Cybersmearing then is clearly on the increase. There have been many incidents at home and abroad. For obvious reasons incidents in the UK attract little publicity with victims being anxious to sweep the issue under the carpet away from the gaze of publicity. Make no mistake, however, incidents like these are happening every day on this side of the Atlantic too.

Search engines   5.11

Search engines work in mysterious ways. There are whole sites (like searchenginewatch.com) devoted to them and to the complex algorithms which they use. Most search engines use some or all of the following to rank sites when searching:

- the text on the web pages;
- the metatags on the site (which are explained below); and
- the site's popularity.

When a website is prepared it is common for the website owner to 'submit' the site to search engines. How he or she does this and how many sites he or she submits to will vary. When contracting with a website designer or a third party, or asking an employee to do search engine submissions, a company should make sure that it knows exactly what it is doing. There are several scams, usually via unsolicited email, promising Top 10 search engine ratings in all of the popular search engines. Guarantees like this are usually worthless. Proper due diligence on the outfit making the submissions should be undertaken and before relying on them guarantees should be put down in writing and made enforceable.

Once the search engine receives a submission it will visit the site using 'spiders' or 'robots' to crawl over the site extracting relevant key words. Most search engines will then store these key words in their databases cross-referencing the word to your site.

Metatags are used in a similar way. A metatag is essentially a signpost hidden in the source code of a web page which directs search engines to the site. Metatags are usually lists of key words which are relevant to the business so, for example, with a law firm the metatags might include the words 'law', 'professional' and 'Europe'.

Search engines generally measure popularity by looking at the number of other sites which link to that site. It is possible to do a reverse link check to see who is linking to a site. It is a useful exercise both to see how each search engine is scoring the site but also as this can quite often be the first signal that someone is about to abuse the site, for example some phising scams will link to the genuine site to add credibility.

What are the legal issues with metatagging? 5.12

Some businesses have been tempted to use their metatags to bring traffic to their site from competitors or use the trademarks of other companies to lead to sales. Many specialist lawyers have always advised against this and the UK's first case on metatagging shows that the courts do not like it either.

In the case of *Roadtech Computer Systems Ltd v Mandata (Management and Data Services) Ltd [2000] ETMR 970* in 2000, the High Court had to decide whether Mandata was entitled to use Roadtech's trademarks as metatags for its website. Roadtech had sued Mandata for doing this but Mandata applied to the court to dismiss the case before a trial as it said the case was 'unwinnable' and a waste of the court's time. In turn, Roadtech applied to the court for judgment before trial on the basis of admissions which it said Mandata had made.

The Master who heard the case (the equivalent of a District Judge) said that the case should not be struck out as Mandata had not replied properly to Roadtech's initial complaint about what it was doing. He also decided that Roadtech was entitled to judgment and ordered Mandata to pay it £15,000 for the metatag infringement.

More recently the UK courts have been grappling with metatag issues in the case of *Reed Executive Plc and Another v Reed Business Information Limited and Others [2004] EWCA Civ 159.* The case concerned the use by Reed Business Information Limited of the word 'Reed' on its website totaljobs.com as a metatag. Trademarks in the UK have to be registered in one of a number of different classes of goods and services. Reed had been registered as a trademark for employment agency services by Reed Executive Plc. Totaljobs.com was a recruitment website run by Reed Business Information Limited, which contained the word Reed both as part of its copyright notice and in metatags.

The court which heard the case initially decided that the unauthorised use of the trademark Reed in the metatags amounted to trademark infringement and passing off, even though the use of the trademark was initially invisible to the public. This decision was appealed on a number of grounds, including the issue of whether or not use of a trademark as part of a metatag constituted trademark infringement.

The Court of Appeal rejected the High Court's decision that the use of the metatag constituted passing off. In all cases where TotalJobs was listed when a search for Reed jobs was made, TotalJobs appeared below the Reed employment website in the results. The Court of Appeal held that there could be no passing off as no one was likely to be misled and no misrepresentation had taken place. This applied whether or not the metatags were visible.

The Court of Appeal's judgment went into some detail in considering whether or not the use of the word Reed as a metatag constituted trademark infringement. Consideration was given to the fact that frequently metatags are invisible to the end user. However, sometimes the metatags might be translated into physical text in the search engine result page. The court decided that there was no trademark infringement as there was simply no confusion. Causing a site to appear in a search result, without anything else happening, does not suggest any connection with anyone else. However, the court reserved its opinion in relation to another type of trademark infringement which deals with trademarks which are identical when the goods and services are also identical. The court said since the services were not identical this type of trademark infringement was irrelevant.

The case would suggest that in the latter type of case – where the goods or services and the trademark are identical – trademark infringement might be found by use of a metatag. The courts are likely to want to look at all of the circumstances of a case and especially the likelihood of the public being misled. The intentions of the alleged infringer will also be of relevance.

Every organisation needs to take a look at the metatags on its website. Often, when the metatags on a company's site are revealed, they show use of their competitors' trademarks in their metatags unlawfully. This has frequently been done without the company's knowledge. It is a sensible precaution for a company to review the metatags on its site and remove any which could be infringements. This exercise should not just be limited to trademarks, however, there maybe other words used in metatags which could be misleading or unlawful and these need to be removed too. Metatag litigation is likely to increase significantly in the next twelve months and the penalties for people who use another firm's trademarks as their metatags could be great.

Why is paid for placement an issue?   5.13

With many search engines cash can also influence their search results. Paid for search engines are on the increase all over the world with some of the larger search engines announcing a move to paid for listings. Major brand owners are becoming increasingly concerned by the practice. The problems are likely to magnify with the acquisition by Overture (one of the leading paid for placement search engines) of the former US search engine of choice Alta Vista. Its subsequent acquisition by Yahoo! is likely to lead to an undiluted Overture listing appearing on both of those search engines. As a sign of the speed with which this sector has grown a recent job advertisement for Overture said it had 'grown from inception in 1997 to revenues over $1 billion in 2003'.

What is paid for placement?   5.14

Paid for placement is the practice of asking for payment for either an enhanced search engine listing or for a listing of any kind. Whilst the method they use to work (and the terms used to describe the practice) vary a search engine may, for example, auction the top five places in a search for any given word with buyers paying something over fifty pence a click to rank in the top five for a well known trademark. Rankings from six onwards would appear with no money changing hands just as most search engines did in the golden days prior to 2002. Search engines which sell listings include US-based Overture and the UK search engine e-spotting. Neither are that well known in the UK – a survey by research consultancy Jupiter MMXI in March 2002 showed reach amongst home users in the UK for Overture of only 3.4 per cent and for e-spotting of 1.8 per cent. So why the problem? All of this is a concern as the results from paid for search engines are likely to influence the majority of UK searches given that listings are effectively bought through the back door in most other search engines. Overture and e-spotting, for example, reportedly supply their results to other search engines including AltaVista, AOL Search, Lycos, HotBot, Netscape Search, msn and Ask Jeeves. Concern has increased since Google, the search engine of choice for many, started its own paid for placement offering Google AdWords in November 2002. These search engines combined dominate – a survey by OneStat in October 2002 showed that 68 per cent of all Internet shopping traffic came via AOL, Google and msn alone whilst another survey by WebSideStory in December 2003 showed those same search engines as being responsible for 67 per cent of all searches. Their power is still on the increase.

The most common business model, and that adopted by both Overture and e-spotting, involves a form of auction with the highest bid per click through winning. So, for example, the search term 'Vodafone' might be sold in a virtual auction at 97p per click to rank first in a search, 94p per click for second place and so on. Just as a good auctioneer encourages participants in the auction to 'bid up', paid for placement sellers use sophisticated software (not unlike that used on eBay) to tell bidders when their last bid has been trumped and, in most cases, to automatically bid up for them up to an agreed ceiling.

Search engine litigation so far   5.15

Search engines have been the subject of litigation in Germany and the US over the way in which adverts appear when a search is returned. The increase in paid for search engines is likely to bring with it more litigation and more dangers for brand owners. In the US the maker of a range of diet products called Body Solution started proceedings against four search engines in a Texas court for auctioning rankings for its brand name to its rivals. It reportedly asked for $10 million in actual damages and $100 million in punitive damages from each company. The company described the practice of paid for placement as 'tantamount to extortion and Internet piracy where trade-marks are involved'. It claimed trademark infringement and dilution, unfair competition and violations of a specific Texas code of commerce.

The practice has also attracted regulatory interest in the US with a complaint being made to the Federal Trade Commission (FTC). The US pressure group, Commercial Alert, filed a deceptive advertising complaint with the FTC against eight major search engines for placing adverts in search engine results. The complaint said that the search engines violate Federal prohibitions against deceptive acts or practices by inserting advertisements in search engine results 'without clear and conspicuous disclosure that the ads are ads'. It goes on to say that this concealment may mislead search engine users to believe that search results are based on relevancy alone. It says that paid for placement is:

'advertising that is outside of the editorial content of the search results, sometimes above or below the editorial content, or in a sidebar.'

It also attacks paid inclusion, which it calls:

'advertising within the editorial content of the search results, though it does not necessarily guarantee a certain position within the results',

and paid submission:

'the practice of requiring payment to speed up the processing of a listing, though it rarely guarantees that a site will in fact be listed by the search engine.'

The complaint is said to seek to protect children and teenagers, in particular saying that they:

'may have limited cognitive abilities and an incomplete understanding of the purpose of advertising. They especially are likely to be deceived by the failure to disclose that listings are paid ads.'

The FTC has also been active on its own account. In June 2002 it issued guidelines about how search engines should disclosure paid content, but a survey by Search Engine Watch after the FTC guidance showed that these guidelines are frequently breached. Both the Body Solution case and the FTC activity are still rumbling on.

AdWords   5.16

More or less the same issues apply with AdWords as with paid for placement. AdWords is an advertising system on the Google search engine which services up advertisements usually on the right hand column of the search results page. The adverts do not appear at random but rather relate in the main to key words in the search itself, for example if searching for 'Ford car Europe' the adverts on the right hand side of the page (as opposed to the search results themselves which will likely appear on the left) will relate to the search and will advertise the sites of people who have 'bought' those key word searches from Google.

At first blush AdWords are not as big a problem as paid for rankings as generally speaking they will be easier to distinguish from the actual search results. Recent litigation in the US and in France has shown the potential issues here too however.

The French case – *Viaticum and Luteciel v Google France (2003)* concerned an Internet travel agency (Viaticum) and a company which managed its site (Luteciel). Both Viaticum and Luteciel hold a number of trademarks including 'bourse de vols' (flight market) and 'bourse des voyage' (travel market). Google sold these search terms as keywords and as a result adverts appeared in the right hand column of search results pages when these terms were searched advertising competitors of Viaticum. Viaticum complained to Google (and incidentally also complained about paid for placement practices eventually settling these disputes with Overture and e-spotting). Google refused settlement and Viaticum and Luteciel issued proceedings in court in Nanterre. As well as arguing trademark infringement it asked the court to decide that Google was guilty of misleading advertising and unfair competition, arguments that are much less likely in the UK.

The court decided that Google France had infringed the trademarks. It rejected Google France's argument that technically its parent company Google, Inc was responsible rather than it. The court decided that Google set up its system to maximise its revenues by the type of matching it offered but said that Viaticum and Luteciel should not suffer for this. Google France was ordered to pay just under £50,000 for its actions plus costs. It was also ordered to remove the links or pay a further £1,045 for each infringement if they remained. It is reported that Google France is currently appealing this decision but nonetheless the decision, which might well be followed by a UK court, shows that the courts are likely also to decide that AdWords can also infringe trademark rights.

In June 2004, the Advertising Standards Commission (ASA) in the UK announced its adjudication of a complaint against Freeserve plc relating to its use of paid for placement.

Freeserve used a search engine powered by results from Overture (see **5.13**). The complainant, Andrew Ellam, MD of a web design company, objected that the search results summary did not make clear that the results included paid for placements and that they were ranked according to the amount of money sponsors paid, not according to their relevance to the search term. Ellam said that he had created around 25,000 websites for small businesses, individuals and charities and that his customers were being pushed to the back of the queue by paid for advertising.

In reply, Freeserve said that it marked the search results being delivered by Overture by a hyperlink at the foot of each sponsored search result. It said that clicking on the hyperlink opened a pop-up box explaining that Overture ranked the search results by the amount each advertiser bid for inclusion in the search. It said, in addition, that the most relevant result always appeared first. Freeserve said it did not believe its website was misleading or its search results were less relevant simply because it showed paid for links first.

The ASA considered that consumers were unlikely to realise that the Overture hyperlink indicated that results were paid for and concluded that consumers could be misled. It asked Freeserve to ensure that paid for links were clearly identified in future.

Ellam said that he now wants the ASA to investigate a number of other search engines and it seems that more ASA activity in this area might follow.

What can be done? 5.17

It is important to stress that there is a distinction to be made between places in a search engine auction and a company not appearing high up in the ranking because its search engine submissions have not been done properly. Every brand owner should conduct regular searches of major search engines to look at its rankings, whether the search engines are taking money to influence the results, whether third parties are influencing the results (for example, by using metatags unlawfully to divert traffic) and what, if any, improvement is needed. Search engine submission is still an involved science and some cases where a company suspects paid for placement have in fact been more easily explained by a poor submission strategy.

If paid for placement is happening there may be a number of options worth exploring.

I. Ask the engine 5.18

In some cases it may be worthwhile to look at the terms and conditions under which listings are sold. Overture's terms include for example:

'ADVERTISER'S RIGHTS AND RESPONSIBILITIES: (a) Advertiser Submissions: *... You represent and warrant that all information, in the listing itself or through the Web site to which the listing links, (i) does not violate any law or regulation; (ii) does not infringe in any manner any copyright, patent, trademark, trade secret or other intellectual property right of any third party; (iii) does not breach any duty toward or rights of any person or entity including, without limitation, rights of publicity or privacy, or has not otherwise resulted in any consumer fraud, product liability, tort, breach of contract, injury, damage or harm of any kind to any person or entity; (iv) is not false or misleading; and/or (v) is neither defamatory, libellous, slanderous or threatening. **. (c) Communications: You agree that regardless of where your listings appear in the Overture Distribution Network, you will direct any communication regarding your listings, your account, the Overture Marketplace or the Overture Marketplace Results directly to Overture and not to any other entity in the Overture Distribution Network.'

2. Monitor Internet activity   5.19

It is important to monitor sites with high rankings in case they have a plan to take away custom or cybersmear. Link popularity checks should be run to see if a concerted strategy is in place. Metatags might also hold other clues.

3. Threaten litigation   5.20

Possible litigation could take a number of forms but there is a need to exercise care and look at each case individually. In some jurisdictions, including the UK, the issuing of a threat to take action in these circumstances could be actionable and US brand owners, including Prince, have already fallen foul of this legislation. It could be wise to explore issues like trademark infringement, passing off, unfair competition rules (for example, in Germany or the Netherlands) as well as more obscure legal remedies.

4. File a complaint with the FTC and other relevant bodies   5.21

As already stated, the FTC is involved in this area and the ASA has recently acted in this area. If the use of paid for placement deceives then other authorities like trading standards in the UK might be interested. Whilst the supporters of paid for placement point to a number of reasons why their results are more reliable than other search engines, it seems clear that for some brand owners paid for placement will be just another of the headaches the Internet brings them. Like many before, however, the trend cannot be ignored and brand owners and their lawyers will need to be vigilant in the coming months as its influence is felt.

Copyright and hotlinking

Background   **5.22**

The first Internet case in the UK – *Shetland Times v Dr Jonathan Wills and Zet News Limited (1996) ITCLR 49* – dealt with a website owner's liability for hotlinking under copyright law. The case concerned two rival news providers on Shetland. The Shetland News, run by Dr Jonathan Wills, increased its news coverage by hotlinking its site to the online news stories of the Shetland Times. The Shetland Times objected and an interdict (the Scottish equivalent of an injunction) was granted. The case settled before the final hearing and Shetland News agreed to put wording on its site when it linked. The agreed wording was:

> 'each link to an individual story shall be acknowledged by the legend "a Shetland Times story" appearing under each headline and of the same or similar size as the headline.'

In the Internet industry this wording has become known as a Shetland Times rider. Cases in Germany, Sweden and the US have also shown the potential liability on website owners for the content of sites they link to. In Germany, an MEP was prosecuted because criminal offences were committed by a site she linked to from her home page. There have also been similar copyright infringement cases on MP3 downloads in Sweden and the US and on photographs copied in breach of copyright in the US.

Additional problems with copyright are highlighted by the American case of Tasini. The Tasini case concerned freelance journalists who had been commissioned to write articles for a paper-based periodical. The contract said nothing about electronic reuse but the articles were reprinted on an Internet site and on CD ROM. The US courts held this to be an infringement of the author's copyright. Whilst this is a US case it is likely that the same reasoning would be followed in the UK. As a result, if work is commissioned that is to be republished digitally, a company should make sure that the terms of reference with the photographer, freelance author or designer allow it to do what it would like to do with the resulting work. Ideally, a company should look for a transfer of the intellectual property rights in the commissioned work to it.

What can be done?   **5.23**

Companies need to control the number of sites they link to. They need a proper linking protocol with procedures in place which must be followed before a link is added to their website. They then need to monitor that protocol. For some companies the scope of their potential liability is amazing. For example, one site had 5343 separate company's websites linked from just one page. No attempt was made to try and exclude liability for any of the sites linked from those pages, nor was it said that no recommendations were to be implied by the fact that the companies listed were linked from the site.

As a minimum a linking policy should include the following:

- A requirement that a proper business case analysis is undertaken before a link is put in place. This would include a thorough investigation into the content of the recipient site and, where necessary, the links that that site linked to in turn. In high risk cases a legal audit could be insisted on, perhaps at the link recipient's expense.

- A linking agreement should include an undertaking from the recipient to give, say, 48 hours prior notice of a material change in its site. It could put out proposed changes on a non-public server to allow a company the opportunity to review the changed site and decide whether to withdraw the link.

- There should also be an auditing system in place to ensure that the policy is being enforced. This may involve, for example, designating one member of staff to review sites that are linked to on a systematic basis and document the fact that those checks have taken place. There needs to be proof that it has a proper policy in place and that that policy is believed.

As far as Tasini type liability is concerned a simple form should be prepared for authors to sign consenting to their materials being reprinted in this way.

Domain names and trademarks

A short history of domain name litigation   5.24

This is probably the area of Internet activity which has occupied the courts the most. The first case, *Harrods v Network Services and Others (1996, BACFI Bulletin July 1998, 'Trade Marks and Domain Name Disputes', p 11)*, concerned trademarks and the Harrods.com domain registered in the US. Harrods already used the harrods.co.uk domain name but said that its trademark registrations entitled it to the harrods.com name too instead of the defendants who had registered the name first as a.com name but without an entitlement to use it. The courts followed a pre-Internet case concerning company names in deciding that Harrods was right and entitled to the.com name. The Harrods case was effectively the first round in the battle against cybersquatters, a battle which has continued since.

Pitman Training Limited v Nominet UK and Pearson Professional Ltd [1997–98] Info. T.L.R. 177 concerned a trademark owner's rights to a domain name and the actions of the domain name regulation authorities. Here, the battle was between two companies, which it is simplest to refer to as Pitman Publishing and Pitman Training. Each had traded as Pitman for many years but they were no longer connected. Pitman Publishing registered pitman.co.uk with Nominet on 21 February 1996 but only made limited use of it. On 15 March 1996, Pitman Training applied to Nominet for the same name and Nominet granted it. Pitman Training used it widely and Pitman Publishing found out what had happened and complained. Nominet returned the domain name to Pitman Publishing on 7 April 1997. Pitman Training sued and obtained an injunction and at the full hearing put its case on the basis of passing off and/or wrongful interference with the contract. The injunctions were discharged at the third interlocutory hearing, the passing off case failing because the judge (Sir Richard Scott) did not feel that there was enough evidence to support passing off (there had been only two email responses to its advertisements) or the contractual claim because, in his opinion, there was no contract between Pitman Training and Nominet.

Since Pitman there have been other cases, including *Prince plc v Prince Sports Group Inc [1998] FSR 21*. Here, Neuberger J effectively decided that whilst the US sports company Prince held US trademarks in its name it could not prevent the UK computer company Prince plc from using prince.com as its domain name. The court decided that Prince Sports had unlawfully threatened Prince plc entitling the UK company to damages.

The most authoritative case on domain names was an attempt by Deputy Judge Jonathan Sumption QC to have a definitive look at the law in this area. The case was appealed to the Court of Appeal and is the precedent most lawyers involved in this area of the law use as the benchmark. In *Marks & Spencer plc and others v One in a Million Ltd and others [1998] FSR 265*, a number of leading companies, including Marks & Spencer plc, Ladbrokes plc, J. Sainsbury plc, Virgin Enterprises Ltd and BT, got together to sue for the return of their domain names. They effectively wanted to clamp down on the sale of Internet domain names and sought injunctions against the defendants (which were registering and offering names for sale), as well as orders for the return of the names and costs. They sued for trademark infringement and passing off. Judgment was granted in the companies' favour in the High Court in November 1997 and the defendants took the case to the Court of Appeal in 1998. The appeal was dismissed. One of the judges, Lord Justice Aldous, said that the domain names:

'were registered to take advantage of the distinctive character and reputation of the marks. That is unfair and detrimental.'

In some respects the Court of Appeal also went further than the judge did in the original trial, notably the decision that in some circumstances the court could grant injunctions against the threat of passing off by registration of a rogue domain name, rather than being able only to grant relief after its use. Additionally, the same judge held that the rogue names were 'instruments of fraud'. He laid down a test to be applied and said that provided that the test is satisfied (essentially intention to appropriate the goodwill of another), an injunction will result. The finding of infringement of the registered trademarks was also upheld. The defendants were ordered in the High Court to pay £65,000 in costs as well as transferring the rogue names over. The case highlights the fact that the courts are prepared to grasp the issues of domain name protection and grant relief. It also puts an end to the view of some in the Internet industry that 'first come first served' is the rule for registration.

A case that came before Mr Justice Rattee after the *One in a Million* case gives another interesting illustration of how the law will be applied. In this case, *French Connection Limited v Sutton (t/a Teleconexus Email [2000] E.T.M.R. 341*, French

Connection sued Sutton for infringement of its registered trademark FCUK and passing off by the defendant's registration of the domain name fcuk.com. French Connection had an extensive advertising campaign from February 1997 using its trademark and in April 1997 Sutton, a self-employed Internet consultant, registered the domain name, the subject of this dispute. French Connection argued, following the *One in a Million case*, that it should be entitled to judgment against Sutton without a full hearing. It argued that Sutton did not have any real defence as FCUK was a household name associated with it. It also said that Sutton had registered the domain name as a means of extorting money from it. Sutton argued that the trademark was a well known alternative to the use of a swear word on the Internet and a means of getting round programmes like Net Nanny which filter out obscene words. He said that he had registered the name to give some sort of kudos to his Internet business and to attract people searching the Internet for pornography. He argued that as a result there was no misrepresentation necessary for French Connection to make out a claim for passing off. The judge only had to work out whether, on the evidence before him, Sutton had no real prospect of successfully defending the claim in passing off. The judge said that the Sutton's arguments were sufficient to allow the matter to go for full trial. He said that Sutton's website consisted of nothing that was remotely similar to French Connection's business as its business consisted of selling clothes and Sutton's website concerned Internet and email consultancy. As a result, French Connection had not established any likelihood of confusion and there was no evidence of actual or likely damage. French Connection's action was dismissed with costs.

Another domain name case has been said by some to illustrate the lengths some people will go to try and make money out of cybersquatting. The case of *WH Smith v Peter Colman trading as Cherished Domains [2001] FSR 9* came before the Court of Appeal in March 2000. Coleman had registered whsmith.com as an Internet domain name and WH Smith sought its return. In the course of putting evidence in the case, Colman referred to a without prejudice letter and he argued that he had transferred the name to a company registered in the Bahamas known as Fernhead and that Fernhead had assigned the name to a private individual called William Harold Smith. WH Smith Limited said that the evidence should remain with the court as Mr Colman had been guilty of 'unambiguous impropriety' and he shouldn't have the benefit of a without prejudice letter. The Court of Appeal said that the letter itself was six pages long and could be described as 'disingenuous, rambling and unrealistic'. It said, however, that it did show that Colman had been trying to settle the case with WH Smith Limited and because there was no evidence of 'unambiguous impropriety', Colman had to be given the benefit of the doubt and should be able to call his letter a without prejudice letter. A similar interim hearing was called for in *Britannia Building Society v Prangley [2000] IP & T 1419* where the building society asked for early judgment against Mr Prangley who had registered BritanniaBuildingSociety.com as a domain name. Britannia owned a trademark for Britannia Building Society and wanted early judgment as it said that Mr Prangley had no real defence to its action against him. Prangley said that he was in the process of establishing a business to provide British building workers to employers in Iran and that the domain name was for that service. The court decided that this argument was not credible and, following the *One in a Million* case, it could intervene and grant an injunction against him.

Scotland has also seen cases broadly following the principles laid down in *One in a Million*. One of the cases in 2002 concerned the Scottish newspaper Business am whose publisher, Bonnier, also published content on a website at www.businessam.co.uk. He also owned another six variations of that domain. Smith was the managing director of Kestral Trading Corporation (KTC) which announced on its website that it had acquired www.businessam.com through which it intended to offer online business advisory services. Bonnier claimed that KTC had registered a further 22 related domains and brought proceedings for passing off and trademark infringement on the basis of what KTC and Smith intended to do. The courts decided that they could intervene on the basis of the threatened harm.

Reputation litigation – what will the future bring?
5.25

The litigation so far has also shown that big business is willing to use the law to protect its pre-existing rights in new media. For example, after the *One in a Million* case BT's draft press release said:

> '...this judgment, in proceedings in which BT has taken a leading role, represents a significant victory on behalf of businesses with valuable trademarks which have been the target of abusive activities by unprincipled domain name pirates and cyber-squatters who seek to take speculative advantage of the goodwill established in well known marks. It reinforces the view that domain names clearly perform a trademark function and that trademark owners can legitimately expect to have their rights protected on the Internet. The message to those who want to register domain names and avoid conflict with trade-marks is "don't imitate, differentiate".'

Following the trend employers continued to be liable for their employees' actions – in January 2003, for example, it was reported that the London law firm which was at the centre of the so-called 'Busty Blonde' email had reached an out of court settlement. The case concerned a legal secretary handing in her notice which led to the request for 'a real fit busty blonde the next time' and the comment 'she cannot be any more trouble and at least it would provide some entertainment.'

The outgoing secretary who read the email took exception and claimed for racial and sexual discrimination. She then launched formal proceedings against the firm but details of the settlement were not announced.

The attack on P2P perhaps reached its peek in March 2003 when the editor of a Swedish newspaper, Aftonbladet, was convicted because of the content of postings left on the newspaper's message board. The conviction relates to some technical problems on the message board in October 2000. Four messages, which should have been moderated, were not deleted from the message board and those messages expressed Nazi sympathies. Charges were brought against the editor for agitation against an ethnic group and he was found guilty and convicted. It would seem as if the judge decided that the posting was illegal even if the messages had appeared on the message board for only a second and had been seen by a few people.

The Dutch courts came to a similar conclusion in May 2003 when at the request of German railway operator, Deutsche Bahn, the President of the District Court of Amsterdam ordered the Dutch ISP XS4All to block two websites created by Radikal, a group of German left-wing activists.

Rise in IP litigation   5.26

In 2002 there was more IP litigation, although in some respects many of the issues in IP, like litigation over domain names, seem to have slowed in prominence as the issues become more certain. However, cases like *Reed* (see **5.12**) over metatagging and Scotland's own Bonnier case (see **5.24**) show that IP cases are still reaching court. The fact that some of the same issues are just coming round again is probably evidenced by the Danish Newsbooster case in July 2002 which has echoes of the *Shetland Times* case from some six years earlier. In the case, Newsbooster.com was a Danish online news service. It was taken to the Danish courts by the Danish Newspaper Publisher's Association (DNPA) for linking directly to the stories of rival news sites. Newsbooster enabled a person to access the latest news by offering links to the headlines on national and international Internet news sites, bypassing the home pages of the newspaper sites. The DNPA consider the use of these deep links as infringements of the individual newspaper's intellectual property rights. Deep linking was likely to affect the value of Internet banner adverts on the newspapers' sites and would cause a downturn in their advertising revenues. Newsbooster, in its defence, said that its service acts like a search engine and that users can put in keywords and are directed to articles that matched their descriptions. In summer 2001, the DNPA won a preliminary interdict against a different defendant who was also charged with infringing copyright law by deep linking. However, the defendant went bankrupt before the case went to trial. This time around the court ruled that Newsbooster was damaging the value of the newspapers' advertisements by providing specific links and that it was in direct competition with the newspapers and granted an interdict accordingly.

Copyright and hotlinking   5.27

The *Shetland Times* case (see **5.22**) concerned hotlinking and copyrighting material on the Internet. The Shetland Times objected, principally it seems, as Shetland News was bypassing the home page which provided a source of advertising revenue. The settlement reached allowed the practice to continue but with an agreed rider.

The Shetland News also agreed to attach, next to any borrowed headlines, a button showing the Shetland Times' masthead and linked to the Shetland Times' pages. Whilst we still await a definitive English ruling, it is clear from the case that copyright will have a role to play in the future development of UK Internet law. The reasoning in the case has since been followed in other jurisdictions around the world, for example in the Danish Newsbooster case in 2002 whose facts were also similar to Shetland Times (see **5.26**).

There are also other dangers with hotlinking which have not yet featured in UK cases but have been seen in litigation overseas. Courts in the US, Germany, France and Sweden have seemed willing to impose liability on a site owner for the content of the sites they link too. If a site links to another site which has copyright infringing music available for download for example, a person could be liable for the copyright infringement. This shows one of the essential dichotomies of the Internet – to make a site more attractive generally the more links the better, yet from a legal perspective with more links the potential liability increases.

Is this just limited to linking?   5.28

Copyright actions on the Internet are not simply limited to hotlinking. The vast swathe of MP3-related actions which occurred in late 2003 and the first few months of 2004 are in essence copyright actions with the music rights owners alleging that their copyright in the recordings has been infringed. Most types of copyright infringement have appeared on the Internet. One of the most significant cases occurred in Germany in June 2002 when Steffi Graf sued Microsoft Germany over fake photographs that were posted on a website which was hosted by Microsoft Germany. The pictures showed Graf's head on another woman's naked body. Graf had asked Microsoft Germany to remove the pictures and although they complied with this request, Microsoft Germany would not sign an undertaking confirming that the images would not appear again. Graf proceeded to take legal action. In a ruling in October 2001, Microsoft Germany were held responsible for the content of the sites it hosted and was ordered to comply with the undertaking. Microsoft Germany appealed this decision but the State Appeals Court in Köln (Cologne) upheld it. In another case in the UK which came before the courts again in 2004 – *Jobserve v Relational Designers Ltd and Ors (Lawtel, 27 February 2004) (unreported elsewhere)* – two of the defendants were held in contempt of court for breaching undertakings given to the court in proceedings which essentially protected the copyright in CVs, albeit by enforcing the terms of use on the website in question rather than a strict application of copyright law.

Checklist

What can be done? 5.29

Companies need to take a proper look at their online reputation. Specialist external counsel will often be part of that process. It is an unenviable task for any business to do this on top of the other day-to-day business tasks. Clever software solutions can be only part of the answer. There is now cybersmearing of one form or another almost every day. Some top tips would be:

✓ Take any incident seriously. From experience the cybersmearer usually starts with a minor attack which many companies just ignore. For many cybersmearers that is just testing the water – do nothing and the battle will commence. Respond appropriately to the initial attack and the cybersmearer might pick on easier prey instead.

✓ Terms and conditions on the site may need to be altered to tell people what they can and cannot do with content from the site, the images and trademarks – this might open the door for a criminal prosecution after any attack.

✓ Employment policies will need to be looked at as quite often cybersmearing, like security, is an inside job.

✓ Relationships with third parties, such as design agencies, need to be reviewed. Some of the more sophisticated cybersmearing attacks have been traced back to agencies and graphic designers who are aggrieved because their claims for payment have been reduced.

✓ Make sure that Internet presence works. If legitimate information about a company dominates the search engine rankings there is less chance of the cybersmearer's sites getting through.

✓ Look at monitoring, especially if customers are allowed to connect with each other online. As well as looking at monitoring and moderating in-house, consider whether it would be better to outsource either or both. There are some specialist moderating companies which may be more appropriate for the operation.

Regrettably, many companies have learned from bitter experience that in these challenging times cybersmearing can significantly hit the bottom line. As the volume of stock traded for some companies, particularly technology companies which are traditionally vulnerable to this type of attack, continues to be low then only a few panic trades after an attack can make the share price plummet – one incident where bad news was posted on an Internet site meant a stock price drop of around eight per cent in an hour.

Chapter 6
Other Communications Risks

Foreword

In the 128 years since Alexander Graham Bell first uttered the line 'Mr Watson, come here, I want you' and the 369 years since King Charles I opened the Royal Mail to the public, the world has changed almost beyond recognition and perhaps the aspect of life that has done most to facilitate this change has been communications.

Today, a plethora of means of communication exist – letter, fax, email, telephone, mobile phone, email over mobile phone – the options available to the modern business are seemingly endless. As new means of communication spring up, then new business avenues are created both in providing the communications infrastructure and in using that infrastructure to provide products and services.

However, with each opportunity comes responsibility. Businesses may be able to take advantage of technology that allows them to contact their employees anywhere in the world, but the business must ensure that the employee's life is not dominated by his or her mobile phone. Text messaging may allow businesses to contact their customers directly, but they must be careful to obtain the consent of the customer. Business must have regard when formulating their strategies to both the surrounding legal and moral position. Companies obviously must ensure that they stay within the law, but the potential for negative publicity should a company be caught doing 'something dodgy' must not be overlooked. This chapter seeks to cover both of these areas and gives a good grounding in both the risks and rewards of the different types of communications.

Introduction   6.1

This section will look at the risks involved in communication. The risks involved in fixed-line communications are generally understood and, given the relative stability of the fixed-line infrastructure in the UK, fairly easy to manage. For most people it will be m-commerce which cases the most problems. In the never-ending debate over whether m-commerce has a future, virtually everybody is missing one critical factor – whether the law in this area might already have severely restricted its growth. What is not beyond doubt is the huge success of basic m-commerce, including texting, ringtones and logos. Texting still continues to grow – UK text messaging figures for March 2004 reached 2.1 billion, an increase of nearly 80 million on February's total according to figures from the Mobile Data Association.

History is littered with ideas that seemed good at the time but perish under the weight of the associated legal problems. In the recent past, a number of e-commerce operations (such as those that sold cut-price cigarettes or contact lenses with the hope of avoiding duty) have fallen by the wayside as their legal compliance was not properly thought through. But m-commerce faces an even bigger threat as regulatory activity accelerates on both sides of the Atlantic. This chapter will look at some of the current applications of m-commerce and some of the issues involved together with some related issues for fixed-line communication.

Location-based data   6.2

One of the main opportunities for m-commerce is the provision of services linked to location. For many m-commerce operations it is the ability to accurately pinpoint a handset around the world that makes this technology so attractive. The most used examples of possible success for pure m-commerce operations, such as incentivising people to enter the restaurant they are just about to walk past, to work out their location and to find them a nearby hotel for the night or even to tell them that the attractive person standing at the other side of the bar is looking for a date, are likely to meet with regulatory disapproval.

Already in the US the picture seems confused. Whilst one regulator, the Federal Communications Commission (FCC), insists on the ability to pinpoint a caller's location as part of its regulatory regime (so that emergency calls can be effectively located), the other, the Federal Trade Commission (FTC), seemed initially to seek to ban it. The FTC called a meeting in Washington in December 2002 with the aim, according to some, of outlawing positioning altogether on privacy grounds. The FTC said that it was concerned because the technology allowed targeted, direct advertising. It could also encroach on privacy rights if people were not given the option of deciding whether they want to be targeted in that way. An outcry in the US forced the FTC to back down at the meeting and adopt a softer line saying that it had no immediate plans for regulation but had called the meeting only 'to educate the Commission about 'what's happening in this space'. The FTC said in its paper published in January 2003 that its aim was to look at m-commerce 'through the lens of consumer protection'. The FTC still says that it is looking to educate itself and that it will not look at enforcement and regulation 'in the short term'. But the spectre of action against geographical positioning remains. Clearly, given the nature of the service itself, any regulation across the Atlantic would have an impact on these shores too.

In the UK the new regime on location-based data came into force on 11 December 2003 as part of the *Privacy and Electronic Communications (EC Directive)*

Regulations 2003 (SI 2003/2426) ('the 2003 Regulations'). The 2003 regulations supplement existing rules on the handling of personal data (see **CHAPTER ONE – SECURITY – WHY BOTHER?** (**1.12**)). The rules distinguish between two types of data – traffic data and location data. The distinction can be confusing as some data could fall into both classes and different rules apply to each category. The rules are especially complicated and a detailed analysis of them is outside the scope of this book. Suffice to say that if location data of any kind is used, for example to track employees, to sell services in a particular locality or simply to provide service in an emergency by tracing the location of a call, extreme caution should be exercised and a detailed review of the regulations made.

In addition to the 2003 Regulations, the Mobile Marketing Association (MMA) has brought in its own Code of Practice. The Code is considered later in more detail (see **6.6**), however, it should be said that it also attempts to regulate the use of location-based data for marketing purposes. The MMA Code says that location-based marketing campaigns may only take place when the recipient has opted in to receive them. In addition, the Code prohibits the use of location-based data for marketing except where:

- the individual cannot be identified from the data used; or

- where the processing is necessary for the provision of a value added service with the consent of the individual.

In addition to regulatory pressure in the UK, commercial and privacy concerns will also come into play. The problems are magnified by the way in which mobile services are sold in the UK. Outside of the employer/employee relationship there is often no meaningful consent obtained to the use of location-based data. Mobile operators which have and sell the data will usually have relied on a third party, such as a mobile phone shop or a supermarket selling pay as you go phones, to bring their terms and conditions to the user's attention. It is easy to see how that might not be a reliable process and how questions will remain as to whether full and meaningful consent is given each time.

The first known litigation over location-based data was issued in Connecticut at the beginning of 2001 but subsequently settled. The Connecticut Department of Consumer Protection brought proceedings against a hire company, Acme, alleging that it had used global positioning to track its cars and that it fined hirers $150 every time they exceeded the speed limit for more than two minutes. In its defence, Acme said that its contract allowed it to fine customers who exceeded speed limits and that it used global positioning to ensure that its safety rules were enforced rather than to make money. The Connecticut authorities argued that even if the contract did allow it this term, it would be void under the US equivalent of the UK's *Unfair Contract Terms Act 1977*.

In the employer/employee environment, employers must make sure they obtain the employee's consent to use location-based data even if they have no current plans to use it. Applications already exist allowing an employer to locate employees via their mobile phones alone using triangulation. Low-cost applications also exist in hire vehicles in the UK and can be factory fitted in some plant and machinery. It is clear that there will be considerable data protection problems to come with global positioning.

Premium Rate Internet   6.3

Premium Rate Internet (PRI) services are still something of a rarity in the UK despite a workable system having existed since 1999. PRI services work by a user requesting a PRI service (such as a long range weather forecast) from an Internet site. The site would then terminate the Internet connection and, after displaying a statutory health warning, reconnect to a private server at a premium rate call charge. The service is worth exploring for many because of the public's reluctance to use credit cards for online transactions and the costs of processing card transactions for low value purchases (known as 'micro payments').

PRI services in the UK are regulated and a host telecoms operator is needed to run the service. PRI services are also more heavily regulated than Internet services and, as well as the statutory warning, a PRI service should be notified to the Independent Committee for the Supervision of Standards of Telephone Information Services (ICSTIS), essentially a self-regulatory body with its own Code of Practice for PRI services. ICSTIS also issued a guideline dealing with PRI (Guideline 11) on 1 January 2004. The Guideline and the Code set out how PRI can be used in the UK. The rules include the need to make consumers aware of what is happening. For example, Guideline 11 says:

> 'The use of any dialler found to activate a premium rate service remotely, without the intervention and informed consent of the consumer, will be in breach of the Code.'

Detailed and specific pricing information must also be given on the website offering the service before connecting to the premium rate server. The call cost must be visible on screen without the need to scroll down to find it. There is more information about ICSTIS and downloads of its Code of Practice and guidelines at www.icstis.org.uk.

Most of the uses of PRI in the UK have been for adult content as ICSTIS' activity against Spanish and German-based providers in November 2002 illustrates. The two cases involved website content promoted by two different service providers, one based in Spain and one in Germany. The promotional material reportedly referred to depraved sexual activity and the PRI server was dialled automatically leading to charges of £1.50 per minute. A number of organisations have had problems with PRI services like this and there are allegations that not only is the switch to PRI automatic but that the host server processes requests deliberately slowly to increase the phone bill.

ICSTIS imposed fines of £75,000 on the Spanish company and £50,000 on the German company and barred access to both services for two years. The companies involved were also instructed to offer redress to complainants and were reported to the UK's National Hi-tech Crime Unit.

As well as showing the significant danger that adult content presents for companies in the UK, the case is disappointing in that it deflects from the real potential that PRI does have, particularly in a business to consumer setting.

Spam   6.4

For many, spam is the big issue of electronic communications. In June 2003, Message Labs estimated that spam cost UK businesses around £3.2 billion each year. Whilst it is hard to see how a figure like that can be calculated, what is certain is that spam is a political hot potato. Ill-advised attempts to pass legislation have left a hotchpotch of confusing and overlapping provisions throughout the world.

New UK legislation on spam   6.5

The main legislation here is also the 2003 Regulations. In the UK now it is unlawful to send unsolicited electronic communications (such as email or SMS) for direct marketing purposes unless the recipient has consented to receiving these communications. There are limited exceptions to the need to obtain consent, including where the recipient's details have been obtained by the sender during the course of the sale or negotiations for the sale of a product or service to that recipient and the direct marketing is for similar products or services (the so-called 'soft opt in)'. Recipients should be able to unsubscribe from electronic marketing communications at any time in a manner that is simple and free (save for the transmission costs).

The 2003 Regulations implement Directive 2002/58/EC on Privacy and Electronic Communications, which was adopted by the EU on 12 July 2002. Member states were required to implement the Directive into their national laws by 31 October 2003. Only six member states managed to inform the European Commission of their transposition provisions by the deadline. The UK managed to be among the select few, even though the 2003 Regulations did not come into force on time. The Commission has decided to begin infringement proceedings against some of the other member states and letters of formal notice of action have been sent to Belgium, Germany, Greece, France, Luxembourg, the Netherlands, Portugal, Finland and Sweden. Whilst some countries like Sweden have made progress, it is likely that the others will face more enforcement action.

The new laws have been criticised for not going far enough in the war against spam. Italy has much tougher anti-spam laws that make spamming a criminal offence punishable with a custodial sentence of up to three years and action has already been taken by the Italian Data Protection Authority. The global perspective is important as UK-based organisations can be prosecuted overseas for marketing campaigns originating from the UK, and similarly UK-based businesses which are the victims of campaigns from overseas will need to know what, if anything, they can do to stop this.

Additional UK regulation   6.6

In addition to the UK law based on the Directive, spam is also regulated by advertising regulations in the UK. The *Electronic Commerce (EC Directive) Regulations 2002 (SI 2002/2013)* provide that spam must be clearly labelled as spam without the need to open it. In addition, the Advertising Standards Authority (known as the ASA) administers the Committee of Advertising Code of Practice (known as the CAP Code), which sets out the rules governing the content of non-broadcast marketing communications. The CAP Code was updated in March 2003 to provide that the explicit consent of a consumer is required prior to marketing by email or SMS, unless the e-marketer can benefit from the 'similar products' exemption which is essentially the same as that in the 2003 Regulations. The ASA has been involved in rulings following on from the CAP Code. In 2003 for example, the ASA ruled against the Training Guild for sending unsolicited marketing emails to individuals and upheld a complaint against a mobile phone retailer following a text message campaign.

In the first case the ASA upheld a complaint against the Training Guild for not obtaining the explicit consent of a customer before sending a marketing email. The email address in question was a personal, rather than a business, one. The Training Guild had sent an email to various customers (including the complainant) for a training seminar with the complainant objecting on the grounds that the necessary consent had not been obtained from him. The Training Guild said that it had bought a list of email addresses that it had thought were for businesses, not individuals. It also thought that the recipients had opted in to receiving information about training by email. The ASA acknowledged that the Training Guild had acted in good faith, but that it was still under an obligation to ensure that all necessary consents had been obtained before sending marketing emails.

In the SMS case, the text message stated: 'For fantastic free handsets, inc up to six months' free line rental or a free DVD player call...'. An individual complained that the text message was sent to him without his consent. The mobile phone retailer explained that an external list provider had sent the messages on its behalf. The list provider had compiled the list using information gathered in a National Shoppers' survey, a copy of which was provided to the ASA. The company argued that the complainant had given permission for his details to be used but after receiving the message asked the list owners to suppress the details.

The ASA acknowledged that the survey offered the respondent the chance to opt out of receiving marketing communications from third parties but the CAP Code requires that marketers have explicit consent before marketing to consumers, in effect a true opt in rather than soft opt in. The company was told to ensure that commercial text messages sent on its behalf in the future were only sent to consumers who had given explicit consent to receive text messages. The CAP Code is not legally binding but the ASA can refer misleading advertisements to the Office of Fair Trading (OFT) and those falling short of the Code will be on the receiving end of bad publicity with the associated risk of damage to their reputation. A breach of the CAP Code is also likely now to be a breach of the 2003 Regulations in most cases.

ICSTIS again have a role to play here with its own Code of Practice. In 2002, ICSTIS used its powers in 36 cases involving the sending of unsolicited SMS messages with fines ranging from £300 to £50,000. The figure rose in 2003 with action being take against 60 companies.

A similar Code of Practice was also issued by the Mobile Marketing Association (MMA) in December 2003. This also requires a user's permission prior to UK firms sending a customer marketing material. It allows soft opt in but suggests that it should be used only to give consumers the opportunity to opt in fully to marketing campaigns. It suggests that if true opt in is not received within 48 hours of the first text the consumer's details should be deleted from the marketing database. The MMA has also set up a service allowing customers to report instances of being spammed. Whilst the code is voluntary, the MMA has said that it will consider banning companies and blacklisting them from SMS networks if they do not comply. MMA members can also be expelled from the MMA for breaches of its Code. The MMA Code can be downloaded from www.mmaglobal.co.uk.

There is also likely to be an increased regulatory focus on SMS spam in particular. ICSTIS said in its annual report for 2002 that complaints about services promoted by SMS increased almost eight fold over 2001 with most complaints involving the use of text message campaigns linked to premium rate numbers as the mechanism for users to reply to the message.

In addition to specific spam legislation, marketing campaigns selling goods will also need to comply with the requirements of the *Consumer Protection (Distance Selling) Regulations 2000 (SI 2000/2334)*. The terms of use imposed by an organisation's Internet Service Provider (ISP) are also likely to include a prohibition on sending spam – the misguided attempts to market by an employee have led to at least one UK company having its service terminated by its ISP and also having proceedings issued by the ISP for the breach. Additional civil or criminal action could also result from spam campaigns, for example for the computing resource required to download spam and the electricity to power the equipment.

The US position on spam   6.7

The US has had a number of attempts to regulate spam with Federal and State legislation. California brought in the 'leave-us-alone legislation' in January 2003 which consisted of three bills prohibiting advertisements via text messages on mobile phones, banning unwanted fax advertisements and making changes to the State's laws governing telemarketing calls. Other States already had legislation in place dealing with other elements of spam including the more common unsolicited emails.

The legislative tidal wave in the US culminated in the Federal CAN-SPAM Act 2003 (passed as Senate Bill S.877) which came into effect on 1 January 2004. By the way in which State and Federal law interact in the US, CAN-SPAM will automatically repeal many of the State laws in this area. As with other US legislation, the full title of the Act seeks to explain the legislative purpose behind it. In this case the full title being Controlling the Assault of Non-Solicited Pornography And Marketing Act. It gives users the right to opt out of commercial spam lists. It also has other provisions, including the requirement that emails which are unsolicited adverts are clearly labelled as such.

The opt-out provisions are contained in *section 5(a)* of CAN-SPAM. This section makes it a criminal offence to omit from a commercial email a functioning means of unsubscribing from future emails. Senders are also required to provide within their email an accurate return postal address. The labelling provisions are in *sections 3(8), 4(c), 5(a)* and *(b)*. They try to get at the worst type of spamming tactics by, for example, prohibiting forged 'sent from' or return addresses, using false or misleading subject lines or using relay servers to disguise the identity of the true sender. Additional provisions of CAN-SPAM place further restrictions on spam of a sexual nature.

CAN-SPAM can be enforced by the FTC and the Attorney General in each State but, significantly, by ISPs as well. The latter route is interesting as some of the larger ISPs have used existing US legislation to attack bulk emailers and have promised to use CAN-SPAM together to the same end.

There has also been litigation in the US too. Motorola, for example, has used trademark litigation to try to stop spam offering a Motorola two-way pager free of charge. Some people who responded to the offer received a different pager from the one advertised in the message, which in some cases was not manufactured by Motorola, and in other cases people received nothing. Motorola received hundreds of complaints from the victims. Motorola said it repeatedly requested the company concerned to stop using the Motorola name in the campaign and its lawyers had received verbal agreements from it agreeing to this. Despite this it seemed the campaign continued and proceedings were issued in Illinois as a result. US trademark law differs from that in the UK but it is likely that a similar approach in the UK could be successful.

It is also perhaps worth making the point that some jurisdictions impose much more strict penalties for spam. In May 2004, Reuters reported that a Chinese court had sentenced two men to jail for using SMS spam messages telling subscribers that they had won lottery prizes. One man now faces eight years in jail while another will spend four years in prison for the crime.

Self help with spam 6.8

In addition to the legislation most organisations would be wise to adopt a policy of self-help to deal with spam. This might include:

- altering the employee acceptable use policy to ask people to exercise more care when giving out their email address in the first place – the most persistent spam often occurs because an email address has been left on a website that the employee should not have been visiting in the first place;

- look at how email addresses are composed in the organisation. Email addresses that are simply firstname.lastname@organisation.com are easy to guess and there has been at least one incident of a university getting mass spam after a spammer obtained its staff list and reconstructed the email addresses which were in this format;

- instruct employees to think carefully before replying to any spam – it is especially unwise with most spam to follow the unsubscribe instructions – this simply verifies that the email address is active and is likely to result in more, not less, spam. The critics of CAN-SPAM cite this as one of the ways in which that legislation is particularly wrong-headed;

- the careful use of key word filters at the email gateway. It could be set up to immediately quarantine any email with certain phrases (like 'get rich quick now', 'spy on your neighbors' or 'no credit check required') or certain words or brand names (like 'Viagra' or 'Nigeria') where it is appropriate to do so given the business. Caution will need to be exercised as it could be the case that some of these emails actually will need to be dealt with or even reported, for example under anti-money laundering legislation in the case of an advanced fee fraud. Online travel company, Holiday Rentals, recently claimed that around ten per cent of its emails to its customers were being blocked. Another example comes from Symantec which sells this type of email filter – it tells of one of its salespeople having his emails to a customer continually blocked as the system had been set up to block the word 'hooker', which happened to be the salesperson's surname;

- look at other technological means – there seems to be a new idea to combat spam every week or so. The reputable computer press in the UK will often feature road tests of new technology available. One solution might be to use technology which profiles legitimate email into the company and only automatically allows through emails which fit that profile; and

- look at the ISP that is used – some have more robust systems than others for filtering out spam.

Voicemail spam   6.9

The problems of unsolicited marketing messages reached a new medium just before Christmas 2002 with the Twentieth Century Fox campaign for the DVD of the Tom Cruise film Minority Report. With marketing similar to spam emails, recorded voicemail messages were sent to a reported 27,000 people on mobile and landline voicemail in the UK given to Twentieth Century Fox under previous promotions.

The ASA received a formal complaint and issued its decision on 12 February 2003. The complaint alleged, amongst other things, that the message was 'inappropriate and offensive'. The complainant was particularly concerned that the caller's number had been withheld making it difficult to understand who had left the message. Twentieth Century Fox said that the campaign had only involved people who had opted in to receive promotional information from the company and that a voiceover at the end of the message made it clear that it was an advertisement. It also said that people who got the message were likely to be familiar with Tom Cruise's voice which, it argued, would mean they were unlikely to be caused undue fear or distress, another of the complaints against it. Additionally, and perhaps a little oddly, it said that most people when they recognised Tom Cruise's voice would realise he was selling something and would not expect him to phone them personally.

The ASA upheld the complaints and 'advised' Twentieth Century Fox to consult it before sending any similar campaigns. It was also advised to make it clear when obtaining opt in that this type of campaign could be used and to specifically tell people that it was likely to cost them to retrieve a voicemail message on their mobile.

As well as the ASA's involvement voicemail campaigns also bring additional regulatory hurdles. In the UK campaigns like this have been regulated since May 1999 under the *Telecommunications (Data Protection and Privacy) (Direct Marketing) Regulations 1998 (SI 1998/3170)* which have now effectively been replaced by *regulation 19* of the 2003 Regulations. *Regulation 19* means that voicemail campaigns using an automated dialling system are not permitted unless the subscriber whose line is being called has previously consented to that type of call. These regulations are intended to protect individuals and in some cases businesses. Even if an opt in has been obtained (as with the Tom Cruise campaign), any marketing campaign needs to be carefully thought through and is likely to also involve clearing the list of numbers to be called against the Telephone Preference Service (TPS) database. Whilst again the TPS database predates the 2003 Regulations its operation is now enshrined in law by *regulation 26* of those regulations. This requires the UK regulator responsible for communications services, OFCOM, to establish a do-not-call register for telephone lines. *Regulation 25* sets up a similar but not identical system, the Fax Preference Service (FPS) for faxes (see **6.10**). Businesses will need to clear their lists against the TPS list regularly – an opt out via the TPS list is effective 28 days after registration. Any business planning a similar voicemail campaign will need to exercise extreme caution to avoid complaints both to the ASA and to the Information Commissioner who polices the 2003 Regulations.

Faxes   6.10

The FPS system for faxes has many similarities with the TPS scheme. Again, a register is maintained under the 2003 Regulations supervised by OFCOM. A major difference between the two is that the FPS register is wider in its scope with, at present, businesses of all kinds able to register under the FPS scheme. This distinction is likely, however, to go very soon – the Government has said that it expects to change the law on 25 June 2004 giving from then on businesses the same right as individuals to block both telephone and fax cold calling. Currently, *regulation 20* of the 2003 Regulations prohibits faxes being used for direct marketing purposes if the number faxed:

- belongs to an individual subscriber unless the subscriber has previously told the faxer that he or she does not object;

- belongs to a corporate subscriber and the subscriber has previously told the faxer not to use the number; and

- is listed on the TPS register.

As with the TPS register the 28-day rule applies for registration on the list which means that fax lists used for direct marketing purposes must be cleaned against the TPS register every four weeks as a minimum. The rules stop both the transmission of the fax and its instigation so if a company asks another to conduct a direct fax campaign on its behalf it is still liable despite the fact that it did not send the faxes itself. Equally, where an employee has sent a direct marketing fax as a normal part of his or her employment it will be reasonable to presume that the employer instigated it unless the sending of direct marketing faxes was expressly prohibited in the employee's contract of employment.

The Information Commissioner has already taken action under the *Telecommunications (Data Protection and Privacy) (Direct Marketing) Regulations 1998* which, as with voice calls, followed much the same format as the 2003 Regulations. In May 2002, 192enquiries.com Ltd and its directors had an enforcement notice served on it for sending unsolicited faxes. Those concerned were alleged to have set up an Internet site that purported to have telephone directory information on it over and above that available from BT. The information was collected in part by sending out unsolicited computer-generated faxes inviting the recipient to send back details using a premium rate fax line. People who received unwanted marketing material from these companies complained to the Information Commissioner. Apparently, the complainants were aggrieved at the cost of wasted fax paper and toner and the disruption caused to them while waiting for faxes to come through and from them coming through to home office numbers in the dead of night. The enforcement notice exposes the directors and the companies concerned to prosecution and the same parties also face investigation and possible enforcement action from the OFT and BT.

Companies sending messages   6.11

Limited companies must additionally consider the impact of *Part XI* of the *Companies Act 1985*. SMS, emails and faxes (and indeed other forms of electronic communication) will need to comply with this legislation. In short, *Part XI* sets out what a limited company's notepaper must contain and the following details have to be included:

- the proper name of the company registered at companies house;

- the place of registration, for example 'registered in England and Wales';

- the company number;

- the address of the registered office;

- the fact that the company is a limited company; and

- either the names of all of the directors or none of them.

As long ago as 1998 Companies House confirmed that it was its unofficial view that *Part XI* applied to electronic communications saying that the Act catches 'the message, not the mode of delivering it'. The consequences of failing to comply with *Part XI* are serious. A prosecution can be brought against any officer of the company or anyone who 'issues or authorises the issue' of publications without the required details. All of this is more concerning when looking at SMS given that the system in the UK only allows messages of a maximum of 160 characters to be sent. When the statutory details required by *Part XI* are put on the bottom of the message the available characters reduce to under 100 – that is only about two dozen words.

Employee problems   6.12

It needs to be remembered that the same type of employee problems discussed in CHAPTER THREE – EMPLOYEE-RELATED RISK also apply in the mobile world. A case in point would be the case of *R v Scott Reid (1999, unreported)*. In this case, Reid worked for a company involved in the lace making industry in Nottingham. He had a dispute with the company and resigned. As he resigned he sent 32,000 text messages telling people that they had won a car. The text message told them that all they needed to do to claim the car was to call a number it gave. That number turned out to be the switchboard number of Reid's former employer. Reid then sent an email with a virus to some of the company's customers. The switchboard was blocked, the employer lost trade and Reid was prosecuted. In court Reid admitted two charges of unlawful modification of computer material and two of unauthorised access to a computer. He also admitted causing annoyance and asked for other offences to be considered. Reid was sentenced by Nottingham Crown Court to three months in prison in August 1999.

Internet domains   6.13

CHAPTER FIVE – ONLINE REPUTATIONAL RISK looked at the issues surrounding Internet domain names. Some of the same issues will apply as selling by mobile means increases especially if systems, like Bango, gain prominence. Bango net Ltd are promoting a similar system to domain names in m-commerce with SMS and WAP applications already available. Bango say that it is difficult to get specific content on the Internet using a WAP phone and conventional URLs are hard to enter on a numeric keypad. Instead, it allocates Bango numbers which can match conventional URLs, users then simply enter the number into their telephone to reach the information they desire. The potential for abuse comes in translating these numbers back into letters. For example, the number 2653 relates on a mobile keyboard to a well-known international brand name. Bango in the past seemed prepared to licence this number on its system for an annual fee of £3,000. In its terms and conditions, it does not have to provide this service if it is unable to because of a court or tribunal order and applicants have to warrant that their application is made in good faith and does not infringe the intellectual property or other rights of a third party. However, similar terms and conditions appear for the registration of conventional domain names and do not appear to deter cybersquatters. Once again, for brand owners there is a judgement call to be made. They will have to decide how important m-commerce is to their future development and how likely systems like Bango are to develop traffic. For many longer numerical combinations, the fee will be less and registration as a result might seem more attractive.

Mobile content issues   6.14

The same content issues apply in the mobile world as they do in the wired world. In some cases the issues will be magnified because of the way in which some aspects of m-commerce have exploded in this country.

An example would be the prevalence of ringtones and logos. If you take text, sound or images over SMS then there is a good chance you have infringed someone else's rights. Whilst royalty paid services have increased in numbers over the past few years for both ringtones and logos, unlicensed copies are certainly still doing the rounds.

As m-commerce gets more sophisticated the same issues will arise with more valuable content. Some of these disputes are likely to be pretty complicated too. For example, in the sports arena it might well be the case that the rights to show goals from football matches on mobile phones involve a complex matrix of rights involving the football clubs, football associations, broadcasters and their licensees. Some of the rights agreements already in place will not have properly predicted new channels for the content and, given the need to recoup their 3G licence spend by the network operators, litigation may well result.

Video-phones   6.15

Content problems of different kinds can emerge from the use of video-phones. As with any piece of new technology scare stories are easy to come by but some of the issues which need to be looked at are:

- pornography – there has been at least one case of indecent images being taken using a camera phone and then transmitted over the public phone network to another handset. Businesses need to make sure that their liability is minimised by adapting the acceptable use policy if they provide camera phones to employees (see **CHAPTER THREE** (**3.6** et seq));

- privacy – there have already been CCTV cases in court where the claimants have alleged that the use of CCTV invades their data protection rights. Similar cases seem likely here – already some schools have prohibited the use of camera phones at school sports days;

- copyright – already some music venues and cinemas ban mobile phones with a camera after bootleg copies taken by camera phones circulated on the Internet;

- industrial espionage – it has been reported in the press that some large organisations, particularly those included with the defence industry, ask visitors to surrender their camera phones on entering the premises; and

- legislation – some US legislators are seeking to ban camera phones at a State and even at a Federal level. Whilst it is still early days for this type of legislation, employers and those carrying camera phones abroad on business or holiday would be wise to check on the progress of legislation like this before they travel with a camera phone.

Wireless LANs   6.16

The commercial use of wireless Local Area Networks (LANs) has increased considerably in the UK since 2001. With analysts and business efficiency gurus touting wireless as the smart way of working and telecoms companies marketing it heavily as a potential new source of revenue, growth is set to be maintained. For those not familiar with the term, a wireless LAN is a Local Area Network (in basic terms a group of computers linked together within a building) that operates without cables. Wireless LANs can also be used to link a number of nearby buildings together, for example three neighbouring office blocks in the City of London. Wireless LANs are also known as WLANs and WiFi (wireless fidelity) networks. WiFi more frequently (though not exclusively) describes a public access facility and wireless LAN an in-house facility and the terms will be used this way in this section.

Similar risk issues are likely to emerge with WiMax, a related technology which started to seriously feature in the technology press in April 2004 having been developed in late 2003. So far a number of technology companies, including Fujitsu and Intel, have been reported as looking at WiMax – effectively a go-faster version of WiFi with a radius of around 30 miles from a single base station. The first WiMax networks are expected to be available in 2005 if the tests prove positive.

Security issues   6.17

In many cases, the demand for wireless LANs seems to have exceeded the supply of specialist installers. Traditionally, cable installers (who clearly see wireless installations as a threat to their business) have often filled the gap. In the UK this led to suspicions of weaknesses, which inspired a major investigation by *The Daily Telegraph* and others in 2001 which found that an empty Pringles crisp tin can be used to help hackers break into insecure wireless LANs. The security firm which carried out the investigation demonstrated that using an empty Pringles tin as an antenna could boost a hacker's chance of picking up a wireless signal by as much as 15 per cent. During a half hour drive around the City of London almost 60 wireless networks were picked up. Around 40 of these had no security – a hacker would be able to use the company's network anywhere he or she liked as well as browse for the information on it.

One of the problems seems to be the default settings on many wireless LANs systems. The default setting is commonly that data will not be secured. Whilst most of the products come with built in encryption capabilities they are simply not switched on.

In April 2002, a second survey was released by the Institute of Information Security (Instis). The 2002 Instis survey involved one operator conducting a survey of the City of London by taxi and by foot using major and some minor roads and then doing the same through five of the surrounding districts in London. A simple laptop and a wireless communication card and some software was used and incredibly the first network was detected on a train on the way into London.

The survey found that in the four-month period between the two surveys the number of highly vulnerable networks in the city of London had increased by 85 per cent. The April 2002 trip showed that 71 per cent of wireless LANs detected were not encrypted compared to 65 per cent four months earlier. One-hundred and eighty five networks were detected in April 2002 compared to 119 in December 2001 and in April 2002 almost half of the networks revealed some information about the company that owned them, such as its name, nature of business, hardware type or geographic location. Only five of the networks detected in December 2001 were not visible the second time around.

A similar survey by the same team and commissioned by RSA Security in January 2004 showed that the problems still exist. The survey shows a 235 per cent growth in wireless networks in London but some of the same mistakes still being made. The survey showed that 34 per cent of access points still lacked encryption. The research also showed that 25 per cent of access points were poorly configured suggesting that rogue employees and departments could be deploying unauthorised wireless networks within their business without the knowledge of IT managers. This is likely given that some basic systems can be bought for as little as £140.

Wireless LANs got a specific mention is the US final version of its National Strategy to Secure Cyberspace (NSSC). Whilst the plan does not have the force of law, even in the UK businesses need to take notice of it. In earlier drafts of the NSSC the problems of wireless security were highlighted and it was suggested that a halt be put on the use of wireless networks in US Federal and civilian agencies until their security was improved. Whilst the final version watered this down (saying only that US Federal agencies should follow wireless security guidelines issued by the US Government), it would be hard for any company to say it was not aware of the issue. The US plan can be downloaded at http://www.whitehouse.gov/pcipb/.

For directors or managers in particular of companies that use wireless LANs the dangers are all too clear. The security obligations imposed by the seventh Data Protection Principle of the *Data Protection Act 1998* are covered in **CHAPTER ONE** (**1.12**). It would seem obvious that not switching on the encryption settings on a wireless LAN, after security breaches have been so well reported, is likely to put any organisation in breach of the principle and leave it and its directors and managers vulnerable to prosecution.

All of the evidence does point to the fact that human error is mostly to blame and that many people in the UK are running properly audited secure wireless LANs systems. The use of properly qualified installers is key.

Other issues
6.18

When buying wireless LANs equipment the specification needs to be checked to ensure that it suits a company's purpose. There are more issues here than just those with conventional IT kits. As well as looking at encryption on installation you need to check that the equipment is legal for use in the UK. Whilst there have been recent changes the radio spectrum is still regulated differently from the US where much of the equipment comes from. There have already been a number of cases in the UK where non-UK specification equipment was used. That is likely to lead to regulatory intervention – made even more likely in one of the cases when it transpired that the equipment sold used a frequency allocated to the Ministry of Defence in the UK.

A company also needs to understand how the equipment will transmit information and check that it is in a suitable area. In one case equipment was installed at a dry dock. It worked well until the dock was flooded. When this happened the superstructure of a vessel in the dock interfered with the workings of the wireless LANs. In another case the outline perimeter of the transmission area of the LANs was set too wide. This meant that a signal was receivable on a public footpath outside the premises the LANs served. This could have been potentially disastrous because of the issues around warchalking which are dealt with in the next section. Whilst many of these problems have been resolved as the market has become more mature this type of system still requires careful thought.

Warchalking
6.19

Warchalking first emerged as a phenomena in July 2002. In short, warchalking is a set of rune-like symbols designed to alert Internet users as to when and where free wireless broadband connectivity is available. As wireless LANs deliver data at high speed with a low level of technology, there is a growing trend of Internet users to seek out new sources of wireless access. This, certainly in the early years of wireless connectivity, was not always an easy thing to do due to the invisibility of wireless 'hotspots' – areas where free wireless access 'spills' into the public domain.

Whilst some of the issues surrounding warchalking would seem to have diminished given the spread of WiFi connectivity in restaurants, hotels and train stations traditionally, in order to locate areas where WiFi was available users would have to rely on Internet sites and word of mouth to notify them of available networks. Warchalking sought to aid this search. With the warchalking system users who discover hotspots use chalk to mark these areas either on pavements or buildings using a system of standardised symbols. These symbols notify the user as to whether the 'node', or wireless access, is open, closed or encrypted with further information as to bandwidth and how to gain access.

A number of sites then began to appear on the Internet to show the standardised symbols used. One site said that it received 60,000 hits within one hour of the news of its existence spreading. The interest ranges from individual members of the public seeking to gain free Internet access on the move to government officials in Utah seeking to use the system for the benefit of policemen. However, despite the large scale of interest that has been created, nothing is known about how widespread rogue use of the networks concerned is. Whatever the case, warchalking has still managed to elicit reactions from certain broadband providers. This reaction has varied from support on the one hand to threatened legal action on the other.

There are clear concerns in relation to warchalking. It could be used to access unprotected wireless LANs to steal information. The concern surrounding drive by hacking of wireless LANs (or war-driving as it is sometimes known) reached its high point towards the end of 2002 with reports of mass hacking events aimed at getting as much information as possible from wireless networks in as short a space of time as possible. One enterprising war-driver in the US even hired a light aircraft to prove that these networks were particularly vulnerable to fly-by hacks. An insecure wireless LAN could also be used by spammers to send unsolicited mail in bulk resulting in law abiding companies being black listed by their ISPs as the mail will be traced to their WLAN network. Gaps in security yet again become an important issue.

Using WiFi for income generation   6.20

It is increasingly common to look at WiFi as a potential revenue stream. As already stated hotels, fast food restaurants, airports, train stations and universities already offer wireless connectivity at a cost on a pay as you go basis. According to a Gartner study featured in *Internet World* in November 2003 there were already 10,000 public hotspots in the world then. Another Gartner study predicts 30 million WiFi users by the end of 2004. In the UK BT alone hopes to have 4,000 hotspots in place by June 2005. These arrangements also have legal implications.

Most organisations will look to bring in a partner to operate the service rather than doing it themselves. A partner will generally provide access, equipment and do the billing. It will also usually have similar agreements with other properties which allow users to roam on wider networks. There are a number of issues that would need to be dealt with in the contract with the partner, including:

- clear specifications of all services, including the integration process if there is a link to the network, subscriber management, service offerings and communications;

- the project plan and timetable;

- clear service levels for support – an organisation would not want to be dealing with customers concerned at the length of time the system is down;

- clear payment and revenue sharing terms – this will include the calculations, accounting mechanism and payment dates;

- who will be responsible for paying additional service providers, such as a fixed line for the wireless network to connect to?

- the length of the relationship and what happens when it comes to an end;

- change of control provisions – the sector will see a lot of consolidation and if the partner is taken over an organisation might want the right to terminate the relationship if the new owner does not pass its due diligence test; and

- escalation and dispute resolution provisions just in case an organisation falls out.

It is important to remember that there is often the scope to negotiate arrangements individually. The market is developing and there will be business models which make more sense for an organisation than others. Some of these agreements allow for the revenue split to change over time, for example the technology provider may take a greater revenue share until the equipment is paid for after which time revenue is split equally. As with any contractual relationship an organisation also needs to do proper due diligence on any potential partner, otherwise it could lose more than its reputation.

Whether a partner is used or the service is provided by the organisation itself, it should also look at how it can reduce its liability to users of the service. For example, one hotel operator has specific terms and conditions covering the use of WiFi in its hotels. Before guests purchase an access card from reception they are given those terms and they are reminded of them when they connect to the network – an on-screen click-through agreement is then put in front of them which they must activate before being allowed onto the network. Another local authority operating a wireless access scheme under the UK Government's New Deal programme provides similar terms and conditions when residents request an access card.

Employment considerations with wireless LANs 6.21

According to research conducted by IDC at the beginning of 2003 the number of workers who spend the majority of their time away from any fixed work station will have doubled by 2007. With figures like this in mind it is not surprising that many employers are looking at WiFi connections as a way of everyday working for their employees. If employees are allowed to use WiFi connections it would be wise to review the employee acceptable use policy (see **CHAPTER THREE (3.6** et seq)). Even if an employer is not prepared to allow employees to use WiFi it might be wise to review its policy to say just that and perhaps to adapt any equipment provided to them to prohibit a WiFi card being installed. If WiFi access is allowed it might also want to consider the following:

- it needs to be clear to employees that the same considerations apply as they would with a fixed-line network, for example if an employer bans access to certain categories of site on the fixed-line network make it clear that these bans also apply with a wireless connection;

- if employees connect to the systems abroad there might be additional considerations and an employer might want to restrict private Internet use even further overseas;

- it might also want to specify which networks an employee can connect up to, for example saying that they may connect to a network where they have consent but that they cannot engage in warchalking;

- there is likely to be a need for additional elements to the policy too, for example an employer might not want employees to edit sensitive documents in public places because of the danger of them being overlooked;

- it might also want to take extra care with health and safety provisions given that it is likely that it will have less direct control over where employees will work and when. For the same reason it might want to take a look at other employment law issues that do not immediately spring to mind, for example it may need waivers if employees exceed a 48-hour working week by connecting to a WiFi network after they leave the office; and

- it might also want to take a look at the process for submitting expense claims – public access hotspots vary considerably in price and there is scope for abuse from unscrupulous employees. It might also want to consolidate its needs with one supplier to benefit from bulk buying.

Checklist for installing a Wireless LAN   6.22

Checklist when installing a wireless LAN:

- ✓ Do due diligence on any potential supplier and partner – some have little track record in the technology and like any new technology some companies are likely to go out of business.

- ✓ Make sure the kit to be installed is legal and fit for its purpose – include appropriate contractual safeguards.

- ✓ Think security – test the partner or technology provider and ensure that there are appropriate contractual safeguards in place.

- ✓ Review employee acceptable use policies prior to implementation.

- ✓ Look at ways to reduce your liability to other end users.

- ✓ Keep abreast of technological change in this area – remember the need to constantly assess new technologies to comply with the seventh Data Protection Principle.

Chapter 7
Managing Operational ICT Risk with Standards and Best Practice

Foreword

By Professor Neil Barrett

Perhaps the most important realisation in the field of information security is that it is not, ideally, concerned primarily with technology. Rather, it is about people. A hacker is a real person, with motives, an objective and a particular level of skill. And their exploits are not purely aimed at breaking the configuration of a particular computer, but at taking advantage of mistakes, oversights or blind spots on the part of the people responsible for managing and maintaining computer systems. Similarly, viruses and worms do not 'mutate': instead, individuals decide that an existing piece of malware code can be altered, improved and retargeted. Computer users make errors or, for personal reasons of their own, deliberately intrude into computer systems. The central tenet of good risk management is, therefore, that information security is threatened by people, bolstered by people or ruined by people; technology merely assists.

Perhaps the most immediate recognition of this feature of information security is embodied in the seventh principle of the UK's *Data Protection Act 1998*, requiring organisations to enact 'adequate technical and organisational methods' to ensure the protection of personal data, ideally through a set of policies and mechanisms broadly equivalent to that of ISO 17799. In this, technology has a role to play, but only one that is subservient to the role of the people involved.

This observation drives the requirement for policies, procedures, education and awareness: ways of 'programming' the staff within an organisation as to how they should act and respond in the light of modern IT dependency. This observation is also recognised in a host of reputable publications: the OECD guidelines of 2002, for example, stress the importance of awareness, responsibility and ethics. Further, the technological measures most successfully

(cont'd)

applied in the modern infrastructure of penetrated perimeters and trusted third parties concentrate on the reliable identification and authorisation of individual users; users who have been informed of the limits of their access rights and who might be trusted to a certain degree. Again, people are the key.

Regulating risk is therefore about understanding the opportunities provided to people to benefit – in financial or reputation terms – from information security weaknesses. As the title of an old DTI survey makes clear, 'Opportunity Makes a Thief'. Good security measures are those which do not merely protect or detect wrongdoing on an information infrastructure, they are those which also act to deter. An intrusion detection system, for example, is an important element of any information security configuration, but an IDS does not deter. An acceptable use policy statement – a formal contract between computer user and owner – does provide a degree of deterrence, but little in the way of protection and detection of wrongdoing. The ideal combination involves all of those measures, but the first and most important step for all organisations to take lies in understanding the level of risk posed by people.

(Professor Neil Barrett BSc PhD CEng CITP MBCS, is visiting professor of computer crime at Cranfield University, and visiting fellow at the University of Glamorgan. Professor Barrett is the author of 'Traces of Guilt' and many articles about computer security and computer crime. He regularly acts as an expert witness for the police in prosecuting computer hackers, Internet paedophiles and computer criminals.)

Introduction   7.1

Information systems risk involves much more than security. But if there is a need for an almost tangible manifestation of risk, and the framework within which to deal with it, then security presents this opportunity. Manage security and you are managing a huge swathe of the issues to do with e-risk, IT governance and data protection (no security, no compliance).

Of course, there is more to information security than IT – there is little point in implementing a technical fortress of firewalls and pass keys and then leaving a copy of a sensitive document on the train. So let us take a broad sweep of the why, how and the what of the issues associated with managing risk and the tools to do so. This chapter will focus on standards and how they are applied to mitigate risks. It will look at the issues in balancing people, technology and processes, taking in:

- standards;
- people;

- firewalls;

- people;

- viruses (and other forms of malicious code);

- people;

- virtual private networks;

- encryption;

- people;

- and a lot more.

On the whole, computers do as they are told. The biggest control issue in information systems is not based on silicon, it is, however, based on its covalent cousin: carbon. In IT, people are so often the problem. It is not the cyberterrorist or hacker whose destructive code is the electronic equivalent of smashing up bus shelters. The biggest threats to date have come from malcontent within the workforce or quite often just clumsy use of an information system (overwriting a file, deleting key records by mistake). In fact, the biggest ally to the hacker is the uneducated operator who clicks on an executable attachment.

This chapter does not discuss which port settings need to be reconfigured to deter hackers. Nor will it explain how to write the all important security policy that will give a security system a manageable framework. It will discuss some threats, some tools and some methods. These include:

- Identification authentication – Knowing who you are dealing with online. Can you trust their digital identity?

- Authorisation – You may know who it is, but what privileges are they allowed and what may they have access to?

- Verification – The structure of digital information is only visible to the initiated. Ask: 'has it been changed?'

- Privacy – With so many businesses outsourcing their network management to the Internet, and information in transit can pass through many different routes and remain on computers for completely unprescribed periods of time, how can you reduce the risk that what you do online is not seen by rest of the world.

- Non–repudiation – How do you make it clear that the person who carried out a transaction online was the person to whom the digital evidence points? What is the risk of losing digital identity to others?

At the core of this chapter is the International Information Security Standard ISO 17799, which is the prime standard to mitigate information and communications technology (ICT) risk.

Standards to mitigate risk   7.2

Businesses face many risks which must be managed or mitigated to avoid undesirable outcomes (Swann, *The Economics of Standardization*, 2000). The lessons learnt by the distillation of best practice and proven tools and techniques encapsulated in standards can support businesses in mitigating these risks. Only 10 per cent of organisations have a formal and well integrated information systems/IT risk management framework (The National Computing Centre, *Risk Management in IT Survey*, 2003).

The ubiquitous and pervasive nature of information systems in business suggests that businesses would be well advised to apply standards to mitigate at least the known risks. There are many standards which can usefully be applied to information systems (see catalogues for BS/CEN/ISO/IEC et al). This would create a beneficial environment for innovation and a stable, sustainable business 'ecosystem' for existing business practices and production to be optimised – weaker links can be strengthened encouraging trust and security.

This has been recognised internationally and has given rise to mitigating policies and processes, such as:

● international standards;

● guidelines from the Organisation for Economic Co-operation and Development (OECD); and

● laws and codes of conduct.

It turns out that hindsight in risk and incident reporting is not applied because there is often no shared data/information source about risk within an organisation and the opportunity is often not taken to connect to, and learn from, wider resources outside the organisation, such as:

● Unified Incident Reporting and Alert Scheme (UNIRAS).

● Warning, Advice and Reporting Point (WARP).

It could be useful to learn lessons from the peripheral industries, for example, from experiences encountered by the insurance industry, which is focused on identifying and catching incidents early (for example, having a culture which encourages openness in reporting risk events or near misses can lead to minor problems being 'nipped in the bud' before they become out of control – a point noted in rogue trader incidents). Issues here for scrutiny include:

● digital risk; and

● corporate governance.

Why standards?   7.3

There appears to be no good reason why standards get such short shrift. After all, they are usually a distillation of best practice prepared by the peers of those who should be glad of their support. The need of the standards to apply to so many 'unique' situations means that some of the advice will be honed down to be generic and inoffensive to all but that makes for polished, pure elements that provide a strong foundation to be built upon.

Standards provide an anchor for all the change that must be managed in an agile business. They are a toolbox that is too often rejected unopened and the tools needed to fix a solution overlooked as proverbial wheels are reinvented.

Standards users need to go in and take what is useful and not deliberate on the irrelevant.

This chapter will identify organisations and standards with an approach to ICT risk, including standards and specifications such as:

- BS 7799 Part 1:2000 – Information technology – Code of practice for information security management (also referred to as ISO 17799 Part 1).

- BS 7799 Part 2:2002 – Information security management – Specification with guidance for use.

- PAS 56:2003 – Guide to business continuity management.

- ISO/IEC TR 13335–1:1996 – Information technology – Guidelines for the management of IT Security – Part 1: Concepts and models for IT Security.

- ISO/IEC TR 13335–2:1997 – Information technology – Guidelines for the management of IT Security – Part 2: Managing and planning IT Security.

- ISO/IEC TR 13335–3:1998 – Information technology – Guidelines for the management of IT Security – Part 3: Techniques for the management of IT Security.

- ISO/IEC TR 13335–4:2000 – Information technology – Guidelines for the management of IT Security – Part 4: Selection of safeguards.

- ISO/IEC TR 13335–5:2001 – Information technology – Guidelines for the management of IT Security – Part 5: Management guidance on network security (available in English only).

- ISO/IEC 15408 Part 1:1999 – Information technology. Security techniques. Evaluation criteria for IT security. Introduction and general model.

- ISO/IEC 15408 Part 2: 1999 – Information technology. Security techniques. Evaluation criteria for IT security. Security functional requirements.

- ISO/IEC 15408 Part 3: 1999 – Information technology. Security techniques. Evaluation criteria for IT security. Security assurance requirements.

- ISO/IEC 21827:2002 Information technology – Systems Security Engineering – Capability Maturity Model.

- ISO/IEC 16085 Standard for Software Life Cycle Processes – Risk Management.

- The eight Desert Island Standards (see **7.13**).

Also, guidance, laws and codes of conduct which set out the whole information security and assurance framework in a managed risk environment, including:

- The Second Basel Accord (commonly referred to as Basel II) from the Basel Committee on Banking Supervision.

- *Section 404* of the *Public Company Accounting Reform and Investor Protection Act of 2002* (commonly referred to as Sarbanes-Oxley).

- Internal Control: Guidance for Directors on the Combined Code from the Institute of Chartered Accountants in England and Wales (commonly referred to as the Turnbull Report).

- The Financial Aspects of Corporate Governance (commonly referred to as the Cadbury Report).

- Review of the role and effectiveness of non-executive directors (commonly referred to as the Higgs Report).

This chapter looks at a generic framework to guide information system users (and providers) through the risk management standards and tools currently available (and upcoming) so that informed choices can be made by users as to:

- What approach to take in managing the operational risk in information systems.

- What tools, methods and standards are available to:

    - identify risks in an organisation;

    - assess those risks;

    - report those risks; and

    - mitigate those risks.

- What codes or standards are they obliged to apply (if any).

- Identify and fill the gaps in their existing internal (and hopefully) integrated risk management framework for information systems.

This is similar (but wider in scope) to the e-Government Interoperability Framework published by the Office of the e-Envoy (Cabinet Office) which catalogues the standards and codes of practice necessary for the interoperability of electronic government systems and, by default, electronic business in general. At the risk of becoming too tied down to labels and epithets, this chapter sets out a 'standard of standards'.

The approach should ensure:

- wheels will not be reinvented;

- new layers of complexity will be avoided;

- old areas of confusion will have paths charted through them;

- the results are embedded within the organisation and not just bolted on; and

- tendency for 'tools' and 'method' owners to 'market' their proprietary information as the weltanschauung rather than the toolbox approach that is needed to recognise the diversity of organisation types, sectors and sizes and the reality that one size does not fit all.

The standards referred to herein should create an open communications platform for trust and confidence between organisations and their auditors, both internal and external, and between the stakeholders in an organisation, including those who may only live in its thrall.

The hierarchy of support – a framework for mitigating operational risk in information systems

What is operational risk? 7.4

The Basel Committee for Banking Supervision defines operational risk as:

'the risk of direct or indirect loss resulting from inadequate or failed internal processes, people and systems or from external events.'

This is a comprehensive and useful definition. The challenge is how to model external events on processes, people and systems with a view to controlling the processes, people and systems and avoid undesirable outcomes.

Mitigating operational risk 7.5

Figure 7.1 shows that there is an awareness of the need to create legislative pressure to invest in ICT risk assessment and mitigation usually at a macro level, such as policies for good governance, and at the specific level with laws regarding data protection and frameworks for electronic signatures (as explained below). These legal pressures are supported from the opposite direction by the soft law of standards which take lessons learnt – from experience or by research – to provide nationally and internationally accredited methods to mitigate risk. However, the love-hate relationship that ICT suppliers and users have with standards suggests that many are not making the connection – or engaging – with standards as the tools to mitigate risk that would otherwise be emergent for many. Figure 7.2 shows how some common risks can be mitigated by the implementation of specific laws, standards and guidelines.

OECD guidelines 7.6

OECD, which is comprised of 30 member nations (with connections to 70 others), first published guidelines for information security in 1992 and revised them in 2002. Titled 'Guidelines for the Security of Information Systems and Networks', the document advocates such principles as awareness, responsibility, ethics, risk assessment and security design and implementation.

Figure 7.1 – Framework for Mitigating Operational Risk in Information Systems (MORFIS)

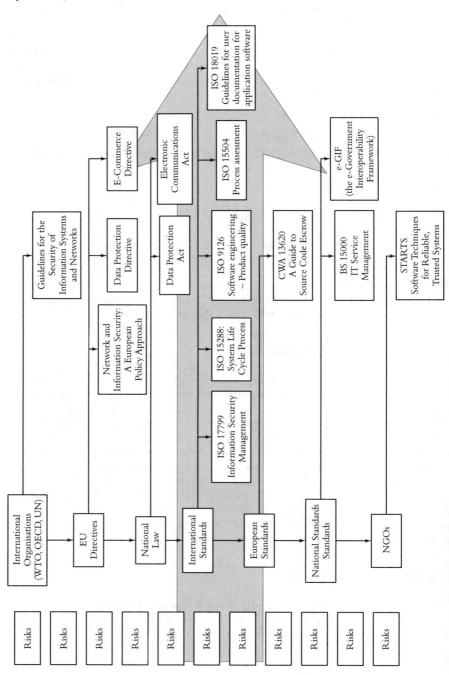

Figure 7.2 – Risks and their mitigating standards from the MORFIS framework

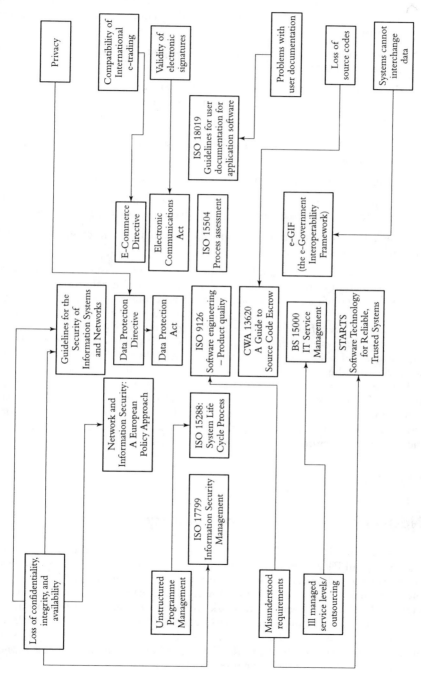

The guidelines are based on nine principles:

1.   Awareness: Participants should be aware of the need for security of information systems and networks and what they can do to enhance security.

2.   Responsibility: All participants are responsible for the security of information systems and networks.

3.   Response: Participants should act in a timely and co-operative manner to prevent, detect and respond to security incidents.

4.   Ethics: Participants should respect the legitimate interests of others.

5.   Democracy: The security of information systems and networks should be compatible with essential values of a democratic society.

6.   Risk assessment: Participants should conduct risk assessments.

7.   Security design and implementation: Participants should incorporate security as an essential element of information systems and networks.

8.   Security management: Participants should adopt a comprehensive approach to security management.

9.   Reassessment: Participants should review and reassess the security of information systems and networks, and make appropriate modifications to security policies, practices, measures and procedures.

The guidelines are a framework to engender greater trust by promoting a culture of security amongst stakeholders in information systems and networks. It is a high-level set of policies to raise awareness of the risks in information systems and networks, and the importance of implementing the policies, practices, measures and procedures available which exist to address those risks. The guidelines are, importantly, for both information system users and providers. They cover the respect for ethical values in the development, deployment and use of information systems and networks to encourage the appropriate environment for co-operation and information sharing.

EU directives

Network and information security   7.7

Security and risk has been the focus of a proposal for a European policy approach. The European Parliament, the Council and the Commission have sought closer European co-ordination on information security by setting up the European Network and Information Security Agency (ENISA) with a view to ensuring a high and effective level of network and information security within the Community, and in order to develop a risk-aware culture of network and information security for the benefit of the citizens, consumers, enterprises and public sector organisations across the European Union. The objective is support for the smooth functioning of the internal market.

The Greece-based agency will be operational for an initial period of five years. It has a budget of €24,300 million for the original 15 member states and a further €9 million for the ten new entrants.

The agency's charter is to:

- support the application of Community measures relating to network and information security, particularly for interoperability of information security functions in networks and information systems; and

- enhance the capability of both Community and member states to respond to network and information security problems.

The agency is intended to play a key role in the security of Europe's networks and information systems and the development of the information society in general. This is brought about by the agency being a central source of expert advice and co-ordinating the gathering and analysis of data on information security. This central view is designed to overcome the lack of a single entity to focus on amongst the many public and private organisations that gather data on IT-incidents and other data relevant to information security. This should lead to a broad co-operation between different stakeholders in the information security field. Such co-operation will be a vital prerequisite for the secure functioning of networks and information systems in Europe. The agency also provides:

- opinions and support for harmonised processes and procedures in the member states when applying technical and legal requirements that affect security; and

- a supportive role in the identification of the relevant standardisation needs and in the promotion of security standards and certification schemes and of their widest possible use by the Commission and the member states in support of the European legislation.

Self regulation of risk

Basel II   7.8

In the mid-seventies, the central banks and financial regulatory authorities of Belgium, Canada, France, Germany, Italy, Japan, Luxembourg, the Netherlands, Spain, Sweden, Switzerland, the UK and the US created the Basel Committee for Banking Supervision. By the late eighties, their first Capital Adequacy Accord was the benchmark for commercial banks to maintain standards to control credit risk. Following major bank collapses where credit risk was the victim of inadequate operational controls, a new accord – popularly known as Basel II – was established to fill the gap.

Basel II comprises three 'pillars':
- minimum capital requirements;
- supervisory review of capital adequacy; and
- public disclosure.

The key difference is the new attention to assess and manage 'operational risk'. Just as IT has learnt much from the banking industry in the management of security, it is likely that the force of Basel II will have spin-off lessons in risk management.

Towards software excellence   7.9

The UK Department of Trade and Industry (DTI) recognised how the software industry has learnt much from developing the programs that lie at the heart of our everyday lives – from controlling traffic lights to running elevators, from powering microwave ovens to flying jumbo jets. When it goes wrong, lives may be lost and businesses can fail. In 1988, a report for the DTI indicated that quality risks in software development could be mitigated by implementing ISO 9000 (BS 5750) for Quality Systems and being independently certificated for it.

A wealth of good practice has been built up from this experience. Ensuring these practices are available to all, especially smaller enterprises, became the heart of the DTI/National Computing Centre (NCC) established scheme: Towards Software Excellence (TSE). The scheme provides self-assessment, advice and support over the Internet aimed at helping smaller software development companies and IT enterprises to understand the capability of their current practices and improve their business processes. It is based on ISO 15504 for Process Assessment.

The overall objective set for TSE, supported not only by UK government but also other industry bodies, enables smaller enterprises in the UK software supplier industry to compare their current approach with best practice. This gives them the knowledge to manage the risk in their software processes and hence maintain or improve their competitiveness.

The scheme operates by providing its users with three key components:

- a route map through best practice, based on international software process standards;

- a self-check tool by which an enterprise can evaluate its current software practice and subsequently measure its progress towards improved processes (and ultimately achieve software excellence); and

- benchmarks and self-certification that suppliers may use to prove to customers and partners their competence, effort and attention to quality.

TSE is designed to manage risk by:

- cutting development times and costs;

- improving market delivery;

- preventing software-related failures;

- ensuring smoother customer relationships; and

- comparing performance with equivalent developers or sectors.

Significantly, TSE is free from the pressures of certification and should be seen as complementing existing schemes such as ISO9001/TickIT and the Capability Maturity Model (CMM) – although it is hoped that it will encourage small medium enterprises (SMEs) to take up such schemes when they feel the time is right and they have the resources available.

State legislation – enforcing responsibility for risk management

Sarbanes-Oxley in the US 7.10

The spectacular collapse of major organisations through fraudulent financial reporting prompted the passing, in the US, of the *Public Company Accounting Reform and Investor Protection Act of 2002* (commonly referred to as Sarbanes-Oxley). *Section 404* requires board level certification of an organisation's financial activity and the effectiveness and status of the organisations internal controls. It is these internal controls that manage operational risk so the implied requirements of good governance are now a statute in the US (with significant implications on foreign subsidiaries and non US firms with listings on Wall Street, NASDAQ etc) rather than implied ethical and moral obligations. As a result, a visible, drains-up approach to operational risk management is needed for auditors to see the effective management process and the subsequent accuracy of the reporting. Deficiencies, weaknesses and acts of fraud must be reported.

Turnbull, Cadbury and Higgs in the UK 7.11

The formalisation of ethics and good governance in the UK, leading to a demand for demonstrable management of operational risk, has largely matured since the last decade. This has been driven by the emergent risks of tardily reported inadequacies in high-level governance, as shown by the Maxwell pension scandal, the fall of the Bank of Credit and Commerce International (BCCI) and the collapse of Polly Peck. The first set of improvements was proposed by Sir Adrian Cadbury, former chairman of the Cadbury chocolate company in 'The Financial Aspects of Corporate Governance'. This was a code of conduct for stock market-listed companies addressing ethical as well as legal questions. The implementation only really became clear when Turnbull prompted attention to risk management.

This evolution of benchmarks for corporate governance was given focus by a working party of the Institute of Chartered Accountants in England and Wales (ICAEW). This was led by Nigel Turnbull and the subsequent document, 'Internal Control: Guidance for Directors on the Combined Code', has become known as the Turnbull Report. Its message is that good corporate governance is achieved by internal controls and risk management. Like Sarbanes-Oxley and Basel II, financial prudence is the driver and a high quality of transparent reporting is a key aspect of compliance. Risks need to be managed and their acceptance must be from the highest level.

The ability to put this into practice has been greatly boosted by the Higgs report which reviewed the roles and effectiveness of non-executive directors in the UK. As a result, the report sets out measures designed to improve the structure and accountability of boardrooms in the UK. This is vital to instil a transparent approach to risk management.

A standards framework to mitigate risk

Desert Island Standards   7.12

In 2003, the NCC published its framework for managing ICT risk in the guise of Desert Island Standards (Guideline 275). This report asks a person to imagine he or she is suddenly called to manage the IT on a desert island and he or she is only allowed to take eight standards to mitigate risk. Which standards would that person take? Just as in the BBC set-up the castaway gets the Bible and the Complete Works of Shakespeare, in this scenario he or she is given:

- ISO 9001 for Quality Management; and

- BS 7799 (or the international version ISO 17799) for Information Security Management.

BS 7799 is pivotal and is described in more detail later (see **7.14** et seq). The other standards selected are:

- ISO 15288: Information Technology – Life Cycle Management – System Life Cycle Processes which creates the management structure for projects from soup to nuts.

- ISO 9126 Software engineering – Product quality which creates a common language for specifying software.

- BS 15000 IT service management which manages the risk to suppliers and users of information system services.

- ISO 15504 Information Technology – Software process assessment which creates the environment for benchmarking and ensuring that risk management initiatives contribute to continuous improvement.

- The *Data Protection Act 1998 (DPA 1998)* which manages the important social risk of privacy that can be compromised so quickly for so many by so few with IT.

- STARTS Software Techniques for Reliable, Trusted Systems which reduces the risks derived from adversarial relationships between suppliers of information systems and their customers.

- e-GIF (the e-Government Interoperability Framework) which reduces the high risk of systems failing to work together.

- ISO 18019 Guidelines for the design and preparation of user documentation for application software which manages the fundamental risk of systems lacking the correct instructions for use.

ISO 9001 for quality management – dealing with emergent risk 7.13

Harmonisation across management standards over the last few years means that a common model has been adopted across many of them to manage risk. The staple of all good management processes is the simple, repeatable plan-do-check-act (PDCA) cycle that can be applied as an overlay to map all processes. This provides a framework to identify and mitigate emergent risk – the risks that were not predicted. Because even with rigorous planning, you must still expect, and deal with, the unexpected (see Figure 7.3).

Figure 7.3 – Plan...Do...Check...Act: The risk management lifecycle

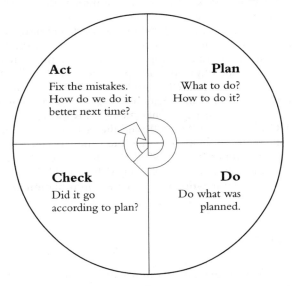

ISO 9001 set the standard for management systems to manage risk by adopting a PDCA life cycle of dealing with known risks (preventive action) and mitigating emergent risk (corrective action):

- Plan: What to do? How to do it?

    Document objectives and processes necessary to deliver results, identifying risks to be mitigated by actions embedded in the processes.

- Do: Do what was planned.

    Implement the processes, mitigate the risk.

- Check: Did it go according to plan?

    Monitor and measure processes and product against policies, objectives and requirements for products and services. Identify emergent risks. Document and report the results.

123

- Act: How do we do it better next time?

  Take actions to continually improve process performance. Deal with emergent risks. Feed the knowledge back to the planning process.

BS 7799 (ISO 17799) for Information Security Management

Provenance   7.14

In 1994, the DTI commissioned the NCC to carry out a security breaches survey which showed that virus attacks, misuse and equipment theft were widespread and cost organisations, on average, £9000 to put right (a recent Forrester report costed downtime as ranging from £50,000 to £500,000 an hour). As a result, the DTI supported the development of a code of practice using the best practices recorded by a group of leading companies. In 1995, the British Standards Institution refined the code of practice and published it as British Standard (BS) number 7799. BS 7799 was refined in 1999 and 2000 to become a two-part standard defining a collection of information security – not IT – controls to select from and build into business management systems. This was again refined in 2002 to reflect the PDCA lifecycle of ISO 9001 and the first part (the code of practice) was issued as an international standard by the International Standards Organisation (ISO) and given the number ISO 17799 Part 1. It is expected that ISO 17799 Part 2 (the management system specification) will be published eventually. BS 7799 (ISO 17799) is a framework within which information security can be assured.

What is in it?   7.15

BS 7799 breaks risk management of information assurance into manageable chunks. In the first part, risk countermeasures are categorised into:

- security policy;
- security organisation;
- asset classification and control;
- personnel security;
- physical and environmental security;
- communications and operations management;
- access control;
- system development and maintenance;
- business continuity management; and
- compliance.

In BS 7799, these issues are dealt with within the context of an Information Security Management System (ISMS) and are discussed in more detail below.

What is the ISMS?   7.16

An ISMS is the implementation of a documented set of policies, processes and procedures that pin down the general requirements of the code of practice to the individual nature of the organisation. Targets are set, controls are put in place to meet them and measurements are made to confirm achievements or initiate improvements.

At the simplest level, this is about the interaction of people, technology and processes within an organisation. First and foremost in the ISMS – which to the merit of many organisations is just the 'Management System' – is the organisation itself. This means how it is arranged in terms of buildings and depots, shops and offices, executive and non-executive boards, all levels of management, project teams, sales force, site services and so on.

The next part of the model – which will vary from size and 'maturity' of the organisation – is a combination of the defined responsibilities (which may manifest themselves in job descriptions) and the procedures for doing whatever it is the organisation does. The latter may be a mature set of instructions that are followed by all staff from switchboard to boardroom. They may be a rather ad hoc affair of success (or otherwise) based on an employee who has been in a company for 25 years and has always done it a particular this way.

Then there is the technology employed to process materials and information that is too often perceived as the management system because of its tangibility. It merely comprises the tools and when defining an ISMS a business must consider whether it has all the tools for the job. The basis for a security management system and a quality management system is the same (as shown in Figure 7.4); the focus is business.

Figure 7.4 – The components of a business management system

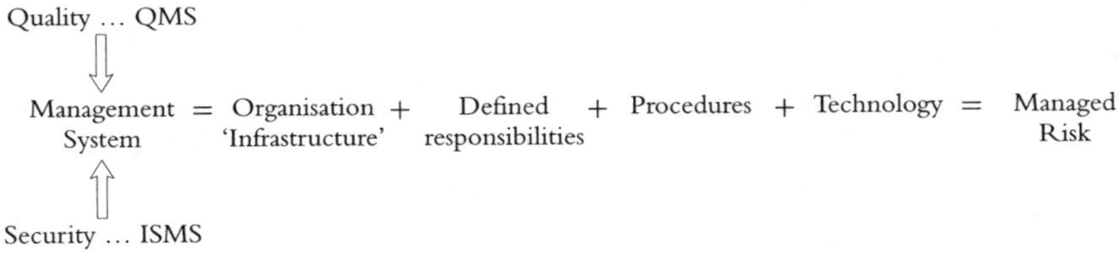

Quality ... QMS

⇩

Management = Organisation + Defined + Procedures + Technology = Managed
System   'Infrastructure'   responsibilities   Risk

⇧

Security ... ISMS

What does the ISMS comprise?   7.17

As discussed above, information security is built on physical and logical controls implemented by people and technology. This section discusses the elements of the ISMS so that as each stage of the implementation project is completed, the elements that have been put in place can be ticked off. However, the greatest threat is complacency. Every aspect will need to be revisited and assessed for suitability for the business and the risks to it as the ISMS is maintained.

Security policy   7.18

The security policy is a published statement that shows management's intent and commitment for managing risk in the organisation. It is based on facts about the criticality of information for business as identified during risk assessment processes. The security policy statement must strongly reflect the management's belief that if information is not secure, the business will suffer. The policy should clearly address issues like:

- Why is information strategically important for the organisation?

- What are business and legal requirements for information security for the organisation?

- What are the organisation's contractual obligation towards security of the information pertaining to business processes, information collected from clients, employees etc?

- What steps will the organisation take to ensure information security?

A clear security policy will provide direction to the information security efforts of the organisation as well as create confidence in the minds of various stakeholders.

Note: Do not confuse the high-level security policy with the detailed controls used for information assurance, for example whether portable devices are permitted, the complexity of passwords, the use of encryption. These are often also referred to as policies.

ISMS scope   7.19

The process of carrying out risk assessments and prioritising the protection requirements for individual business areas, based on business impact, should highlight a good measure of the critical processes that comprise the ISMS. Describing these processes will define the scope for ISMS for the organisation. Subsequent efforts will be to assure the security of these business activities within the framework of BS 7799 and applying the appropriate controls to each. A BS 7799 certificate will be specific to this scope. If more physical locations or business processes are added that change the scope, the scope of a business' BS 7799 certificate will have to be extended.

ISMS processes and procedures   7.20

Just as policies set out what a business wants to achieve – a secure, risk managed, working environment, a brand with integrity, well-trained and motivated staff – processes and procedures set out how to achieve it. To a degree, the nomenclature is a matter of preference but the de facto standard is to have one or more policies which are implemented by one or more processes. These processes may be enacted by carrying out all, or parts of, several procedures. To meet the requirements of the procedures, a business may need to use values derived from one or more standards (such as the Desert Island set – see **7.13**). This may need some very detailed work instructions to the level of what buttons to press and so on. These documents may also deliver reports to confirm that the actions in the processes and procedures have been successfully completed. This hierarchy is shown in Figure 7.5.

Figure 7.5 – The documentary components of a business management system

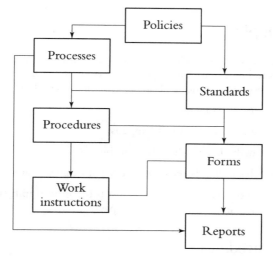

Risk assessment report   7.21

This is a report which contains the results of looking at risks to the optimum business environment. This is sometimes categorised, in the least, in terms of employment, legislation, security, competition and financial risks, and their effects on the confidentiality, integrity and availability (C-I-A) to information assets. *BS IEC 62198:2001 – Project risk management – Application guidelines* goes further to break up the classification into:

- economic;
- human;
- technical;
- legal;
- dependability;
- financial;

- social;
- market;
- environmental;
- political; and
- emergent/unclassified.

It is usual to calculate risks in terms of what information assets are at risk, what could go wrong (the risk), the likelihood of something going wrong and the impact of the problem if it does. Reports are usually returned in terms of risks being high, medium or low, or a relative value assigned.

Risk treatment plan   7.22

A risk treatment plan is the extension of the risk assessment report and covers the tools and methods to be deployed to mitigate the risks. Risks are usually mitigated in terms of what is going to be done about them, which could be:

- prevention – stop it happening;
- reduction – reduce the effect if it happens;
- transference – make it someone else's problem;
- contingency – have plan B ready to roll when all goes pear shaped; or
- acceptance – recognise that the risk is just too costly to mitigate and so the organisation will carry the risk and its impact.

Operational procedures   7.23

These are the 'how tos' that describe the best practices within the organisation. They cover everything from management planning processes to fulfilling orders and the measurement and review processes in between.

Records   7.24

Records are the evidence of the work being done to assure the confidentiality, integrity and availability of the information. Records will include backup and firewall logs, incident reports, management reviews and risk assessments.

Statement of applicability   7.25

The success of BS 7799 implementation is getting the scope of a management system right – relevant, sufficiently comprehensive, achievable – and the controls that need to be put in place to address the risks within that scope. The statement of applicability defines:

- the controls of BS 7799;
- where each control is implemented; and
- if a control is not implemented then a justification of why not.

The statement of applicability could be a fairly static document prepared for the sake of internal audits and external assessments. It can be made into a useful knowledge management tool by including:

- the tools and methods used to implement each control;
- notes and comments about related risk controls; and
- action (by whom, by when to complete implementation), review effectiveness, decommission unrequired equipment etc.

Business continuity plan   7.26

The business continuity plan is closely linked to the risk assessment and treatment plan that identify the events that can cause interruptions to business processes. Once these threats are identified, the business continuity plan specifies the roles and actions to maintain or restore business operations in the required timescales following the interruption. The plan must be tested and maintained to account for changes to the business. It must reflect the priorities identified in the risk assessment.

Management activity

Management responsibility   7.27

The key to perpetuate the effort put in by the grass roots risk management practitioners which makes all stakeholders aware of security management and give them the wherewithal to comply with security policies is the demonstration of management commitment. This can manifest itself in the chief executive's signature on top level missions and policies, the top-down briefings to all staff and the atmosphere of 'do as we do' rather than the too often found 'do as we say'.

Resource management   7.28

Resource management is often an indicator of how much the management is committed to security. Good security management requires equipment commensurate with the assets to be protected. It requires time to learn the techniques and implement the tools. It requires adequate prioritisation with what may seem more obvious first line duties. Good management practice will 'tool up' to the job in hand and be prepared to release and redeploy people and equipment to the most effective positions.

Management review   7.29

The management review is a process wherein the ISMS is periodically reviewed for its suitability and effectiveness in implementing an organisation's security policy and objectives. Plan formal review meetings at reasonable intervals. The frequency may need to vary depending on circumstances, such as changes in management, significant issues arising from internal or external audit, exceptional security incidents and so on. The agenda for the review would cover:

- results of internal audits;
- corrective action/security issues statistics;
- second/third party audit report/findings;
- policy and objectives review;
- security policy;
- scope of certification;
- risk management;
- legal and regulatory issues;
- actions for improvement; and
- acceptance of risk.

Internal audit   7.30

Internal audits are the mainstay of any management initiative. They give the underlying consistent push to the management launch and give the management information as to what is successful, what is not and what just simply needs reinforcement (in memoranda, briefings, or formal training).

The internal audits need to cover as many of the activities of as many of the functions in the management system as possible. Some processes will be audited as part of regular operations. For example:

- ongoing password checks;
- firewall event logging;
- software license checks;
- virus tool reports; and
- vulnerability audits.

Continuous improvement   7.31

The information that is collected about security incidents and the results of internal audits will be the mainstay of how a business gauges its success in continuously improving its management system. It will need to decide on the appropriate measures and set achievable, realistic targets within defined time boxes. Measures may include:

- numbers of security incidents;

- severity of security incidents;

- time taken to successfully resolve security incidents; and

- the number of repeated incidents (that is, how effective was the preventive action in eliminating or reducing recurrence).

Corrective action   7.32

Management systems are not the panacea for all ills but they do provide a calming framework in which to put right what does not go to plan or how to manage the unexpected. Corrective action is the way of dealing with the problems that will arise. The aim of corrective action is to:

- solve the problem;

- solve it effectively; and

- only make new mistakes.

Preventive action   7.33

Preventive action takes the longer view. Preventive action takes the knowledge and resources available to prevent security incidents from happening. These may include procedures or new or strengthened logical and physical controls.

Managing risk within the BS 7799 framework   7.34

BS 7799 groups mitigating controls into the ten areas listed above (**7.15**). This section will discuss some of the practical implementation of these controls in an organisation to provide a constant, cultural safety net to mitigate information-based risks.

Unfortunately, many who are not familiar with the structure of BS 7799 do not consider it to have a primary focus on risk assessment. However, that is exactly how the standard is designed to be implemented as the organisations which go the extra step to be externally reviewed by the likes of LRQA, BSI and other accredited bodies know. There is evidence (*Risk Management in IT Survey*) of this lack of awareness of how to use the standard in the organisations which frequently claim BS 7799 compliance without third-party assessment and the other organisations which claim that the standard is either too difficult (read 'expensive') to achieve or 'not secure enough' for their business. These last two diversions are missing the point of the standard entirely. The standard is about risk assessment. It is not too expensive to implement because an organisation is only expected to implement the security controls which are relevant to its business; if it does not implement the controls to match the risks then its governance is at question. Those who claim they need more security are merely doing the risk assessment that BS 7799 expects and coming to the conclusions that they need very stringent controls. Both schools of thought have a scalable framework in BS 7799. Part 1 is a checklist of controls, Part 2 is a framework of how to select and deploy these controls in a classic PDCA cycle.

Security policy   7.35

First and foremost is the top level security policy which acts as a demonstration of commitment to a stakeholder and a metaphorical knot in the handkerchief of those who carry out the organisation's business. It is a microcosm of all the other parts of the organisation's approach to risk management. The security policy will touch on the use and distribution of the organisation's information, the respect for its intellectual property and who has access to it. It will allude as to how access to buildings and equipment is controlled and how technical constraints are applied. It is to be promulgated like a mission statement.

Security organisation   7.36

Responsibility and authority is all important (the people angle again). If the disaster recovery plan shows the requirement for duplicate kit then the authority to purchase that kit is needed. Information security requires constant vigilance and updating processes and equipment to match changing circumstances. The organisation must reflect the structure to:

- manage information security within the company; and
- maintain the security where activities are outsourced or involve third parties.

The organisation must have a panel or forum that can set policy for endorsement by senior management. The panel's responsibilities include gathering, maintaining and protecting information from risk by giving advice on best practice. It needs to create a culture of co-operation so that there is a transient, virtual organisation that always has risk management on the agenda.

The panel provides an independent source of review of the acceptability of risks detected by audits, vulnerability scanning, penetration testing and general awareness. Policy setting and interpretation as to how risks are managed goes through the panel. For example, the panel will determine the constraints on contractors' access and which risks can be confidently transferred or outsourced.

Asset classification and control   7.37

An early step of risk management is knowing what is threatened so that controls can be put in place to mitigate the general and specific threats at a cost-effective level (not overspending to provide resilience to an easily replaceable asset while recognising the complexity of intellectual property developed using, or stored on, those assets). Examples of two types of asset are shown in the table below:

Information Assets Physical (off the shelf)	Information Assets Logical (created)
PCs	Databases
Phones	Research papers
PDAs	Training material
Routers	Email
Servers	Personnel records
Software (eg COTS)	Tax records

These assets need to be classified to simplify the decision processes as to how they should be handled. This helps to put risk management into context as the impact of risk is clear when the classification of the asset is known. It is really up to the respective organisations to determine a common vocabulary or nomenclature for classifying assets. It is worth pointing out here that risks will vary during the lifecycle of information. A document destined for the public domain – for example a press release – is likely to require a classification reflecting a high degree of confidentiality whilst it is being written. However, once released, its status will change to allow it a high level of availability. Risk assessment formulae can deliver the appropriate level of classification which may be selected from a subset of:

- Unclassified.
- Classified.
- Restricted.
- Confidential.
- Private.
- Commercial in confidence.

- Personal.
- Important.
- Secret.
- Top secret.
- Addressee only.
- Cosmic top secret.

Personnel security   7.38

It turns out that the greatest risks come from a business' own staff, not just from malcontents making malicious attacks or finding opportunities to steal, but from indiscretion with information (not least passwords) or mistakes such as accidental deletion of information. BS 7799 recognises the importance of training, education and continuing awareness in reducing risks of human error, theft, fraud or misuse of facilities. The NCC *Survey of Information Security Policy and Practice 2004* shows the need for, and effectiveness of, persistent formal or informal security awareness campaigns to:

- make users aware of information security threats and concerns;

- enable staff to realise the corporate security policy in the normal course of their work;

- minimise the damage from security incidents through corrective action; and

- learn from incidents and take preventive action.

Never underestimate the people issues. Access to information should still be granted only on a need to know basis and the process to take away access from staff leaving or changing roles is just as important. Staff only require the information to do their jobs so beware of pressure to allow too much access merely as a comfort or just in case.

Be consistent. Apply the same level of integrity and risk management across:

- fixed networks;

- teleworkers;

- mobile computing devices; and

- contract/temporary staff.

Give staff the facilities and encouragement to report security incidents (without blame).

Physical and environmental security   7.39

Given the interconnectedness of security issues, BS 7799 does well to compartmentalise the controls (in Part 1 of the standard). With the emphasis made on personnel security, the focus shifts to practical activity and considerations to prevent unauthorised access, damage and interference to business premises and information; to prevent loss, damage or compromise of assets and interruption to business activities and to prevent compromise or theft of information and information processing facilities. The standard requires some modelling best approached using sound engineering principles to assess risks and decide:

- Who do you let in?

- How do you keep control once they are in.

Risk management is not only an enabler but it also helps to decide on the how little or how many measures need to be put in place. It allows the wider picture to be assessed so that where an organisation may have steel doors, if the dividing walls are hardboard or raised floors or lowered ceilings leave gaps below or above then that security measure can be by-passed. The risk assessment needs to develop a practical picture of how many countermeasures are required. As so much, as already discussed, relies on staff, then the levels of trust must be applied. For example, if a terminal is activated with a smart card and password, can staff be relied on to remove the card when out of the office or must it, say, be attached by a cord to a belt to force its removal when moving from a desk.

Can staff remember changing key pad codes for doors or does a business need to invest in key fobs? Can staff be relied on to look after the fobs or is a biometrics measure, such as an iris scan or handprint, the enabler for access. (Does this endanger staff? One report concerned a thief who stole a laptop and severed the thumb of the victim to enable it.) Perhaps electronic and mechanical protection is not enough and well-vetted security guards need to be in place.

A business needs to keep a watch on how it protects the most vulnerable spots, such as loading areas. Even the rubbish can be a risk if cardboard boxes left outside premises advertises the arrival of new equipment to thieves who are often looking to steal on demand.

Once in the secure areas, a business needs to consider the access of visitors, and different levels of staff authorisation, to information so practices such as clear desks, clear screens when unattended and locked cabinets may need to be enforced.

Communications and operations management   7.40

Communications are the life essence of management systems. It is important to write down the how tos – how the organisation approaches risk in PDCA cycles. When these documented processes are followed by staff with varying responsibilities they create 'gestalts' by dividing sensitive tasks amongst different roles. This is often necessary so that there is no single picture holder. For example, procedures will make sure that a customer's PIN number cannot be pieced together by a single call-centre operative.

Procedures need to have the route to destroying sensitive 'waste'; this means all media – paper, magnetic and optical, both fixed and portable.

Backups must be carried out to set schedules which suit the results of risk assessments. The schedules need to determine how many generations of backup are taken and where they are stored – how far away from the source. The longevity of some media is questionable. Again the risk provides the amount of work to be done. Backup processes are incomplete without verification so the schedules must include periodic restoration tests. Beware backing up or restoring problems, particularly after a security incident such a virus.

Email is now a key communications mechanism for many but it still needs strict rules for what can and can't be sent. Risk assessment must ask whether it is a drain for confidential data. Staff need reminding that its content must be legal, decent, honest, moral and truthful. This is where the balance of risks must be made as to what technologies and processes are deployed. Make sure that the mutual rights of employers and employees are respected by the requirements of the *Regulation of Investigatory Powers Act 2000 (RIPA 2000)*.

Even a well-managed virus protection regime can be susceptible to the constant barrage of malicious code. Beware attachments and preview panes and think about the cost of SPAM. Use the delete key. Virus protection means installing the latest additions of anti-virus software and opening nothing doubtful. With the ability of code to 'spoof' identities, in the world of email trust no one. If an attack still occurs, follow the right instructions – not the ones the virus gives (although most viruses will give the impression of not having had an effect whilst they embed themselves and begin to replicate, deleting or altering files and so on).

Not all alerts are real so hoaxes will also need to be managed. One warning recommended users to look for certain signs of having been infected by one of these viruses that has no visible effect on opening the email or extension. If (and it gave the name of) a filename in a specific directory was there then the computer was infected and deleting the file would fix the problem. Users diligently made this correction in the satisfaction of having done something technical and clever. However, there was no virus. The file was a legitimate component of the prevalent version of Microsoft Windows. Deleting it meant that uses became restricted to filenames of eight characters or less.

There are several variations on the theme of malicious code. Worms permeate computer systems, changing code and erasing files. They are difficult to trace and stop. Macro viruses hide within applications files such as spreadsheets or word processor documents and their damage can extend well beyond the application. Trojan Horses, like their legendary namesake, hold hidden problems within an otherwise innocent looking file. They breakdown defences to enable unauthorised access to the network.

Many of these malicious programs exploit vulnerabilities in existing software. They issue commands through the software enabling defacing of websites and the controlling of a computer. Sometimes these vulnerabilities are used directly allowing hackers to retrieve files, place keyboard logging software on a computer to record credit card and PIN numbers, passwords and other confidential and often lucrative information that permits identity theft. Vulnerabilities are now an unavoidable result of the complexity not only of single operating system but also the interaction of operating systems and multiple applications. An NCC survey of vulnerabilities (*Testing the Effectiveness of Security Measures*, 2002) from 144 penetration testing campaigns in 80 organisations over two years showed that not only were more than fifty per cent of vulnerable services accessible, none of the organisations tested has a suitable level of corrective software patches to close up the gaps.

Some users confuse vulnerability scanning with penetration testing. Scanning involves the automated detection of vulnerabilities-effectively one computer testing another (although the programs may be activated by a person). For this to happen, the vulnerabilities in question must have a number of characteristics:

- they must be known about in advance;

- they must be simple and predictable, recognisable by a 'signature'; and

- they must usually be a single step.

This is not dissimilar to the way a virus checker works. It has a library of signatures relating to viruses that are known to exist. Files are checked for these signatures and if found, action can be taken. Virus checkers can't detect new viruses because they do not have the signatures.

Penetration testing is a far more comprehensive activity than vulnerability scanning. Whereas vulnerability surveys can be done effectively with good automated tools, penetration testing is an art which really needs expert human intervention to identify the appropriate combination of attempts to crack passwords, war dialling, vulnerability scanning, internal testing and so on. The price reflects this. Actions from vulnerability scanning (a few hundreds pounds) can lock out 90 per cent plus of attackers. Actions from penetration testing (thousands of pounds) locks out 99 per cent.

Penetration testing is an organised process of assessing the full threats to an organisation and attempting to infiltrate the IT systems taking on roles such as malicious hacker or disgruntled employee.

Access control 7.41

It is no longer appropriate to rely on a single yes/no approach to allowing access to information systems. Different kinds of users need different privileges or levels of access and the differing communities of users present different risks. This is where the importance of the completeness of risk management is clear. Not only must staff roles be assessed, but also the types of individual. The placing of access is important. Is the limited access of a receptionist's PC an open door to the network when unattended? What is the efficacy of access control during office hours if cleaning staff prop open security doors whilst taking out rubbish in the evening. Who vetted the cleaning staff in the first place? Is the risk managed by trust in the agency to vet them or must the business do it? These are serious issues, which must be addressed for temporary and contract staff. How does an organisation get the flexibility for giving quick access for productivity whilst not compromising the risk assessment that it has carried out?

The basic military policy of need to know is still a valid approach. To support it a business needs mechanisms to give access when the risks are acceptable and take it away when they are not. Sometimes risk mitigation is a continuous activity to keep control once they are in. Sometimes it is done by trust with clearly labelled areas where only authorised staff may be admitted – where psychological contracts are enough – and at other times an appropriate mix of technology, such as key pad, key fobs, or biometrics is needed. The need to manage privileges means that an organisation is often controlling the risks associated with access to the assets of a transient virtual organisation. It must establish onion skin-like layers of trust.

Risk assessment is a decision making tool for how and when a business allows access to its assets. It points to whether it needs a technological fix to control passwords ensuring that they are alphanumeric mixes of at least eight characters and changed frequently. It enables it to make the choice between outsourcing its network management to the Internet or whether leased lines are needed for a less vulnerable communications channel. Similarly, for remote or mobile access, the choice between the modem dial-in or the virtual private network (VPN) for teleworking and the need to create a VPN for a credibly secure wireless network is supported by the outcomes of risk assessment.

Knowing the risks gives a business the opportunity to assess what or who it may be letting in as a result of the interoperability of different software applications. It may need to limit the risks by having a time-out or limited connection time to ensure that if undesirable connections are made, they are not permanent. This is where it is important to consider the synchronisation of computer clocks, especially where an organisation is spread over several time zones.

The headings in this chapter are often so interrelated that it is difficult to nail down some solutions to certain problems. Systems access control is a huge topic relating to, for example, what the cleaners may get up to trying to have a surreptitious surf of the Internet through to a competitor who wants to find out what a business' unique product is going to be. And it is getting more complex and difficult to control. It has progressed from securing fixed machines in known locations to the era of mobile computing. Hard wired connections are difficult enough to secure but wireless computing and the cross over between ICTs are positively broadcasting secrets far and wide.

So it is vital to have a policy in place with supporting processes and procedure and properly trained staff (never underestimate the people issues) to:

- ensure the need to know principle is not compromised and staff get the right level of information to do their jobs;

- make sure that those with no business to know do not get access;

- make sure that the integrity of the network and the resources it supports is not compromised;

- highlight when things that shouldn't be going on are detected and stopped; and

- apply the same level of integrity and risk management across fixed networks, teleworkers and mobile computing devices.

Keeping them out and us in-firewalls 7.42

Risk management, as mentioned above (see **7.41**), is akin to onions – there is layer upon layer of issues to be dealt with. Use this as a strength and take advantage of structure. Identify the empire and, like Hadrian, set up the defence of the perimeter. For years an isolated network was safe, but as soon as a business wants to take advantage of the defrayed cost of connecting its network to others using the Internet, it is opening a door with a welcome mat if it is not careful. The villagers of Eysham put out vinegar to protect their neighbours from plague but a business can't rely on neighbours to protect its interests so it needs a way of controlling the gateway between the internal network and the Internet. This is what a firewall is for – a software system that controls what can enter and leave the network. But beware, this is not a matter of buying a box and inserting the right CD ROM. The firewall needs to be supported by a clear security policy with sufficient detail to ensure that when implemented, the policy makes sure that the firewall is not bypassed by an isolated modem elsewhere on the network connected to the Internet and open to let in all that the firewall is designed to keep out.

The firewall may be a single PC checking the incoming packets of information for acceptability according to predetermined rules. It may comprise a honeycomb of computers checking a range of inputs and outputs from the company network. It may separate the day-to-day operational network from a company web server, or it may be a component of a larger system where an internal firewall protects the privacy of accounts or personnel records.

Firewalls operate any one of, or a combination of, activities, or can be set up in different configurations for effectiveness. Four examples are:

- Stateful Inspection where nothing comes in that wasn't asked for.

- Packet Filter or screening router which checks specific Internet Provider addresses or applications.

- Proxy Server which represents the network from the perspective of the Internet and vice versa.

- Network Address Translation (NAT) where the network appears as a single machine to the rest of the Internet.

The firewall should be complemented with intrusion detection software. One of its functions is to register the normal, legitimate activity of traffic into the network and use pattern checking to alert administrators when activity outside a normal range is detected. This is true for the corporate firewall and must be scaled accordingly for the personal or desktop firewall.

Treating attacks like the army – the demilitarised zone 7.43

The demilitarised zone (DMZ) is the next layer of protection to complement the firewall. Firewalls are only one line of defence and combining the firewall with a DMZ greatly increases protection from outside attack. It is essentially like having another network between a business and the firewall. The DMZ stops the external Internet from making a direct connection with the internal network. Place web servers in the DMZ. A DMZ may also be used internally to isolate sensitive data on a particular machine. It can be used for, say, collecting credit card details over the Internet and making sure that those details are stored in an isolated area so that they can only be accessed by the internal network.

Establishing the DMZ is only one step. There are additional security hardening activities that can be taken. For example, when the web server is placed in the DMZ, consider having two network cards – one for outward bound traffic and one for traffic that is inward bound. Use different login patterns in the DMZ so if a hacker gets that far, he or she can't get to the next stage – the internal company network – using the information gleaned from the DMZ.

Virtual private networks   7.44

When connecting to a corporate resource using a VPN, the connection is real, not virtual – using the Internet as a 'backbone' – and it is not really a network but more of a tunnel between two places.

So why use VPNs? When using the Internet, you are outsourcing network maintenance very cheaply – paying just the phone bills and Internet Service Provider (ISP) charges, if any. The view of a corporate network is the same as if logging on, on-site at a permanent connection. Establishing a VPN sets up a tunnel and tunnels keep intruders out by controlling what can (and can't) come in at each end. The process for the remote user is as follows:

- dial up the ISP and log on;

- then log on to the corporate network;

- the software on the PC opens a tunnel between it and the network;

- the corporate network authenticates the user details and opens the other end of the tunnel to allow access to the corporate network; and

- information travelling in the tunnel is encrypted and only decoded at either end.

Using VPNs provides an easily scalable way of increasing or reducing users on the fixed network without compromising performance. However, it is not uncommon for staff to use the VPN line for both company and private business and this is prevalent in small office/home office (SOHO) applications. It allows sending (external) mail, faxing, and browsing using the ISP's mail servers without routing data through the company servers. This raises problems of billing and security as work can be done outside the tunnel bypassing security measures.

Signatures and public key infrastructures   7.45

Identity theft – particularly by organised crime – is on the rise. This is why non-repudiation has become a basic security criterion, with confidentiality, integrity and availability. One of the mitigants against this is to use digital signatures which have been made admissible evidence by the *Electronic Communications Act 2000 (ECA 2000)*.

Do not confuse a digital signature with a digitised signature which has been scanned in or added with a stylus. A digital signature is a mathematical piece of software which takes the document to be signed – such as an online form or a letter – and wraps around it some coding which shows that:

- the document was signed by whosoever has the password or other access method(s) to the software that adds the signature; and

- no unauthorised change has been made to the document.

Digital signatures are essentially an electronic identity that is granted to users by signature service providers or Trusted Third Parties (TTP). The issue being how much a TTP will do to authenticate the identity of who is asking for a signature to use online.

Digital signatures are useful for protecting transactions and it is a good idea to restrict dealings to organisations which offer the facility. The marked problem is that the majority of sites have very weak authentication and of course will not know about a business' decision not to use them.

Another problem is the quality of digital signature – what are the criteria for handing them out and how secure is the software that implements them? As part of the *ECA 2000*, the Government recognised this and requires at least some industry self-regulation to avoid mandatory licensing of TTPs. For this, the scheme was established and its existence highlights the dilemma that the common acceptability of electronic signatures in the European Commission's Electronic Signatures Directive 1999 (1999/93/EC) means that in terms of admissibility a signature from a certificated TTP in the UK may have the same weight of evidence as one from an unregulated signature from a TTP elsewhere in the Commission.

Public key infrastructures   7.46

A Public Key Infrastructure (PKI) combines authentication software, encryption technologies and services designed to help enterprises protect the security of communications across the Internet. The key to PKI is the digital certificate, which is often compared to a passport (the original kind of passport). Like a passport, the digital certificate identifies its bearer and makes certain guarantees about the bearer's status. In any secure transaction, an exchange of such certificates must precede the business itself if all the parties concerned are to be assured of the identity and status of the others.

The 'infrastructure' refers to the creation and distribution of two pieces of software – the public and the private key. First, the public key. It is accessible to all who use the PKI system. It allows users to select the equivalent of an electronic padlock to add to a message. Once added, only the holder of the corresponding private key can unlock that message and read it. The process of adding the public key to a message actually encrypts the message in a 'virtually' unbreakable code. Virtually because enough computing power over enough millennia will eventually be able to decrypt the message. This is unbreakable to all practical intents and purposes.

The private key has two uses. It allows the user to unlock messages that he or she may receive as just discussed. It also allows the user, when sending a message, to make it as certain as possible – barring sophisticated theft of a digital persona – that the message has been sent by him or her. The private key adds a tamper-proof digital signature to the information.

PKI is intended to protect data and secure transactions at every stage in the process.

The public and private keys are allocated in pairs by a certificate authority which takes the responsibility of identifying the users before allocating the keys. This is a significant issue as the efficacy of the system depends on whether a key pair may be obtained by completing an online form or whether some other proof of identity is required first. This is where levels of risk are dependent on trust, not on security.

System development and maintenance 7.47

Security is a basic requirement, as much as the end-user requirements for the functions of a system. There is nothing better than the practice of building security in rather than bolting it on afterwards. Build the systems so that they do no permit users or unauthorised access that would result in loss, modification or misuse of the software of its data.

The amount of effort and how the system deals with security issues should be determined by risk assessment. System design can, at the outset, enforce certain complexities of password, divide responsibilities up so that more that one authenticated user is required to complete a transaction, or ensure, as far as possible, that the interoperability of a new application with another does not introduce new vulnerabilities. The integrity element of risk can be mitigated by quality and accuracy checks of data. The risks in the deperimeterisation of information systems can be mitigated by authentication, authorisation and encryption to reduce the risk of the interception or corruption of the information in transit.

Not all risks are mitigatable by attention to technical detail. The risks need to be mitigated well in advance in the recruitment of those with the authority to change systems and access to the mechanisms to do so. Similar attention to the risks of temporary staff and contractors as those made when vetting permanent staff is required. The change of staff from one area to another also needs scrutiny. Strict risk treatment policies have been bypassed, such as private information being 'creamed off' by contractors using covert or Trojan code.

Getting the system desired requires solid, structured systems engineering principles. There is no short cut to application security and users must be assisted to manage risks by:

- explicitly stating security requirements;
- controlling outsourced development; and
- taking acceptance test procedures seriously.

Ecclesiastes recognised that there is nothing new under the sun and the mechanisms for users and suppliers to work together is well defined in programmes such as STARTS (Software Techniques Applied to Reliable Trusted Systems) which explicitly dealt with risk, security, as well as safety critical issues, well before the implementation of tools to effect risk management such as digital signatures and public key infrastructures.

Availability of the source code for the systems being developed and maintained is a risk issue in itself and one that can be mitigated by source code escrow. This is a good example of contrasting quality in risk management as escrow can be initiated with insufficient controls leaving the released code unusable. This is one of many examples where standards are in place to manage the risks and compliance with the principles of *CWA 13620 – Escrowguide* from the Committee for European Standardisation (CEN) which can save many an investment.

Business continuity management   7.48

When the computer goes down, the business can go down with it. What about desk space and a telephone in the event of a fire? Business continuity plans – tested plans to make sure that it can reload a backup tape, get in touch with key personnel who are off site etc – are the foundation to keeping business going through minor interruptions through to major disasters.

Consider that statistics from the University of Texas reveal that of companies suffering a catastrophic data loss, 43 per cent never reopened and 51 per cent closed within two years. Only six per cent survived. Risk conjures up images of fire, flooding or, now more so than ever, bombing, but it is far more common for telephone lines to fail, servers to crash or for a local builder to cut through the mains electricity with a digger. And then there is the fifth column. Look not to the hacker but to the carelessness of a business' own staff or the maliciousness of an ex-employee. No wonder that there is talk not just of selecting technological controls but also building a human firewall too (see **7.38**). The foundations for this are going to be deep rooted. Current European proposals (see the discussion of ENISA in **7.8**) point to education in 'respect for information' to begin at school level. There is no horizon to be avoided in countering risk.

Business continuity planning warrants a complete section of the ISMS standard because they are fundamental to the cycle of risk management (as shown in Figure 7.6).

Reading a business continuity plan should give a clear picture of the effectiveness of the risk assessment that has done. The business continuity plan is where it takes the assessment of threats and balances risk against the cost of reduction or prevention. It provides strategy and guidance for an organisation to continue to satisfy expectations. From an ICT point of view, the focus is on, but usually not restricted to, maintaining levels of IT services, as in the IT service management standard BS 15000 (see **7.12**).

Figure 7.6 – The managed cycle of ICT risk

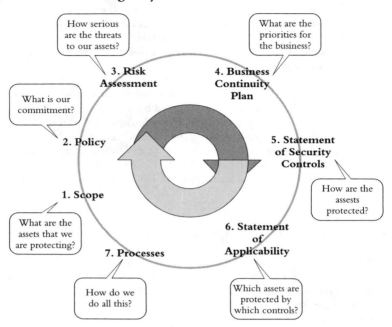

Business continuity plans can't pre-empt every eventuality (or emergent risk) but they should provide a framework of tools, contacts and personnel (such as a disaster recovery team) to deal with almost anything, based on the probability (risk) of incidents. The plan defines the correct sequence of actions, from the beginning of an event to getting everything up and running again. Such planning must fit hand in glove with the risk treatment plan.

Business continuity plans need to be easy to use in an emergency situation when risks are realised. They need to hold no surprises and a business should have some reasonable expectations based on rehearsals and tests. There is of course a limit to how much testing can be done; live end-to-end tests are difficult to create. Therefore, learn the lessons from incidents which do occur, measure recovery times and compare them against a preset target for acceptability. Carry out desktop walkthroughs of major, minor and mixed incidents. Some additional prethought may not really mitigate the risk but it can soften the blow with business continuity insurance or managing the expectations of stakeholders.

Compliance   7.49

Regulations are usually taken to be a constraint but they can be used as a positive set of requirements for information systems. Do this and a by-product will be the avoidance of breaches of criminal or civil law, statutory, regulatory and contractual obligations.

This filters down to the internal processes and procedures and manifests itself in the organisational security policies and standards. As a result, compliance and audit processes can become part of the regular business activity rather than an add-on or parallel activity.

Keep abreast of (at least) the following acts of parliament:

- Civil contingencies.
- Companies.
- Computer misuse.
- Copyright designs and patents.
- Data protection.

- Electronic communications.
- Freedom of information.
- Human rights.
- Regulation of investigatory powers.

Liability and standards   7.50

Standards, as a barrister colleague once said, should be regarded as soft law. The liability of the standards implementers is interesting. They certainly have more to do with mitigating the operational risk of failure rather than underwriting liabilities. This is shown in the way that:

- regulators encourage the use of standards rather than draw up their own (for example, the Information Commissioner recommends BS 7799 as an enabler for the seventh principle of Data Protection); and

- standards can lay down baseline requirements of quality, care and skill but note that a ruling has referred to a standard establishing a minimum requirement which is not admissible if the state of knowledge at the time permitted better performances.

Compliance with standards is widely interpreted as a necessary but insufficient condition to avoid liability.

Implementing an ISMS   7.51

BS 7799 is the framework for an ISMS but like many other standards it does not prescribe how to implement an ISMS or keep it up to date. This section will look briefly at a method created by the NCC, which published the original security breaches surveys that brought ICT risk into sharp relief.

The method comprises thirteen stages. Many organisations which mitigate risk with or without recognising that they have an ISMS will find the steps familiar. Even those who have not intended to put their level of governance at risk and fail to create a formal ISMS will find that they have some parts already in place. This is an iterative model.

(1)   Senior management acceptance and endorsement of security.

No matter where an idea comes from – staff, customers or the company board – it must carry the approval of senior management to ensure that it receives the resources needed and remains at the right level in the priorities list. This stage collects any issues identified to date, presents the business case for the implementation of the ISMS and hands the baton to those who will see it through the forthcoming stages defined below.

(2)   Information security organisation and infrastructure.

After the security policy statement has been issued, establish structure for managing security within the organisation. This is necessary to ensure an organisation's involvement in identifying and implementing various security measures.

The implementation of the ISMS will need the buy-in from the whole organisation, not just initially, but also when threats are identified or incidents occur. A mechanism will be needed whereby an organisation can collect a holistic view of the impact of security issues and a channel for disseminating the information and actions. An information security panel that represents the make up of the organisation is needed.

(3)   High level security policy.

This is where the information security panel works with senior management to set the scope of the management system and high-level security policy.

(4)   Staff training and education – creating security awareness.

Information security will involve every member of the organisation be they responsible for designing products, delivering services or maintaining the areas in which the designers work. Information security touches the whole organisation whether they are ICT users or not. Each person has the capability of sabotaging the information security through ignorance or with malicious intent. A careless comment about a customer may do expensive or irredeemable damage to the organisation's brand.

Education and training is needed to explain each individual's role in maintaining the information security and his or her responsibilities towards every information asset that he or she handles or has access to. Education and training should be comprehensive and adequate to ensure that each person clearly understands the security policies of the organisation, various security risks and threats, the processes and procedures to be followed and, finally, consequences of not abiding by the security procedures.

(5)   Identify and classify the assets.

It is difficult to protect what an organisation does not know it has. The purpose of this phase is to identify the organisation's information assets – which may vary from computers, databases, or printed and hand-written documents – and know something about these assets. Once something is known about what it has, the information security panel can make sensible decisions about the level of protection required to keep public information accessible and private information available to those who need to know.

(6) Risk assessment.

Once there is a comprehensive list of all the critical assets whose failure could impact a business and the C-I-A rating for each, the business needs to identify and assess risks to these assets. This will involve an analysis of the gap between the current state of the protection and the threats that need mitigating. This stage will identify all the gaps and inadequacies in the current security set up and present it to the information security panel with a cost-benefit analysis so that when security controls are adopted, they are fit for the intended purpose.

(7) Risk treatment plan.

The risks have been identified, now it needs to be decided how to mitigate their impact (or make the business decision to live with them). The options for risk management are based on a cost-benefit analysis of various options available to handle or accept the risk.

(8) Security standards document (control measures).

This stage is where the nitty gritty and day-to-day rules that realise the objectives of the security policy are developed.

(9) Statement of applicability.

So far, the risk management approach has been taken for identifying and mitigating the risks. Now check the selection of controls against the 127 controls defined by BS 7799. As explained, these controls are described in very general terms and no specific interpretation has been provided. There is no 'how to implement a control' defined anywhere. Entire emphasis is on selection of appropriate controls based on the risk assessment. This will create a statement of applicability which matches the business of the organisation.

(10) System security plans and procedures.

Each policy in the statement of controls will be supported by appropriate plans, processes, procedures, instructions and guidelines based on selected practices and, in some instances, products.

Note: Many documented processes will cover several policies or parts of policies. Do not tie the ISMS in knots by trying to maintain a 1:1 relationship between policy and procedure, although a business must be able to map one on to the other (and this will probably be apparent in the statement of applicability).

The procedures should be detailed and unambiguous enough for every person to follow. These will explain how to assure the security of the business.

(11) Monitor and review the ISMS performance.

The ISMS is not a marketing tool (although it can help); it is a serious, integrated part of the business processes required to assure the information that is handled. Implementing the ISMS is not a one-off job. It needs to be constantly monitored and reviewed to make sure that it remains faithful to the business objectives.

(12)   Maintain the ISMS and ensure continuous improvement.

Implementing ISMS will not ensure sudden improvement in the information assurance of an organisation. It provides an opportunity to monitor the security in an organised manner and ensure continuous improvement. Ensure that the continuous improvement actually takes place.

(13)   Extending the scope of the security management system.

Businesses will change. In fact, a complex business may implement an ISMS in phases by concentrating on certain areas or processes and then extending the scope until it is suitably comprehensive. The ISMS must manage change and integrate new scenarios and business activities into current practices or extend those practices as necessary.

Mitigating risks within the BS 7799 framework

The risk register   7.52

There is little that can be understated about the importance of having a risk register as a repository of known pitfalls. However, this needs to be tempered with the risk of:

- encountering an emergent risk that wasn't considered;

- not keeping the risk register up to date; and

- not referring to the register when planning.

The risk register – which may sometimes be referred to as a loss database – sets out the known risks but must be kept open for the emergent risks. It is not just a one-off exercise but part of a positive feedback loop (as shown in diagram 7.6: The managed cycle of ICT risk (see **7.48**)). A good approach to risk is the connection of the risk register to risk treatment plans with the policy to 'only make new mistakes'.

The attention to risk needs targets of levels of risk which are honestly set – this is wholly commensurate with the expectation of the Turnbull report (see **7.11**). Do not become oversensitive to high impact/low probability. Similarly, do not gloss over the risks when first considering the possibilities – 'dredge first/hedge later'.

A selection of risks (this is *not* an exhaustive list) faced by the modern ICT operation includes:

Available sockets and power supply are adequate for the IT installed.	Loss of company documents.	Major virus infiltration.
Continuous telephone use without a headset.	Loss of Customer Relationship Management System.	Mobile phone used while driving.
Damage to IT equipment.	Loss of desktop services.	Potential danger to third parties – whether other household members or visitors not managed.
Equipment is not safe.	Loss of digital communications.	Power outage.
Health and Safety at Work Act 1974 not applied.	Loss of equipment.	Record of work-related accidents, injuries and incidents not recorded and reported.
Interception of confidential material during transmission.	Loss of fax machines.	Rogue programming.
Loss of ABC organisation internal servers.	Loss of forum/ development servers.	Room temperature and ventilation inadequately controlled.
Loss of ABC organisation web server (content).	Loss of Internet connection.	Screens (VDUs) regulations not applied.
Loss of ABC organisation web server (operation).	Loss of key personnel (general).	Server may not be available in time to test.
Loss of building access (long term).	Loss of printer/servers.	Trailing cables that might constitute a danger.
Loss of building access (short term).	Loss of work during transmission.	Working Time Directive 1993 (93/104/EC) or screen breaks not implemented.

What to do with this information 7.53

The BS 7799 framework establishes the security framework for mitigating risk to information assurance (see diagram 7.6 (**7.48**)). Other standards, such as the Desert Island selection, mitigate other risks in the register. See Figure 7.2 – Risks and their mitigating standards from the MORFIS framework (**7.5**) as a risk treatment suggestion – standards to mitigate risk.

The risk register should be a growing resource.

Getting started: how to manage risk and a business at the same time 7.54

Managing a business is about managing risk. Remember, ICT can allow things to go wrong with the same alarming speed that we expect it to apply to the efficiency of our business processes.

The apocryphal 'my boss' story tells of the manager who demanded that every problem he or she was told of must be accompanied by the recommendation of at least one solution – to prove that the informant wasn't part of the problem. Risk management is a bit like this. If you are not careful, you may sound like you want to go out of your way to find out why an enterprise won't work. But risk management is about turning inevitable problems into positive supports to push the business forward. Can a business risk its competitors being more prepared than it?

This final section of the chapter takes a quick look at how to get started (a general look at the risk management process) and then gives some pointers about how to get a bit more sophisticated (asset-based risk management).

Step one is analysis. There is no getting away from it, but it needn't cost huge consultancy fees. This step is all about thinking about what may stop delivery being on time, getting the customer's order right and putting more money into the bank account than spending it. So, make a list, or get staff to make a list, of issues. Do not worry about completeness the first time through – experience and memory will help add to the list with time.

Now look at what has been listed and consider how likely each showstopper or stumbling block is to crop up. Think about what will be the impact on the business if it does? Add these details to the list – make a table – now prioritise. All risks are bad but some are worse than others. They can be prioritised. What will have the biggest impact and what is most likely to happen. This will result in a list of the major business risks.

Step two is to consider what can a business can afford to do to stop the stoppers? This is the positive part – risk mitigation.

Look at each risk and consider what is likely to stop it happening? One of the key, background thoughts is to think about how much the business might spend and how much the risk would cost to put right if it occurred. Remember not to spend thousands to protect an asset that would only cost hundreds to restore or replace. Keep this in mind; it will help to keep plans in perspective.

Next, some more detail. The key word in the paragraph above is *asset*. Risk management should be asset-based. Rather than think generally about the risks (above), first think about what it is the business is trying to protect. Consider the business' assets – this could be extended down to the paper clips but should be restricted to information assets. This is where ICT risk management is often misplaced. It is relatively easy to replace hardware but the information stored thereon may have taken years to design or accumulate.

Depending on the size of a business, it may be worthwhile to list the 'owner' of each information asset to make sure that there is ownership for managing the risks associated with them. This will be key to identifying the real risks and what to do about them. Soft systems practitioners will be well aware of the importance of modelling different views.

Information assets may include:

- financial records;
- software source code;
- customer web content;
- personnel records;
- software products;
- contact database;
- agreements with suppliers/third parties;
- project data/products;
- quality/security management system documents;
- company web pages;
- software tools (office infrastructure);
- customer licenses, contracts and agreements;
- email;
- software tools (development and support);
- business plans;
- publications;
- working files;
- asset register; and
- fax machines/printers.

For each asset, list each risk, its relative value, the probability of this risk happening and the severity or impact of the effects. Use judgement to score a relative value, probability and impact. One simple, but effective, way of scoring is to use values ranging from one to five (one=low, five=high). Now calculate the business' exposure by multiplying importance, probability and severity together to derive a joint value.

On the basis that the most valuable asset scores a top mark of five, and if the risk of losing its desired confidentiality, integrity and availability is up to a mark of five, and that an event which causes that to happen gets five, if it is very likely means that there is a real problem. So in this model the worst mark is 125/125, ie 100 per cent. The more that is done to mitigate a risk, the less likely it becomes and so the probability score comes down. If there are good plans in place then a business can mitigate its effects and so the impact score drops.

The options are:

- prevent the risk – stop it happening;

- reduce the risk – reduce the impact if it does happen; and

- transfer the risk – bluntly put, make it someone else's problem (this does not just mean outsourcing).

Then there is contingency – because it is so likely to happen, be prepared. Finally there is acceptance of the risk. Some risks a business will have to accept – it is unlikely that it will be able to double up all staff skills and competencies etc and will doubling up be enough? Where does it end?

The icing on the risk management cake is to assign trigger dates by which the mitigation plans will be set in place. This, with the mitigation plan (what is going to be done about this risk?) gives a business the point of control and reduces the surprises. Finally, remember to manage change and introduce review dates for checking that the mitigation plans are still up to date and appropriate. With these ticking over, a business can have the assurance that it is doing its best while it gets on with the business. Once it has got used to it, managing the risks – or even taking the risks – becomes one with the business.

Checklists

People

High priority   7.55

✓ Make a high level policy of security compliance with explicit support from senior management.

✓ Put security responsibilities, including web and email use constraints, into job descriptions, terms and conditions and employee's contracts. Make it clear that there are disciplinary sanctions for infringement.

✓ Make sure users keep their passwords secret and implement a policy of no sharing of logon IDs and passwords.

✓ Careless talk costs jobs: think about who is in earshot if you mention business, password, or access codes.

✓   Audit and enforce detailed security policies. For example, email preview panes can trigger malicious code. Make sure that users haven't switched them back on since the last check.

✓   Never open attachments that were not expected without verifying their provenance with the originator. Be particularly wary of file names ending in.vb,.vbs,.exe, and.scr.

✓   Treat email with the same respect as you would business letters between organisations and individuals. Have strict rules for what can/can't be sent. Make sure that it is not a drain for confidential data.

✓   Make sure that staff know how to identify a security incident, report it adequately and how to react.

✓   Appoint someone – separate from the IT operations manager whose primary responsibility is security – with the authority to enforce security policies.

Medium priority   7.56

✓   Cover security issues during induction procedures and keep staff aware with a programme of briefings and bulletins.

✓   Classify information (with 'For internal use only', 'Commercial in confidence' etc). Not least as a reminder as to how careful a business must be with information assets.

✓   Be aware of more vulnerable times: events, exhibitions, or opening facilities for others.

✓   Be responsible for your own personal possessions.

✓   If staff leave the office for a coffee, a meeting, fire drill or even the toilet, make sure they lock their screen or set a password-protected screensaver to come in after no more than three minutes. They may only intend to step out for a minute but....

✓   Be careful not to switch off any security features, such as personal firewalls or virus scanners.

✓   any equipment based at home is protected to the same standard as equipment at the office.

✓   Always close the Internet browser after use and do not use facilities which remember the passwords.

Important   7.57

✓   Consider issuing all staff with identity badges which must be carried at all times. They do not always deter intruders but they can be useful reminders for staff to uphold their security responsibilities.

✓ Know the warning signs of a security breach:

- the computer begins to behave abnormally;
- the computer runs slower than usual;
- some files change size or become corrupted inexplicably;
- the computer will not boot up normally;
- strange messages or graphics appear;
- unknown files or directories appear; and
- less memory is available than usual.

Process

High priority 7.58

✓ Manage security within the ten-point framework of the ISO 17799 Code of Practice for Information Security. Select from the controls which give the business a return on investment and reduce risks to desired level.

✓ Undertake regular risk analysis of systems. Prepare and maintain a risk treatment plan to keep up with the business.

✓ Investigate all security incidents and learn the lessons either for assurance of having adequate countermeasures or the need to implement new preventive activities.

✓ Maintain a complete register of assets. For information assets include databases, drawings and technical documents. For equipment include memory and hard disc capacities if you do not know you have got it, you are unlikely to miss it if it disappears. For software, practice software asset management for legal compliance and cost-effective licensing.

✓ Ensure that activities comply with the *DPA 1998* (especially when transferring information to third parties), *Computer Misuse Act 1990* and the *RIPA 2000* at least.

✓ Create a thorough business continuity plan. Keep it rehearsed, tested and up to date. Use reports of security incidents as tests of the plan. Align the plan with the importance of the assets in the asset register. Evaluate the business' information assets according to values based on confidentiality, integrity and availability.

✓ Quarantine new software – know what it is being tested for and have acceptable results before rolling it out to live systems.

✓ Protect intellectual property vigorously with trademarks, patents and security-savvy non-disclosure agreements with partners, contractors and the relevant parts of the supply chain. Build data protection into procedures whereby customer information or personnel records are checked as a matter of course and incorrect or outdated information removed.

✓ Think Business Continuity Planning (BCP), not Disaster Recovery (DR).

Medium priority 7.59

✓ Implement a policy for Internet and dial out and dial in access. Make sure that the systems administrator has the appropriate control procedures.

✓ Conduct risk assessment workshops with staff to list and prioritise their perceived threats and vulnerabilities. Factor in the likelihood of occurrence then calculate the actual values for risks and costed countermeasures. Get management to quantify the acceptable levels of risk.

✓ Make insurance an integral part of the business continuity plan and keep the insurers informed of any changes in the risk covered.

✓ Use the Common Criteria (ISO 15408) as a measure for product security and for specifying security requirements throughout the procurement process.

✓ Make security requirements explicit in contracts and schedule security tests into acceptance test plans. Retest these requirements after any upgrade.

✓ Keep software and manuals secure: it costs a pretty penny to keep licenses up to date and compliant, why should someone else benefit illegally?

✓ Consider what is safe in the bin and what should be shredded. You may have reprinted a page with a missing comma but all those other sensitive details are ripe for the picking if the last version is just dropped in the bin.

✓ Lock away company documents at night – if it is highly sensitive, put it out of sight over lunch time or extended time away from the desk.

✓ Follow the TrustUK-approved codes of practice relevant to the sector for the electronic business activities.

Important 7.60

✓ Do not confuse security with trust. Make business information secure as a basis for trust. Maintain:

- confidentiality – restrict access to information to those whom the user wishes to impart the information, authentication is therefore of paramount importance;

- ontegrity – verify the accuracy of collected and processed information before it is released;

- availability – make sure that security restrictions or technology constraints do not restrict the access of genuine users (those with a need to know).

✓ Make source code escrow is a stipulation for bespoke software and externally managed websites. Select an escrow agent that complies with TickIT and CWA 13620.

✓ Ensure that the supply-chain partners are aware of and adhere to the security standards.

✓ Treat information security as the foundation of good corporate governance.

✓ Review third party contracts for clauses relating to loss of service.

Technology

High priority   7.61

✓ Keep up-to-date checks in place for malicious programs, like viruses, on all servers and personal computers. Screen email leaving and coming in. Keep firewalls up to date with practical rules and virus check tools with latest updates.

✓ Protect key equipment with surge protectors, uninterruptible power supplies (UPS) and make provision for a standby generator.

✓ Carry out regular vulnerability assessments to close known vulnerabilities (note that this is not the same as penetration testing).

✓ Backup regularly depending on the frequency of change and the importance of the information. Regularly check that original systems and data can be restored from the backup media.

✓ Enforce sufficiently strong passwords. Review password systems regularly for compliance to the business' policy. Do not enable remember me/password facilities, keeping security tokens separate from machines.

✓ Encrypt sensitive information with technology of a complexity commensurate with the sensitivity.

✓ Install physical security devices on critical system equipment.

✓ If not using a facility, close it or delete it. Close unused firewall ports. Make the default policy 'disabled'.

✓ If the business enjoys the freedom of wireless networks, do not skimp on the additional security considerations.

✓ Laptops, mobile phones and PDAs are ever attractive. Keep them with you or locked up. Encrypt what is important and make sure that passwords are set and comply with password policy.

✓ If you think that the business has been a victim of e-crime – including misuse of IT by staff – you may need a computer forensics service. Touch nothing! Even switching on a PC or viewing a file will corrupt the evidence.

✓ Physically remove sensitive information from laptops, including cleansing cookies regularly.

Medium priority   7.62

✓ Take expert advice – use CLAS approved advisers or consultants with a track record that can be trusted.

✓ Change factory-set password and privileges. Do not rely on factory default settings for door locks and software – especially the firewall. Remove the 'Guest' user IDs supplied with the system.

✓ Review the logs from firewalls, intrusion detection systems and door entry systems. Use the information recorded to ensure that there is adequate security measures in place.

✓ Do not leave evidence of recently purchased equipment on view for thieves to see (for example, packing cases left outside the building for disposal).

✓ Review the control of PCs and portable equipment for security risks (many laptop users forget the true value of their equipment and data and can leave it unattended), carry out periodic checks to see what laptop owners have added.

✓ Engage CESG CHECK-approved penetration testing to ensure that the optimum security arrangements are made for the network.

✓ Use digital signature facilities from a supplier certificated under tScheme.

✓ Make use of UNIRAS/CERT/SANS to keep abreast of current vulnerabilities for the defined systems patch where appropriate.

✓ Periodically check published information available on the website to reduce information that could direct undesirable attention to otherwise concealed network-sensitive information.

Important   7.63

✓ Reduce the number of email addresses on the website to limit SPAM and reduce unwanted email.

✓ Minimise the amount of information processing outside the firewall. Use 'server side' processing and demark personal information from identifying information.

✓ Make security part of the architecture where ever possible.

✓ Wipe, do not just delete, the contents of equipment that is being disposed. Do this also for transfers of equipment from one department to another.

✓ Aim for a minimum of two lines of defence.

Appendix I
A Summary of the General Principles Binding a Director in the Companies Bill

1. Obeying the constitution and other lawful decisions

A director must act in accordance with the company's constitution and any decisions taken under the constitution and must exercise his or her powers for a proper purpose.

2. Promotion of company's objectives

A director must act in a way which will promote the success of the company for the benefit of its members, taking into account all 'material' factors ('material' factors mean the long and short-term consequences of his or her actions that a person of skill and care would consider relevant and all other factors a person of skill and care would consider relevant), including relationships with employees, suppliers and customers, impact on affected communities and the environment, the company's need to maintain a reputation for high standards of business conduct and to achieve fairness between members.

3. Delegation and independence of judgement

A director must not delegate any powers he or she is not authorised to or fail to exercise independent judgement in relation to exercising those powers.

4. Care, skill and diligence

A director must exercise a level of care, skill and diligence which would be expected of a reasonably diligent person with both the knowledge, skill and experience which may reasonably be expected of a director in his or her position and, importantly, any additional knowledge, skill and experience which he or she has. As is the case under the existing law, directors with special skills, such as in IT, will therefore need to pay greater attention to their areas of speciality than their fellow directors.

5. Transactions involving conflict of interest

A director must not enter into transactions where he or she has a conflict of interest which has not been disclosed.

6. Personal use of the company's property, information or opportunity

A director or former director must not use company property, information or opportunities for his or her own or anyone else's benefit unless the company has sanctioned it or the board has authorised it. Where the board authorises use (in the case of a private company), the constitution must not invalidate its use; (in the case of a public company) the constitution must positively enable the board to authorise use.

7. Benefits of a third party

No director or former director can receive any benefit as a result of his or her position unless the company has consented to the benefit or it is necessarily incidental to the performance of his or her functions as director. It is difficult to imagine many cases coming under this exception.

Appendix 2
Sample Technical
Precautions

1. Firewalls and security

The obvious way to avoid exposure to risks in the use of IT and e-commerce systems is to ensure that there is adequate security in place. This will depend on how secure a system needs to be, for example with individuals' data being processed and where financial transactions are involved.

Companies need to ensure that they have firewalls which are immune to penetration. A firewall is a collection of hardware and/or software or a system which sits between the Internet and the local network through which all traffic from inside to outside and vice versa must pass. It is designed to ensure that only authorised traffic is allowed to pass through it.

2. Password controls

This is the most basic form of prevention and protection and it is, therefore, sensible to ensure that all employees use passwords to protect the information contained on a company's database. In most cases, a minimum two factor authentication should be considered, for example the combination of a password with a smart key without which the computer will not work.

3. Electronic signatures

Another topical and developing area related to e-commerce, consumer and business to business transactions is how the security of such transactions can be maintained. The public's lack of faith in the Internet as a secure place for commerce has long been regarded as one of the most limiting factors for its growth. Sites need to feel secure to end users to allow them to trade online. To be comparable to a hand-written signature, an electronic signature must be unique to its signatory, created using a method within the signatory's sole control and capable of being linked to the relevant document or data in such a way that subsequent changes to the document or data will be detectable.

4. Encryption

This is basically a mathematical process of securing text or data, making it unintelligible to all but the intended recipient. Whilst this is an involved topic in itself, there is insufficient space to deal with this here. Directors should consider the extent to which encryption can be used in their business.

Appendix 3
Data Protection Act 1998

The text below is selected extracts from the *Data Protection Act 1998*.

Data Protection Act 1998

1998 CHAPTER 29

An Act to make new provision for the regulation of the processing of information relating to individuals, including the obtaining, holding, use or disclosure of such information.

[16th July 1998]

BE IT ENACTED by the Queen's most Excellent Majesty, by and with the advice and consent of the Lords Spiritual and Temporal, and Commons, in this present Parliament assembled, and by the authority of the same, as follows:–

PART I

PRELIMINARY

I   Basic interpretative provisions

(1)   In this Act, unless the context otherwise requires–
'data' means information which–

    (a)   is being processed by means of equipment operating automatically in response to instructions given for that purpose,

    (b)   is recorded with the intention that it should be processed by means of such equipment,

    (c)   is recorded as part of a relevant filing system or with the intention that it should form part of a relevant filing system, *or*

    (d)   does not fall within paragraph (a), (b) or (c) but forms part of an accessible record as defined by section 68; [or

    (e)   is recorded information held by a public authority and does not fall within any of paragraphs (a) to (d);]

'data controller' means, subject to subsection (4), a person who (either alone or jointly or in common with other persons) determines the purposes for which and the manner in which any personal data are, or are to be, processed;

'data processor', in relation to personal data, means any person (other than an employee of the data controller) who processes the data on behalf of the data controller;

'data subject' means an individual who is the subject of personal data;

'personal data' means data which relate to a living individual who can be identified–

    (a)   from those data, or

    (b)   from those data and other information which is in the possession of, or is likely to come into the possession of, the data controller,

163

and includes any expression of opinion about the individual and any indication of the intentions of the data controller or any other person in respect of the individual;

'processing', in relation to information or data, means obtaining, recording or holding the information or data or carrying out any operation or set of operations on the information or data, including—

    (a) organisation, adaptation or alteration of the information or data,

    (b) retrieval, consultation or use of the information or data,

    (c) disclosure of the information or data by transmission, dissemination or otherwise making available, or

    (d) alignment, combination, blocking, erasure or destruction of the information or data;

['public authority' has the same meaning as in the Freedom of Information Act 2000;]

'relevant filing system' means any set of information relating to individuals to the extent that, although the information is not processed by means of equipment operating automatically in response to instructions given for that purpose, the set is structured, either by reference to individuals or by reference to criteria relating to individuals, in such a way that specific information relating to a particular individual is readily accessible.

(2) In this Act, unless the context otherwise requires—

    (a) 'obtaining' or 'recording', in relation to personal data, includes obtaining or recording the information to be contained in the data, and

    (b) 'using' or 'disclosing', in relation to personal data, includes using or disclosing the information contained in the data.

(3) In determining for the purposes of this Act whether any information is recorded with the intention—

    (a) that it should be processed by means of equipment operating automatically in response to instructions given for that purpose, or

    (b) that it should form part of a relevant filing system,

it is immaterial that it is intended to be so processed or to form part of such a system only after being transferred to a country or territory outside the European Economic Area.

(4) Where personal data are processed only for purposes for which they are required by or under any enactment to be processed, the person on whom the obligation to process the data is imposed by or under that enactment is for the purposes of this Act the data controller.

[(5) In paragraph (e) of the definition of 'data' in subsection (1), the reference to information 'held' by a public authority shall be construed in accordance with section 3(2) of the Freedom of Information Act 2000.

(6) Where section 7 of the Freedom of Information Act 2000 prevents Parts I to V of that Act from applying to certain information held by a public authority, that information is not to be treated for the purposes of paragraph (e) of the definition of 'data' in subsection (1) as held by a public authority.]

2   Sensitive personal data

In this Act 'sensitive personal data' means personal data consisting of information as to—
    (a) the racial or ethnic origin of the data subject,

    (b) his political opinions,

    (c) his religious beliefs or other beliefs of a similar nature,

    (d) whether he is a member of a trade union (within the meaning of the Trade Union and Labour Relations (Consolidation) Act 1992,

    (e) his physical or mental health or condition,

    (f) his sexual life,

    (g) the commission or alleged commission by him of any offence, or

    (h) any proceedings for any offence committed or alleged to have been committed by him, the disposal of such proceedings or the sentence of any court in such proceedings.

3   The special purposes

In this Act 'the special purposes' means any one or more of the following—

    (a) the purposes of journalism,

    (b) artistic purposes, and

    (c) literary purposes.

4   The data protection principles

(1) References in this Act to the data protection principles are to the principles set out in Part I of Schedule 1.

(2) Those principles are to be interpreted in accordance with Part II of Schedule 1.

(3) Schedule 2 (which applies to all personal data) and Schedule 3 (which applies only to sensitive personal data) set out conditions applying for the purposes of the first principle; and Schedule 4 sets out cases in which the eighth principle does not apply.

(4) Subject to section 27(1), it shall be the duty of a data controller to comply with the data protection principles in relation to all personal data with respect to which he is the data controller.

5   Application of Act

(1) Except as otherwise provided by or under section 54, this Act applies to a data controller in respect of any data only if–

  (a) the data controller is established in the United Kingdom and the data are processed in the context of that establishment, or

  (b) the data controller is established neither in the United Kingdom nor in any other EEA State but uses equipment in the United Kingdom for processing the data otherwise than for the purposes of transit through the United Kingdom.

(2) A data controller falling within subsection (1)(b) must nominate for the purposes of this Act a representative established in the United Kingdom.

(3) For the purposes of subsections (1) and (2), each of the following is to be treated as established in the United Kingdom–

  (a) an individual who is ordinarily resident in the United Kingdom,

  (b) a body incorporated under the law of, or of any part of, the United Kingdom,

  (c) a partnership or other unincorporated association formed under the law of any part of the United Kingdom, and

  (d) any person who does not fall within paragraph (a), (b) or (c) but maintains in the United Kingdom–

    (i) an office, branch or agency through which he carries on any activity, or

    (ii) a regular practice;

and the reference to establishment in any other EEA State has a corresponding meaning.

6 The Commissioner and the Tribunal

[(1) For the purposes of this Act and of the Freedom of Information Act 2000 there shall be an officer known as the Information Commissioner (in this Act referred to as 'the Commissioner').]

[(3) For the purposes of this Act and of the Freedom of Information Act 2000 there shall be a tribunal known as the Information Tribunal (in this Act referred to as 'the Tribunal').]

Part II
Rights of Data Subjects and Others

7 Right of access to personal data

(1) Subject to the following provisions of this section and to *sections 8 and 9* [sections 8, 9 and 9A], an individual is entitled–

  (a) to be informed by any data controller whether personal data of which that individual is the data subject are being processed by or on behalf of that data controller,

  (b) if that is the case, to be given by the data controller a description of–

    (i) the personal data of which that individual is the data subject,

    (ii) the purposes for which they are being or are to be processed, and

    (iii) the recipients or classes of recipients to whom they are or may be disclosed,

  (c) to have communicated to him in an intelligible form–

    (i) the information constituting any personal data of which that individual is the data subject, and

    (ii) any information available to the data controller as to the source of those data, and

(d) where the processing by automatic means of personal data of which that individual is the data subject for the purpose of evaluating matters relating to him such as, for example, his performance at work, his creditworthiness, his reliability or his conduct, has constituted or is likely to constitute the sole basis for any decision significantly affecting him, to be informed by the data controller of the logic involved in that decision-taking.

(2) A data controller is not obliged to supply any information under subsection (1) unless he has received–

(a) a request in writing, and

(b) except in prescribed cases, such fee (not exceeding the prescribed maximum) as he may require.

[(3) Where a data controller–

(a) reasonably requires further information in order to satisfy himself as to the identity of the person making a request under this section and to locate the information which that person seeks, and

(b) has informed him of that requirement,

the data controller is not obliged to comply with the request unless he is supplied with that further information.]

(4) Where a data controller cannot comply with the request without disclosing information relating to another individual who can be identified from that information, he is not obliged to comply with the request unless–

(a) the other individual has consented to the disclosure of the information to the person making the request, or

(b) it is reasonable in all the circumstances to comply with the request without the consent of the other individual.

(5) In subsection (4) the reference to information relating to another individual includes a reference to information identifying that individual as the source of the information sought by the request; and that subsection is not to be construed as excusing a data controller from communicating so much of the information sought by the request as can be communicated without disclosing the identity of the other individual concerned, whether by the omission of names or other identifying particulars or otherwise.

(6) In determining for the purposes of subsection (4)(b) whether it is reasonable in all the circumstances to comply with the request without the consent of the other individual concerned, regard shall be had, in particular, to–

(a) any duty of confidentiality owed to the other individual,

(b) any steps taken by the data controller with a view to seeking the consent of the other individual,

(c) whether the other individual is capable of giving consent, and

(d) any express refusal of consent by the other individual.

(7) An individual making a request under this section may, in such cases as may be prescribed, specify that his request is limited to personal data of any prescribed description.

(8) Subject to subsection (4), a data controller shall comply with a request under this section promptly and in any event before the end of the prescribed period beginning with the relevant day.

(9) If a court is satisfied on the application of any person who has made a request under the foregoing provisions of this section that the data controller in question has failed to comply with the request in contravention of those provisions, the court may order him to comply with the request.

(10) In this section–

'prescribed' means prescribed by the [Secretary of State] by regulations;

'the prescribed maximum' means such amount as may be prescribed;

'the prescribed period' means forty days or such other period as may be prescribed;

'the relevant day', in relation to a request under this section, means the day on which the data controller receives the request or, if later, the first day on which the data controller has both the required fee and the information referred to in subsection (3).

(11) Different amounts or periods may be prescribed under this section in relation to different cases.

8 Provisions supplementary to section 7

(1) The [Secretary of State] may by regulations provide that, in such cases as may be prescribed, a request for information under any provision of subsection (1) of section 7 is to be treated as extending also to information under other provisions of that subsection.

(2) The obligation imposed by section 7(1)(c)(i) must be complied with by supplying the data subject with a copy of the information in permanent form unless–

(a) the supply of such a copy is not possible or would involve disproportionate effort, or

(b) the data subject agrees otherwise;

and where any of the information referred to in section 7(1)(c)(i) is expressed in terms which are not intelligible without explanation the copy must be accompanied by an explanation of those terms.

(3) Where a data controller has previously complied with a request made under section 7 by an individual, the data controller is not obliged to comply with a subsequent identical or similar request under that section by that individual unless a reasonable interval has elapsed between compliance with the previous request and the making of the current request.

(4) In determining for the purposes of subsection (3) whether requests under section 7 are made at reasonable intervals, regard shall be had to the nature of the data, the purpose for which the data are processed and the frequency with which the data are altered.

(5) Section 7(1)(d) is not to be regarded as requiring the provision of information as to the logic involved in any decision-taking if, and to the extent that, the information constitutes a trade secret.

(6) The information to be supplied pursuant to a request under section 7 must be supplied by reference to the data in question at the time when the request is received, except that it may take account of any amendment or deletion made between that time and the time when the information is supplied, being an amendment or deletion that would have been made regardless of the receipt of the request.

(7) For the purposes of section 7(4) and (5) another individual can be identified from the information being disclosed if he can be identified from that information, or from that and any other information which, in the reasonable belief of the data controller, is likely to be in, or to come into, the possession of the data subject making the request.

9 Application of section 7 where data controller is credit reference agency

(1) Where the data controller is a credit reference agency, section 7 has effect subject to the provisions of this section.

(2) An individual making a request under section 7 may limit his request to personal data relevant to his financial standing, and shall be taken to have so limited his request unless the request shows a contrary intention.

(3) Where the data controller receives a request under section 7 in a case where personal data of which the individual making the request is the data subject are being processed by or on behalf of the data controller, the obligation to supply information under that section includes an obligation to give the individual making the request a statement, in such form as may be prescribed by the [Secretary of State] by regulations, of the individual's rights–

    (a) under section 159 of the Consumer Credit Act 1974 , and

    (b) to the extent required by the prescribed form, under this Act.

[9A Unstructured personal data held by public authorities]

[(1) In this section 'unstructured personal data' means any personal data falling within paragraph (e) of the definition of 'data' in section 1(1), other than information which is recorded as part of, or with the intention that it should form part of, any set of information relating to individuals to the extent that the set is structured by reference to individuals or by reference to criteria relating to individuals.

(2) A public authority is not obliged to comply with subsection (1) of section 7 in relation to any unstructured personal data unless the request under that section contains a description of the data.

(3) Even if the data are described by the data subject in his request, a public authority is not obliged to comply with subsection (1) of section 7 in relation to unstructured personal data if the authority estimates that the cost of complying with the request so far as relating to those data would exceed the appropriate limit.

(4) Subsection (3) does not exempt the public authority from its obligation to comply with paragraph (a) of section 7(1) in relation to the unstructured personal data unless the estimated cost of complying with that paragraph alone in relation to those data would exceed the appropriate limit.

(5) In subsections (3) and (4) 'the appropriate limit' means such amount as may be prescribed by the [Secretary of State] by regulations, and different amounts may be prescribed in relation to different cases.

(6) Any estimate for the purposes of this section must be made in accordance with regulations under section 12(5) of the Freedom of Information Act 2000.]

10 Right to prevent processing likely to cause damage or distress

(1) Subject to subsection (2), an individual is entitled at any time by notice in writing to a data controller to require the data controller at the end of such period as is reasonable in the circumstances to cease, or not to begin, processing, or processing for a specified purpose or in a specified manner, any personal data in respect of which he is the data subject, on the ground that, for specified reasons–

    (a) the processing of those data or their processing for that purpose or in that manner is causing or is likely to cause substantial damage or substantial distress to him or to another, and

    (b) that damage or distress is or would be unwarranted.

(2) Subsection (1) does not apply—

(a) in a case where any of the conditions in paragraphs 1 to 4 of Schedule 2 is met, or

(b) in such other cases as may be prescribed by the [Secretary of State] by order.

(3) The data controller must within twenty-one days of receiving a notice under subsection (1) ('the data subject notice') give the individual who gave it a written notice—

(a) stating that he has complied or intends to comply with the data subject notice, or

(b) stating his reasons for regarding the data subject notice as to any extent unjustified and the extent (if any) to which he has complied or intends to comply with it.

(4) If a court is satisfied, on the application of any person who has given a notice under subsection (1) which appears to the court to be justified (or to be justified to any extent), that the data controller in question has failed to comply with the notice, the court may order him to take such steps for complying with the notice (or for complying with it to that extent) as the court thinks fit.

(5) The failure by a data subject to exercise the right conferred by subsection (1) or section 11(1) does not affect any other right conferred on him by this Part.

11 Right to prevent processing for purposes of direct marketing

(1) An individual is entitled at any time by notice in writing to a data controller to require the data controller at the end of such period as is reasonable in the circumstances to cease, or not to begin, processing for the purposes of direct marketing personal data in respect of which he is the data subject.

(2) If the court is satisfied, on the application of any person who has given a notice under subsection (1), that the data controller has failed to comply with the notice, the court may order him to take such steps for complying with the notice as the court thinks fit.

[(2A) This section shall not apply in relation to the processing of such data as are mentioned in paragraph (1) of regulation 8 of the Telecommunications (Data Protection and Privacy) Regulations 1999 (processing of telecommunications billing data for certain marketing purposes) for the purposes mentioned in paragraph (2) of that regulation.]

(3) In this section 'direct marketing' means the communication (by whatever means) of any advertising or marketing material which is directed to particular individuals.

12 Rights in relation to automated decision-taking

(1) An individual is entitled at any time, by notice in writing to any data controller, to require the data controller to ensure that no decision taken by or on behalf of the data controller which significantly affects that individual is based solely on the processing by automatic means of personal data in respect of which that individual is the data subject for the purpose of evaluating matters relating to him such as, for example, his performance at work, his creditworthiness, his reliability or his conduct.

(2) Where, in a case where no notice under subsection (1) has effect, a decision which significantly affects an individual is based solely on such processing as is mentioned in subsection (1)—

(a) the data controller must as soon as reasonably practicable notify the individual that the decision was taken on that basis, and

(b) the individual is entitled, within twenty-one days of receiving that notification from the data controller, by notice in writing to require the data controller to reconsider the decision or to take a new decision otherwise than on that basis.

(3) The data controller must, within twenty-one days of receiving a notice under subsection (2)(b) ('the data subject notice') give the individual a written notice specifying the steps that he intends to take to comply with the data subject notice.

(4) A notice under subsection (1) does not have effect in relation to an exempt decision; and nothing in subsection (2) applies to an exempt decision.

(5) In subsection (4) 'exempt decision' means any decision—

(a) in respect of which the condition in subsection (6) and the condition in subsection (7) are met, or

(b) which is made in such other circumstances as may be prescribed by the [Secretary of State] by order.

(6) The condition in this subsection is that the decision—

(a) is taken in the course of steps taken—

(i) for the purpose of considering whether to enter into a contract with the data subject,

(ii) with a view to entering into such a contract, or

(iii) in the course of performing such a contract, or

(b) is authorised or required by or under any enactment.

(7) The condition in this subsection is that either–

    (a) the effect of the decision is to grant a request of the data subject, or

    (b) steps have been taken to safeguard the legitimate interests of the data subject (for example, by allowing him to make representations).

(8) If a court is satisfied on the application of a data subject that a person taking a decision in respect of him ('the responsible person') has failed to comply with subsection (1) or (2)(b), the court may order the responsible person to reconsider the decision, or to take a new decision which is not based solely on such processing as is mentioned in subsection (1).

(9) An order under subsection (8) shall not affect the rights of any person other than the data subject and the responsible person.

[12A Rights of data subjects in relation to exempt manual data]

[(1) A data subject is entitled at any time by notice in writing–

    (a) to require the data controller to rectify, block, erase or destroy exempt manual data which are inaccurate or incomplete, or

    (b) to require the data controller to cease holding exempt manual data in a way incompatible with the legitimate purposes pursued by the data controller.

(2) A notice under subsection (1)(a) or (b) must state the data subject's reasons for believing that the data are inaccurate or incomplete or, as the case may be, his reasons for believing that they are held in a way incompatible with the legitimate purposes pursued by the data controller.

(3) If the court is satisfied, on the application of any person who has given a notice under subsection (1) which appears to the court to be justified (or to be justified to any extent) that the data controller in question has failed to comply with the notice, the court may order him to take such steps for complying with the notice (or for complying with it to that extent) as the court thinks fit.

(4) In this section 'exempt manual data' means–

    (a) in relation to the first transitional period, as defined by paragraph 1(2) of Schedule 8, data to which paragraph 3 or 4 of that Schedule applies, and

    (b) in relation to the second transitional period, as so defined, data to which paragraph 14 of that Schedule applies.

(5) For the purposes of this section personal data are incomplete if, and only if, the data, although not inaccurate, are such that their incompleteness would constitute a contravention of the third or fourth data protection principles, if those principles applied to the data.]

13 Compensation for failure to comply with certain requirements

(1) An individual who suffers damage by reason of any contravention by a data controller of any of the requirements of this Act is entitled to compensation from the data controller for that damage.

(2) An individual who suffers distress by reason of any contravention by a data controller of any of the requirements of this Act is entitled to compensation from the data controller for that distress if–

    (a) the individual also suffers damage by reason of the contravention, or

    (b) the contravention relates to the processing of personal data for the special purposes.

(3) In proceedings brought against a person by virtue of this section it is a defence to prove that he had taken such care as in all the circumstances was reasonably required to comply with the requirement concerned.

14 Rectification, blocking, erasure and destruction

(1) If a court is satisfied on the application of a data subject that personal data of which the applicant is the subject are inaccurate, the court may order the data controller to rectify, block, erase or destroy those data and any other personal data in respect of which he is the data controller and which contain an expression of opinion which appears to the court to be based on the inaccurate data.

(2) Subsection (1) applies whether or not the data accurately record information received or obtained by the data controller from the data subject or a third party but where the data accurately record such information, then–

    (a) if the requirements mentioned in paragraph 7 of Part II of Schedule 1 have been complied with, the court may, instead of making an order under subsection (1), make an order requiring the data to be supplemented by such statement of the true facts relating to the matters dealt with by the data as the court may approve, and

    (b) if all or any of those requirements have not been complied with, the court may, instead of making an order under that subsection, make such order as it thinks fit for securing compliance with those requirements with or without a further order requiring the data to be supplemented by such a statement as is mentioned in paragraph (a).

(3) Where the court

  (a) makes an order under subsection (1), or

  (b) is satisfied on the application of a data subject that personal data of which he was the data subject and which have been rectified, blocked, erased or destroyed were inaccurate,

it may, where it considers it reasonably practicable, order the data controller to notify third parties to whom the data have been disclosed of the rectification, blocking, erasure or destruction.

(4) If a court is satisfied on the application of a data subject–

  (a) that he has suffered damage by reason of any contravention by a data controller of any of the requirements of this Act in respect of any personal data, in circumstances entitling him to compensation under section 13, and

  (b) that there is a substantial risk of further contravention in respect of those data in such circumstances,

the court may order the rectification, blocking, erasure or destruction of any of those data.

(5) Where the court makes an order under subsection (4) it may, where it considers it reasonably practicable, order the data controller to notify third parties to whom the data have been disclosed of the rectification, blocking, erasure or destruction.

(6) In determining whether it is reasonably practicable to require such notification as is mentioned in subsection (3) or (5) the court shall have regard, in particular, to the number of persons who would have to be notified.

PART III
NOTIFICATION BY DATA CONTROLLERS

16 Preliminary

(1) In this Part 'the registrable particulars', in relation to a data controller, means–

  (a) his name and address,

  (b) if he has nominated a representative for the purposes of this Act, the name and address of the representative,

  (c) a description of the personal data being or to be processed by or on behalf of the data controller and of the category or categories of data subject to which they relate,

  (d) a description of the purpose or purposes for which the data are being or are to be processed,

  (e) a description of any recipient or recipients to whom the data controller intends or may wish to disclose the data,

  (f) the names, or a description of, any countries or territories outside the European Economic Area to which the data controller directly or indirectly transfers, or intends or may wish directly or indirectly to transfer, the data,

  [(ff) where the data controller is a public authority, a statement of that fact,] and

  (g) in any case where–

    (i) personal data are being, or are intended to be, processed in circumstances in which the prohibition in subsection (1) of section 17 is excluded by subsection (2) or (3) of that section, and

    (ii) the notification does not extend to those data,

  a statement of that fact.

(2) In this Part–

'fees regulations' means regulations made by the [Secretary of State] under section 18(5) or 19(4) or (7);

'notification regulations' means regulations made by the [Secretary of State] under the other provisions of this Part;

'prescribed', except where used in relation to fees regulations, means prescribed by notification regulations.

(3) For the purposes of this Part, so far as it relates to the addresses of data controllers–

  (a) the address of a registered company is that of its registered office, and

  (b) the address of a person (other than a registered company) carrying on a business is that of his principal place of business in the United Kingdom.

17 Prohibition on processing without registration

(1) Subject to the following provisions of this section, personal data must not be processed unless an entry in respect of the data controller is included in the register maintained by the Commissioner under section 19 (or is treated by notification regulations made by virtue of section 19(3) as being so included).

(2) Except where the processing is assessable processing for the purposes of section 22, subsection (1) does not apply in relation to personal data consisting of information which falls neither within paragraph (a) of the definition of 'data' in section 1(1) nor within paragraph (b) of that definition.

(3) If it appears to the [Secretary of State] that processing of a particular description is unlikely to prejudice the rights and freedoms of data subjects, notification regulations may provide that, in such cases as may be prescribed, subsection (1) is not to apply in relation to processing of that description.

(4) Subsection (1) does not apply in relation to any processing whose sole purpose is the maintenance of a public register.

18 Notification by data controllers

(1) Any data controller who wishes to be included in the register maintained under section 19 shall give a notification to the Commissioner under this section.

(2) A notification under this section must specify in accordance with notification regulations–

    (a) the registrable particulars, and

    (b) a general description of measures to be taken for the purpose of complying with the seventh data protection principle.

(3) Notification regulations made by virtue of subsection (2) may provide for the determination by the Commissioner, in accordance with any requirements of the regulations, of the form in which the registrable particulars and the description mentioned in subsection (2)(b) are to be specified, including in particular the detail required for the purposes of section 16(1)(c), (d), (e) and (f) and subsection (2)(b).

(4) Notification regulations may make provision as to the giving of notification–

    (a) by partnerships, or

    (b) in other cases where two or more persons are the data controllers in respect of any personal data.

(5) The notification must be accompanied by such fee as may be prescribed by fees regulations.

(6) Notification regulations may provide for any fee paid under subsection (5) or section 19(4) to be refunded in prescribed circumstances.

19 Register of notifications

(1) The Commissioner shall–

    (a) maintain a register of persons who have given notification under section 18, and

    (b) make an entry in the register in pursuance of each notification received by him under that section from a person in respect of whom no entry as data controller was for the time being included in the register.

(2) Each entry in the register shall consist of–

    (a) the registrable particulars notified under section 18 or, as the case requires, those particulars as amended in pursuance of section 20(4), and

    (b) such other information as the Commissioner may be authorised or required by notification regulations to include in the register.

(3) Notification regulations may make provision as to the time as from which any entry in respect of a data controller is to be treated for the purposes of section 17 as having been made in the register.

(4) No entry shall be retained in the register for more than the relevant time except on payment of such fee as may be prescribed by fees regulations.

(5) In subsection (4) 'the relevant time' means twelve months or such other period as may be prescribed by notification regulations; and different periods may be prescribed in relation to different cases.

(6) The Commissioner–

    (a) shall provide facilities for making the information contained in the entries in the register available for inspection (in visible and legible form) by members of the public at all reasonable hours and free of charge, and

    (b) may provide such other facilities for making the information contained in those entries available to the public free of charge as he considers appropriate.

(7) The Commissioner shall, on payment of such fee, if any, as may be prescribed by fees regulations, supply any member of the public with a duly certified copy in writing of the particulars contained in any entry made in the register.

20 Duty to notify changes

(1) For the purpose specified in subsection (2), notification regulations shall include provision imposing on every person in respect of whom an entry as a data controller is for the time being included in the register maintained under section 19 a duty to notify to the Commissioner, in such circumstances and at such time or times and in such form as may be prescribed, such matters relating to the registrable particulars and measures taken as mentioned in section 18(2)(b) as may be prescribed.

(2) The purpose referred to in subsection (1) is that of ensuring, so far as practicable, that at any time—

   (a) the entries in the register maintained under section 19 contain current names and addresses and describe the current practice or intentions of the data controller with respect to the processing of personal data, and

   (b) the Commissioner is provided with a general description of measures currently being taken as mentioned in section 18(2)(b).

(3) Subsection (3) of section 18 has effect in relation to notification regulations made by virtue of subsection (1) as it has effect in relation to notification regulations made by virtue of subsection (2) of that section.

(4) On receiving any notification under notification regulations made by virtue of subsection (1), the Commissioner shall make such amendments of the relevant entry in the register maintained under section 19 as are necessary to take account of the notification.

21 Offences

(1) If section 17(1) is contravened, the data controller is guilty of an offence.

(2) Any person who fails to comply with the duty imposed by notification regulations made by virtue of section 20(1) is guilty of an offence.

(3) It shall be a defence for a person charged with an offence under subsection (2) to show that he exercised all due diligence to comply with the duty.

22 Preliminary assessment by Commissioner

(1) In this section 'assessable processing' means processing which is of a description specified in an order made by the [Secretary of State] as appearing to him to be particularly likely—

   (a) to cause substantial damage or substantial distress to data subjects, or

   (b) otherwise significantly to prejudice the rights and freedoms of data subjects.

(2) On receiving notification from any data controller under section 18 or under notification regulations made by virtue of section 20 the Commissioner shall consider—

   (a) whether any of the processing to which the notification relates is assessable processing, and

   (b) if so, whether the assessable processing is likely to comply with the provisions of this Act.

(3) Subject to subsection (4), the Commissioner shall, within the period of twenty-eight days beginning with the day on which he receives a notification which relates to assessable processing, give a notice to the data controller stating the extent to which the Commissioner is of the opinion that the processing is likely or unlikely to comply with the provisions of this Act.

(4) Before the end of the period referred to in subsection (3) the Commissioner may, by reason of special circumstances, extend that period on one occasion only by notice to the data controller by such further period not exceeding fourteen days as the Commissioner may specify in the notice.

(5) No assessable processing in respect of which a notification has been given the Commissioner as mentioned in subsection (2) shall be carried on unless either—

   (a) the period of twenty-eight days beginning with the day on which the notification is received by the Commissioner (or, in a case falling within subsection (4), that period as extended under that subsection) has elapsed, or

   (b) before the end of that period (or that period as so extended) the data controller has received a notice from the Commissioner under subsection (3) in respect of the processing.

(6) Where subsection (5) is contravened, the data controller is guilty of an offence.

(7) The [Secretary of State] may by order amend subsections (3), (4) and (5) by substituting for the number of days for the time being specified there a different number specified in the order.

23 Power to make provision for appointment of data protection supervisors

(1) The [Secretary of State] may by order—

   (a) make provision under which a data controller may appoint a person to act as a data protection supervisor responsible in particular for monitoring in an independent manner the data controller's compliance with the provisions of this Act, and

(b) provide that, in relation to any data controller who has appointed a data protection supervisor in accordance with the provisions of the order and who complies with such conditions as may be specified in the order, the provisions of this Part are to have effect subject to such exemptions or other modifications as may be specified in the order.

(2) An order under this section may–

(a) impose duties on data protection supervisors in relation to the Commissioner, and

(b) confer functions on the Commissioner in relation to data protection supervisors.

24 Duty of certain data controllers to make certain information available

(1) Subject to subsection (3), where personal data are processed in a case where–

(a) by virtue of subsection (2) or (3) of section 17, subsection (1) of that section does not apply to the processing, and

(b) the data controller has not notified the relevant particulars in respect of that processing under section 18,

the data controller must, within twenty-one days of receiving a written request from any person, make the relevant particulars available to that person in writing free of charge.

(2) In this section 'the relevant particulars' means the particulars referred to in paragraphs (a) to (f) of section 16(1).

(3) This section has effect subject to any exemption conferred for the purposes of this section by notification regulations.

(4) Any data controller who fails to comply with the duty imposed by subsection (1) is guilty of an offence.

(5) It shall be a defence for a person charged with an offence under subsection (4) to show that he exercised all due diligence to comply with the duty.

PART IV
EXEMPTIONS

27 Preliminary

(1) References in any of the data protection principles or any provision of Parts II and III to personal data or to the processing of personal data do not include references to data or processing which by virtue of this Part are exempt from that principle or other provision.

(2) In this Part 'the subject information provisions' means–

(a) the first data protection principle to the extent to which it requires compliance with paragraph 2 of Part II of Schedule 1, and

(b) section 7.

(3) In this Part 'the non-disclosure provisions' means the provisions specified in subsection (4) to the extent to which they are inconsistent with the disclosure in question.

(4) The provisions referred to in subsection (3) are–

(a) the first data protection principle, except to the extent to which it requires compliance with the conditions in Schedules 2 and 3,

(b) the second, third, fourth and fifth data protection principles, and

(c) sections 10 and 14(1) to (3).

(5) Except as provided by this Part, the subject information provisions shall have effect notwithstanding any enactment or rule of law prohibiting or restricting the disclosure, or authorising the withholding, of information.

(b) in a case where the proceedings were stayed on the making of a claim, that the claim is withdrawn.

(6) For the purposes of this Act 'publish', in relation to journalistic, literary or artistic material, means make available to the public or any section of the public.

34 Information available to the public by or under enactment

Personal data are exempt from–

(a) the subject information provisions,

(b) the fourth data protection principle and [sections 12A and 14(1) to (3)], and

(c) the non-disclosure provisions,

if the data consist of information which the data controller is obliged by or under any enactment [other than an enactment contained in the Freedom of Information Act 2000] to make available to the public, whether by publishing it, by making it available for inspection, or otherwise and whether gratuitously or on payment of a fee.

35 Disclosures required by law or made in connection with legal proceedings etc

(1) Personal data are exempt from the non-disclosure provisions where the disclosure is required by or under any enactment, by any rule of law or by the order of a court.

(2) Personal data are exempt from the non-disclosure provisions where the disclosure is necessary–

(a) for the purpose of, or in connection with, any legal proceedings (including prospective legal proceedings), or

(b) for the purpose of obtaining legal advice,

or is otherwise necessary for the purposes of establishing, exercising or defending legal rights.

36 Domestic purposes

Personal data processed by an individual only for the purposes of that individual's personal, family or household affairs (including recreational purposes) are exempt from the data protection principles and the provisions of Parts II and III.

38 Powers to make further exemptions by order

(1) The [Secretary of State] may by order exempt from the subject information provisions personal data consisting of information the disclosure of which is prohibited or restricted by or under any enactment if and to the extent that he considers it necessary for the safeguarding of the interests of the data subject or the rights and freedoms of any other individual that the prohibition or restriction ought to prevail over those provisions.

(2) The [Secretary of State] may by order exempt from the non-disclosure provisions any disclosures of personal data made in circumstances specified in the order, if he considers the exemption is necessary for the safeguarding of the interests of the data subject or the rights and freedoms of any other individual.

Part V
Enforcement

40 Enforcement notices

(1) If the Commissioner is satisfied that a data controller has contravened or is contravening any of the data protection principles, the Commissioner may serve him with a notice (in this Act referred to as 'an enforcement notice') requiring him, for complying with the principle or principles in question, to do either or both of the following–

(a) to take within such time as may be specified in the notice, or to refrain from taking after such time as may be so specified, such steps as are so specified, or

(b) to refrain from processing any personal data, or any personal data of a description specified in the notice, or to refrain from processing them for a purpose so specified or in a manner so specified, after such time as may be so specified.

(2) In deciding whether to serve an enforcement notice, the Commissioner shall consider whether the contravention has caused or is likely to cause any person damage or distress.

(3) An enforcement notice in respect of a contravention of the fourth data protection principle which requires the data controller to rectify, block, erase or destroy any inaccurate data may also require the data controller to rectify, block, erase or destroy any other data held by him and containing an expression of opinion which appears to the Commissioner to be based on the inaccurate data.

(4) An enforcement notice in respect of a contravention of the fourth data protection principle, in the case of data which accurately record information received or obtained by the data controller from the data subject or a third party, may require the data controller either–

(a) to rectify, block, erase or destroy any inaccurate data and any other data held by him and containing an expression of opinion as mentioned in subsection (3), or

(b) to take such steps as are specified in the notice for securing compliance with the requirements specified in paragraph 7 of Part II of Schedule 1 and, if the Commissioner thinks fit, for supplementing the data with such statement of the true facts relating to the matters dealt with by the data as the Commissioner may approve.

(5) Where–

(a) an enforcement notice requires the data controller to rectify, block, erase or destroy any personal data, or

(b) the Commissioner is satisfied that personal data which have been rectified, blocked, erased or destroyed had been processed in contravention of any of the data protection principles,

an enforcement notice may, if reasonably practicable, require the data controller to notify third parties to whom the data have been disclosed of the rectification, blocking, erasure or destruction; and in determining whether it is reasonably practicable to require such notification regard shall be had, in particular, to the number of persons who would have to be notified.

(6) An enforcement notice must contain—

(a) a statement of the data protection principle or principles which the Commissioner is satisfied have been or are being contravened and his reasons for reaching that conclusion, and

(b) particulars of the rights of appeal conferred by section 48.

(7) Subject to subsection (8), an enforcement notice must not require any of the provisions of the notice to be complied with before the end of the period within which an appeal can be brought against the notice and, if such an appeal is brought, the notice need not be complied with pending the determination or withdrawal of the appeal.

(8) If by reason of special circumstances the Commissioner considers that an enforcement notice should be complied with as a matter of urgency he may include in the notice a statement to that effect and a statement of his reasons for reaching that conclusion; and in that event subsection (7) shall not apply but the notice must not require the provisions of the notice to be complied with before the end of the period of seven days beginning with the day on which the notice is served.

(9) Notification regulations (as defined by section 16(2)) may make provision as to the effect of the service of an enforcement notice on any entry in the register maintained under section 19 which relates to the person on whom the notice is served.

(10) This section has effect subject to section 46(1).

41 Cancellation of an enforcement notice

(1) If the Commissioner considers that all or any of the provisions of an enforcement notice need not be complied with in order to ensure compliance with the data protection principle or principles to which it relates, he may cancel or vary the notice by written notice to the person on whom it was served.

(2) A person on whom an enforcement notice has been served may, at any time after the expiry of the period during which an appeal can be brought against that notice, apply in writing to the Commissioner for the cancellation or variation of that notice on the ground that, by reason of a change of circumstances, all or any of the provisions of that notice need not be complied with in order to ensure compliance with the data protection principle or principles to which that notice relates.

42 Request for assessment

(1) A request may be made to the Commissioner by or on behalf of any person who is, or believes himself to be, directly affected by any processing of personal data for an assessment as to whether it is likely or unlikely that the processing has been or is being carried out in compliance with the provisions of this Act.

(2) On receiving a request under this section, the Commissioner shall make an assessment in such manner as appears to him to be appropriate, unless he has not been supplied with such information as he may reasonably require in order to—

(a) satisfy himself as to the identity of the person making the request, and

(b) enable him to identify the processing in question.

(3) The matters to which the Commissioner may have regard in determining in what manner it is appropriate to make an assessment include—

(a) the extent to which the request appears to him to raise a matter of substance,

(b) any undue delay in making the request, and

(c) whether or not the person making the request is entitled to make an application under section 7 in respect of the personal data in question.

(4) Where the Commissioner has received a request under this section he shall notify the person who made the request—

(a) whether he has made an assessment as a result of the request, and

(b) to the extent that he considers appropriate, having regard in particular to any exemption from section 7 applying in relation to the personal data concerned, of any view formed or action taken as a result of the request.

43 Information notices

(1) If the Commissioner–

- (a) has received a request under section 42 in respect of any processing of personal data, or

- (b) reasonably requires any information for the purpose of determining whether the data controller has complied or is complying with the data protection principles,

he may serve the data controller with a notice (in this Act referred to as 'an information notice') requiring the data controller, within such time as is specified in the notice, to furnish the Commissioner, in such form as may be so specified, with such information relating to the request or to compliance with the principles as is so specified.

(2) An information notice must contain–

- (a) in a case falling within subsection (1)(a), a statement that the Commissioner has received a request under section 42 in relation to the specified processing, or

- (b) in a case falling within subsection (1)(b), a statement that the Commissioner regards the specified information as relevant for the purpose of determining whether the data controller has complied, or is complying, with the data protection principles and his reasons for regarding it as relevant for that purpose.

(3) An information notice must also contain particulars of the rights of appeal conferred by section 48.

(4) Subject to subsection (5), the time specified in an information notice shall not expire before the end of the period within which an appeal can be brought against the notice and, if such an appeal is brought, the information need not be furnished pending the determination or withdrawal of the appeal.

(5) If by reason of special circumstances the Commissioner considers that the information is required as a matter of urgency, he may include in the notice a statement to that effect and a statement of his reasons for reaching that conclusion; and in that event subsection (4) shall not apply, but the notice shall not require the information to be furnished before the end of the period of seven days beginning with the day on which the notice is served.

(6) A person shall not be required by virtue of this section to furnish the Commissioner with any information in respect of–

- (a) any communication between a professional legal adviser and his client in connection with the giving of legal advice to the client with respect to his obligations, liabilities or rights under this Act, or

- (b) any communication between a professional legal adviser and his client, or between such an adviser or his client and any other person, made in connection with or in contemplation of proceedings under or arising out of this Act (including proceedings before the Tribunal) and for the purposes of such proceedings.

(7) In subsection (6) references to the client of a professional legal adviser include references to any person representing such a client.

(8) A person shall not be required by virtue of this section to furnish the Commissioner with any information if the furnishing of that information would, by revealing evidence of the commission of any offence other than an offence under this Act, expose him to proceedings for that offence.

(9) The Commissioner may cancel an information notice by written notice to the person on whom it was served.

(10) This section has effect subject to section 46(3).

44 Special information notices

If the Commissioner–

- (a) has received a request under section 42 in respect of any processing of personal data, or

- (b) has reasonable grounds for suspecting that, in a case in which proceedings have been stayed under section 32, the personal data to which the proceedings relate–

  - (i) are not being processed only for the special purposes, or

  - (ii) are not being processed with a view to the publication by any person of any journalistic, literary or artistic material which has not previously been published by the data controller,

he may serve the data controller with a notice (in this Act referred to as a 'special information notice') requiring the data controller, within such time as is specified in the notice, to furnish the Commissioner, in such form as may be so specified, with such information as is so specified for the purpose specified in subsection (2).

(2) That purpose is the purpose of ascertaining–

- (a) whether the personal data are being processed only for the special purposes, or

- (b) whether they are being processed with a view to the publication by any person of any journalistic, literary or artistic material which has not previously been published by the data controller.

(3) A special information notice must contain–

- (a) in a case falling within paragraph (a) of subsection (1), a statement that the Commissioner has received a request under section 42 in relation to the specified processing, or

- (b) in a case falling within paragraph (b) of that subsection, a statement of the Commissioner's grounds for suspecting that the personal data are not being processed as mentioned in that paragraph.

(4) A special information notice must also contain particulars of the rights of appeal conferred by section 48.

(5) Subject to subsection (6), the time specified in a special information notice shall not expire before the end of the period within which an appeal can be brought against the notice and, if such an appeal is brought, the information need not be furnished pending the determination or withdrawal of the appeal.

(6) If by reason of special circumstances the Commissioner considers that the information is required as a matter of urgency, he may include in the notice a statement to that effect and a statement of his reasons for reaching that conclusion; and in that event subsection (5) shall not apply, but the notice shall not require the information to be furnished before the end of the period of seven days beginning with the day on which the notice is served.

(7) A person shall not be required by virtue of this section to furnish the Commissioner with any information in respect of–

- (a) any communication between a professional legal adviser and his client in connection with the giving of legal advice to the client with respect to his obligations, liabilities or rights under this Act, or

- (b) any communication between a professional legal adviser and his client, or between such an adviser or his client and any other person, made in connection with or in contemplation of proceedings under or arising out of this Act (including proceedings before the Tribunal) and for the purposes of such proceedings.

(8) In subsection (7) references to the client of a professional legal adviser include references to any person representing such a client.

(9) A person shall not be required by virtue of this section to furnish the Commissioner with any information if the furnishing of that information would, by revealing evidence of the commission of any offence other than an offence under this Act, expose him to proceedings for that offence.

(10) The Commissioner may cancel a special information notice by written notice to the person on whom it was served.

45 Determination by Commissioner as to the special purposes

(1) Where at any time it appears to the Commissioner (whether as a result of the service of a special information notice or otherwise) that any personal data–

- (a) are not being processed only for the special purposes, or

- (b) are not being processed with a view to the publication by any person of any journalistic, literary or artistic material which has not previously been published by the data controller,

he may make a determination in writing to that effect.

(2) Notice of the determination shall be given to the data controller; and the notice must contain particulars of the right of appeal conferred by section 48.

(3) A determination under subsection (1) shall not take effect until the end of the period within which an appeal can be brought and, where an appeal is brought, shall not take effect pending the determination or withdrawal of the appeal.

46 Restriction on enforcement in case of processing for the special purposes

(1) The Commissioner may not at any time serve an enforcement notice on a data controller with respect to the processing of personal data for the special purposes unless–

- (a) a determination under section 45(1) with respect to those data has taken effect, and

- (b) the court has granted leave for the notice to be served.

(2) The court shall not grant leave for the purposes of subsection (1)(b) unless it is satisfied–

- (a) that the Commissioner has reason to suspect a contravention of the data protection principles which is of substantial public importance, and

- (b) except where the case is one of urgency, that the data controller has been given notice, in accordance with rules of court, of the application for leave.

(3) The Commissioner may not serve an information notice on a data controller with respect to the processing of personal data for the special purposes unless a determination under section 45(1) with respect to those data has taken effect.

47 Failure to comply with notice

(1) A person who fails to comply with an enforcement notice, an information notice or a special information notice is guilty of an offence.

(2) A person who, in purported compliance with an information notice or a special information notice—

    (a) makes a statement which he knows to be false in a material respect, or

    (b) recklessly makes a statement which is false in a material respect,

is guilty of an offence.

(3) It is a defence for a person charged with an offence under subsection (1) to prove that he exercised all due diligence to comply with the notice in question.

48 Rights of appeal

(1) A person on whom an enforcement notice, an information notice or a special information notice has been served may appeal to the Tribunal against the notice.

(2) A person on whom an enforcement notice has been served may appeal to the Tribunal against the refusal of an application under section 41(2) for cancellation or variation of the notice.

(3) Where an enforcement notice, an information notice or a special information notice contains a statement by the Commissioner in accordance with section 40(8), 43(5) or 44(6) then, whether or not the person appeals against the notice, he may appeal against—

    (a) the Commissioner's decision to include the statement in the notice, or

    (b) the effect of the inclusion of the statement as respects any part of the notice.

(4) A data controller in respect of whom a determination has been made under section 45 may appeal to the Tribunal against the determination.

(5) Schedule 6 has effect in relation to appeals under this section and the proceedings of the Tribunal in respect of any such appeal.

49 Determination of appeals

(1) If on an appeal under section 48(1) the Tribunal considers—

    (a) that the notice against which the appeal is brought is not in accordance with the law, or

    (b) to the extent that the notice involved an exercise of discretion by the Commissioner, that he ought to have exercised his discretion differently,

the Tribunal shall allow the appeal or substitute such other notice or decision as could have been served or made by the Commissioner; and in any other case the Tribunal shall dismiss the appeal.

(2) On such an appeal, the Tribunal may review any determination of fact on which the notice in question was based.

(3) If on an appeal under section 48(2) the Tribunal considers that the enforcement notice ought to be cancelled or varied by reason of a change in circumstances, the Tribunal shall cancel or vary the notice.

(4) On an appeal under subsection (3) of section 48 the Tribunal may direct—

    (a) that the notice in question shall have effect as if it did not contain any such statement as is mentioned in that subsection, or

    (b) that the inclusion of the statement shall not have effect in relation to any part of the notice,

and may make such modifications in the notice as may be required for giving effect to the direction.

(5) On an appeal under section 48(4), the Tribunal may cancel the determination of the Commissioner.

(6) Any party to an appeal to the Tribunal under section 48 may appeal from the decision of the Tribunal on a point of law to the appropriate court; and that court shall be—

    (a) the High Court of Justice in England if the address of the person who was the appellant before the Tribunal is in England or Wales,

    (b) the Court of Session if that address is in Scotland, and

    (c) the High Court of Justice in Northern Ireland if that address is in Northern Ireland.

(7) For the purposes of subsection (6)–

    (a) the address of a registered company is that of its registered office, and

    (b) the address of a person (other than a registered company) carrying on a business is that of his principal place of business in the United Kingdom.

PART VI
MISCELLANEOUS AND GENERAL

Functions of Commissioner

51 General duties of Commissioner

(1) It shall be the duty of the Commissioner to promote the following of good practice by data controllers and, in particular, so to perform his functions under this Act as to promote the observance of the requirements of this Act by data controllers.

(2) The Commissioner shall arrange for the dissemination in such form and manner as he considers appropriate of such information as it may appear to him expedient to give to the public about the operation of this Act, about good practice, and about other matters within the scope of his functions under this Act, and may give advice to any person as to any of those matters.

(3) Where–

    (a) the [Secretary of State] so directs by order, or

    (b) the Commissioner considers it appropriate to do so,

the Commissioner shall, after such consultation with trade associations, data subjects or persons representing data subjects as appears to him to be appropriate, prepare and disseminate to such persons as he considers appropriate codes of practice for guidance as to good practice.

(4) The Commissioner shall also–

    (a) where he considers it appropriate to do so, encourage trade associations to prepare, and to disseminate to their members, such codes of practice, and

    (b) where any trade association submits a code of practice to him for his consideration, consider the code and, after such consultation with data subjects or persons representing data subjects as appears to him to be appropriate, notify the trade association whether in his opinion the code promotes the following of good practice.

(5) An order under subsection (3) shall describe the personal data or processing to which the code of practice is to relate, and may also describe the persons or classes of persons to whom it is to relate.

(6) The Commissioner shall arrange for the dissemination in such form and manner as he considers appropriate of–

    (a) any Community finding as defined by paragraph 15(2) of Part II of Schedule 1,

    (b) any decision of the European Commission, under the procedure provided for in Article 31(2) of the Data Protection Directive, which is made for the purposes of Article 26(3) or (4) of the Directive, and

    (c) such other information as it may appear to him to be expedient to give to data controllers in relation to any personal data about the protection of the rights and freedoms of data subjects in relation to the processing of personal data in countries and territories outside the European Economic Area.

(7) The Commissioner may, with the consent of the data controller, assess any processing of personal data for the following of good practice and shall inform the data controller of the results of the assessment.

(8) The Commissioner may charge such sums as he may with the consent of the [Secretary of State] determine for any services provided by the Commissioner by virtue of this Part.

(9) In this section–

    'good practice' means such practice in the processing of personal data as appears to the Commissioner to be desirable having regard to the interests of data subjects and others, and includes (but is not limited to) compliance with the requirements of this Act;

    'trade association' includes any body representing data controllers.

53 Assistance by Commissioner in cases involving processing for the special purposes

(1) An individual who is an actual or prospective party to any proceedings under section 7(9), 10(4), 12(8)[, 12A(3)] or 14 or by virtue of section 13 which relate to personal data processed for the special purposes may apply to the Commissioner for assistance in relation to those proceedings.

(2) The Commissioner shall, as soon as reasonably practicable after receiving an application under subsection (1), consider it and decide whether and to what extent to grant it, but he shall not grant the application unless, in his opinion, the case involves a matter of substantial public importance.

(3) If the Commissioner decides to provide assistance, he shall, as soon as reasonably practicable after making the decision, notify the applicant, stating the extent of the assistance to be provided.

(4) If the Commissioner decides not to provide assistance, he shall, as soon as reasonably practicable after making the decision, notify the applicant of his decision and, if he thinks fit, the reasons for it.

(5) In this section–

    (a) references to 'proceedings' include references to prospective proceedings, and

    (b) 'applicant', in relation to assistance under this section, means an individual who applies for assistance.

(6) Schedule 10 has effect for supplementing this section.

Unlawful obtaining etc of personal data

55 Unlawful obtaining etc of personal data

(1) A person must not knowingly or recklessly, without the consent of the data controller–

    (a) obtain or disclose personal data or the information contained in personal data, or

    (b) procure the disclosure to another person of the information contained in personal data.

(2) Subsection (1) does not apply to a person who shows–

    (a) that the obtaining, disclosing or procuring–

        (i) was necessary for the purpose of preventing or detecting crime, or

        (ii) was required or authorised by or under any enactment, by any rule of law or by the order of a court,

    (b) that he acted in the reasonable belief that he had in law the right to obtain or disclose the data or information or, as the case may be, to procure the disclosure of the information to the other person,

    (c) that he acted in the reasonable belief that he would have had the consent of the data controller if the data controller had known of the obtaining, disclosing or procuring and the circumstances of it, or

    (d) that in the particular circumstances the obtaining, disclosing or procuring was justified as being in the public interest.

(3) A person who contravenes subsection (1) is guilty of an offence.

(4) A person who sells personal data is guilty of an offence if he has obtained the data in contravention of subsection (1).

(5) A person who offers to sell personal data is guilty of an offence if–

    (a) he has obtained the data in contravention of subsection (1), or

    (b) he subsequently obtains the data in contravention of that subsection.

(6) For the purposes of subsection (5), an advertisement indicating that personal data are or may be for sale is an offer to sell the data.

(7) Section 1(2) does not apply for the purposes of this section; and for the purposes of subsections (4) to (6), 'personal data' includes information extracted from personal data.

(8) References in this section to personal data do not include references to personal data which by virtue of section 28 [or 33A] are exempt from this section.

Records obtained under data subject's right of access

56 Prohibition of requirement as to production of certain records

(1) A person must not, in connection with–

    (a) the recruitment of another person as an employee,

    (b) the continued employment of another person, or

    (c) any contract for the provision of services to him by another person,

require that other person or a third party to supply him with a relevant record or to produce a relevant record to him.

(2) A person concerned with the provision (for payment or not) of goods, facilities or services to the public or a section of the public must not, as a condition of providing or offering to provide any goods, facilities or services to

another person, require that other person or a third party to supply him with a relevant record or to produce a relevant record to him.

(3) Subsections (1) and (2) do not apply to a person who shows–

(a) that the imposition of the requirement was required or authorised by or under any enactment, by any rule of law or by the order of a court, or

(b) that in the particular circumstances the imposition of the requirement was justified as being in the public interest.

(4) Having regard to the provisions of Part V of the Police Act 1997 (certificates of criminal records etc), the imposition of the requirement referred to in subsection (1) or (2) is not to be regarded as being justified as being in the public interest on the ground that it would assist in the prevention or detection of crime.

(5) A person who contravenes subsection (1) or (2) is guilty of an offence.

(6) In this section 'a relevant record' means any record which–

(a) has been or is to be obtained by a data subject from any data controller specified in the first column of the Table below in the exercise of the right conferred by section 7, and

(b) contains information relating to any matter specified in relation to that data controller in the second column,

and includes a copy of such a record or a part of such a record.

TABLE

Data controller	Subject-matter
1 Any of the following persons–	(a) Convictions.
(a) a chief officer of police of a police force in England and Wales.	(b) Cautions.
(b) a chief constable of a police force in Scotland.	
(c) the [Chief Constable of the Police Service of Northern Ireland].	
(d) the Director General of the National Criminal Intelligence Service.	
(e) the Director General of the National Crime Squad.	
2 The Secretary of State.	(a) Convictions.
	(b) Cautions.
	(c) His functions under [section 92 of the Powers of Criminal Courts (Sentencing) Act 2000], section 205(2) or 208 of the Criminal Procedure (Scotland) Act 1995 or section 73 of the Children and Young Persons Act (Northern Ireland) 1968 in relation to any person sentenced to detention.
	(d) His functions under the Prison Act 1952, the Prisons (Scotland) Act 1989 or the Prison Act (Northern Ireland) 1953 in relation to any person imprisoned or detained.
	(e) His functions under the Social Security Contributions and Benefits Act 1992, the Social Security Administration Act 1992 or the Jobseekers Act 1995.
	(f) His functions under Part V of the Police Act 1997.
3 The Department of Health and Social Services for Northern Ireland.	Its functions under the Social Security Contributions and Benefits (Northern Ireland) Act 1992, the Social Security Administration (Northern Ireland) Act 1992 or the Jobseekers (Northern Ireland) Order 1995.

[(6A) A record is not a relevant record to the extent that it relates, or is to relate, only to personal data falling within paragraph (e) of the definition of 'data' in section 1(1).]

(7) In the Table in subsection (6)–

'caution' means a caution given to any person in England and Wales or Northern Ireland in respect of an offence which, at the time when the caution is given, is admitted;

'conviction' has the same meaning as in the Rehabilitation of Offenders Act 1974 or the Rehabilitation of Offenders (Northern Ireland) Order 1978.

(8) The [Secretary of State] may by order amend–

(a) the Table in subsection (6), and

(b) subsection (7).

(9) For the purposes of this section a record which states that a data controller is not processing any personal data relating to a particular matter shall be taken to be a record containing information relating to that matter.

(10) In this section 'employee' means an individual who–

(a) works under a contract of employment, as defined by section 230(2) of the Employment Rights Act 1996, or

(b) holds any office,

whether or not he is entitled to remuneration; and 'employment' shall be construed accordingly.

57 Avoidance of certain contractual terms relating to health records

(1) Any term or condition of a contract is void in so far as it purports to require an individual–

(a) to supply any other person with a record to which this section applies, or with a copy of such a record or a part of such a record, or

(b) to produce to any other person such a record, copy or part.

(2) This section applies to any record which–

(a) has been or is to be obtained by a data subject in the exercise of the right conferred by section 7, and

(b) consists of the information contained in any health record as defined by section 68(2).

Information provided to Commissioner or Tribunal

58 Disclosure of information

No enactment or rule of law prohibiting or restricting the disclosure of information shall preclude a person from furnishing the Commissioner or the Tribunal with any information necessary for the discharge of their functions under this Act [or the Freedom of Information Act 2000].

59 Confidentiality of information

(1) No person who is or has been the Commissioner, a member of the Commissioner's staff or an agent of the Commissioner shall disclose any information which–

(a) has been obtained by, or furnished to, the Commissioner under or for the purposes of [the information Acts],

(b) relates to an identified or identifiable individual or business, and

(c) is not at the time of the disclosure, and has not previously been, available to the public from other sources,

unless the disclosure is made with lawful authority.

(2) For the purposes of subsection (1) a disclosure of information is made with lawful authority only if, and to the extent that–

(a) the disclosure is made with the consent of the individual or of the person for the time being carrying on the business,

(b) the information was provided for the purpose of its being made available to the public (in whatever manner) under any provision of [the information Acts],

(c) the disclosure is made for the purposes of, and is necessary for, the discharge of–

(i) any functions under [the information Acts], or

(ii) any Community obligation,

(d) the disclosure is made for the purposes of any proceedings, whether criminal or civil and whether arising under, or by virtue of, [the information Acts] or otherwise, or

(e) having regard to the rights and freedoms or legitimate interests of any person, the disclosure is necessary in the public interest.

(3) Any person who knowingly or recklessly discloses information in contravention of subsection (1) is guilty of an offence.

[(4) In this section 'the information Acts' means this Act and the Freedom of Information Act 2000.]

General provisions relating to offences

60 Prosecutions and penalties

(1) No proceedings for an offence under this Act shall be instituted–

   (a) in England or Wales, except by the Commissioner or by or with the consent of the Director of Public Prosecutions;

   (b) in Northern Ireland, except by the Commissioner or by or with the consent of the Director of Public Prosecutions for Northern Ireland.

(2) A person guilty of an offence under any provision of this Act other than [section 54A and] paragraph 12 of Schedule 9 is liable–

   (a) on summary conviction, to a fine not exceeding the statutory maximum, or

   (b) on conviction on indictment, to a fine.

(3) A person guilty of an offence under [section 54A and] paragraph 12 of Schedule 9 is liable on summary conviction to a fine not exceeding level 5 on the standard scale.

(4) Subject to subsection (5), the court by or before which a person is convicted of–

   (a) an offence under section 21(1), 22(6), 55 or 56,

   (b) an offence under section 21(2) relating to processing which is assessable processing for the purposes of section 22, or

   (c) an offence under section 47(1) relating to an enforcement notice,

may order any document or other material used in connection with the processing of personal data and appearing to the court to be connected with the commission of the offence to be forfeited, destroyed or erased.

(5) The court shall not make an order under subsection (4) in relation to any material where a person (other than the offender) claiming to be the owner of or otherwise interested in the material applies to be heard by the court, unless an opportunity is given to him to show cause why the order should not be made.

61 Liability of directors etc

(1) Where an offence under this Act has been committed by a body corporate and is proved to have been committed with the consent or connivance of or to be attributable to any neglect on the part of any director, manager, secretary or similar officer of the body corporate or any person who was purporting to act in any such capacity, he as well as the body corporate shall be guilty of that offence and be liable to be proceeded against and punished accordingly.

(2) Where the affairs of a body corporate are managed by its members subsection (1) shall apply in relation to the acts and defaults of a member in connection with his functions of management as if he were a director of the body corporate.

(3) Where an offence under this Act has been committed by a Scottish partnership and the contravention in question is proved to have occurred with the consent or connivance of, or to be attributable to any neglect on the part of, a partner, he as well as the partnership shall be guilty of that offence and shall be liable to be proceeded against and punished accordingly.

Amendments of Consumer Credit Act 1974

62 Amendments of Consumer Credit Act 1974

(1) In section 158 of the Consumer Credit Act 1974 (duty of agency to disclose filed information)–

   (a) in subsection (1)–

     (i) in paragraph (a) for 'individual' there is substituted 'partnership or other unincorporated body of persons not consisting entirely of bodies corporate', and

     (ii) for 'him' there is substituted 'it',

   (b) in subsection (2), for 'his' there is substituted 'the consumer's', and

   (c) in subsection (3), for 'him' there is substituted 'the consumer'.

(2) In section 159 of that Act (correction of wrong information) for subsection (1) there is substituted–

183

'(1) Any individual (the 'objector') given–

    (a) information under section 7 of the Data Protection Act 1998 by a credit reference agency, or

    (b) information under section 158,

who considers that an entry in his file is incorrect, and that if it is not corrected he is likely to be prejudiced, may give notice to the agency requiring it either to remove the entry from the file or amend it.'.

(3) In subsections (2) to (6) of that subsection–

    (a) for 'consumer', wherever occurring, there is substituted 'objector', and

    (b) for 'Director', wherever occurring, there is substituted 'the relevant authority'.

(4) After subsection (6) of that section there is inserted–

'(7) The Data Protection Commissioner may vary or revoke any order made by him under this section.

(8) In this section 'the relevant authority' means–

    (a) where the objector is a partnership or other unincorporated body of persons, the Director, and

    (b) in any other case, the Data Protection Commissioner.'.

(5) In section 160 of that Act (alternative procedure for business consumers)–

    (a) in subsection (4)–

        (i) for 'him' there is substituted 'to the consumer', and

        (ii) in paragraphs (a) and (b) for 'he' there is substituted 'the consumer' and for 'his' there is substituted 'the consumer's', and

    (b) after subsection (6) there is inserted–

'(7) In this section 'consumer' has the same meaning as in section 158.'.

General

63 Application to Crown

(1) This Act binds the Crown.

(2) For the purposes of this Act each government department shall be treated as a person separate from any other government department.

(3) Where the purposes for which and the manner in which any personal data are, or are to be, processed are determined by any person acting on behalf of the Royal Household, the Duchy of Lancaster or the Duchy of Cornwall, the data controller in respect of those data for the purposes of this Act shall be–

    (a) in relation to the Royal Household, the Keeper of the Privy Purse,

    (b) in relation to the Duchy of Lancaster, such person as the Chancellor of the Duchy appoints, and

    (c) in relation to the Duchy of Cornwall, such person as the Duke of Cornwall, or the possessor for the time being of the Duchy of Cornwall, appoints.

(4) Different persons may be appointed under subsection (3)(b) or (c) for different purposes.

(5) Neither a government department nor a person who is a data controller by virtue of subsection (3) shall be liable to prosecution under this Act, but *section* [sections 54A and] 55 and paragraph 12 of Schedule 9 shall apply to a person in the service of the Crown as they apply to any other person.

[63A Application to Parliament]

[(1) Subject to the following provisions of this section and to section 35A, this Act applies to the processing of personal data by or on behalf of either House of Parliament as it applies to the processing of personal data by other persons.

(2) Where the purposes for which and the manner in which any personal data are, or are to be, processed are determined by or on behalf of the House of Commons, the data controller in respect of those data for the purposes of this Act shall be the Corporate Officer of that House.

(3) Where the purposes for which and the manner in which any personal data are, or are to be, processed are determined by or on behalf of the House of Lords, the data controller in respect of those data for the purposes of this Act shall be the Corporate Officer of that House.

(4) Nothing in subsection (2) or (3) is to be taken to render the Corporate Officer of the House of Commons or the Corporate Officer of the House of Lords liable to prosecution under this Act, but section 55 and paragraph 12 of Schedule 9 shall apply to a person acting on behalf of either House as they apply to any other person.]

64 Transmission of notices etc by electronic or other means

(1) This section applies to

(a) a notice or request under any provision of Part II,

(b) a notice under subsection (1) of section 24 or particulars made available under that subsection, or

(c) an application under section 41(2),

but does not apply to anything which is required to be served in accordance with rules of court.

(2) The requirement that any notice, request, particulars or application to which this section applies should be in writing is satisfied where the text of the notice, request, particulars or application—

(a) is transmitted by electronic means,

(b) is received in legible form, and

(c) is capable of being used for subsequent reference.

(3) The [Secretary of State] may by regulations provide that any requirement that any notice, request, particulars or application to which this section applies should be in writing is not to apply in such circumstances as may be prescribed by the regulations.

SCHEDULE I
The Data Protection Principles

Section 4(1) and (2)

PART I
THE PRINCIPLES

1 Personal data shall be processed fairly and lawfully and, in particular, shall not be processed unless—

(a) at least one of the conditions in Schedule 2 is met, and

(b) in the case of sensitive personal data, at least one of the conditions in Schedule 3 is also met.

2 Personal data shall be obtained only for one or more specified and lawful purposes, and shall not be further processed in any manner incompatible with that purpose or those purposes.

3 Personal data shall be adequate, relevant and not excessive in relation to the purpose or purposes for which they are processed.

4 Personal data shall be accurate and, where necessary, kept up to date.

5 Personal data processed for any purpose or purposes shall not be kept for longer than is necessary for that purpose or those purposes.

6 Personal data shall be processed in accordance with the rights of data subjects under this Act.

7 Appropriate technical and organisational measures shall be taken against unauthorised or unlawful processing of personal data and against accidental loss or destruction of, or damage to, personal data.

8 Personal data shall not be transferred to a country or territory outside the European Economic Area unless that country or territory ensures an adequate level of protection for the rights and freedoms of data subjects in relation to the processing of personal data.

PART III
NTERPRETATION OF THE PRINCIPLES IN PART I

The first principle

1 (1) In determining for the purposes of the first principle whether personal data are processed fairly, regard is to be had to the method by which they are obtained, including in particular whether any person from whom they are obtained is deceived or misled as to the purpose or purposes for which they are to be processed.

(2)   Subject to paragraph 2, for the purposes of the first principle data are to be treated as obtained fairly if they consist of information obtained from a person who–

    (a)   is authorised by or under any enactment to supply it, or

    (b)   is required to supply it by or under any enactment or by any convention or other instrument imposing an international obligation on the United Kingdom.

2   (1)   Subject to paragraph 3, for the purposes of the first principle personal data are not to be treated as processed fairly unless–

    (a)   in the case of data obtained from the data subject, the data controller ensures so far as practicable that the data subject has, is provided with, or has made readily available to him, the information specified in sub-paragraph (3), and

    (b)   in any other case, the data controller ensures so far as practicable that, before the relevant time or as soon as practicable after that time, the data subject has, is provided with, or has made readily available to him, the information specified in sub-paragraph (3).

(2)   In sub-paragraph (1)(b) 'the relevant time' means–

    (a)   the time when the data controller first processes the data, or

    (b)   in a case where at that time disclosure to a third party within a reasonable period is envisaged–

        (i)   if the data are in fact disclosed to such a person within that period, the time when the data are first disclosed,

        (ii)   if within that period the data controller becomes, or ought to become, aware that the data are unlikely to be disclosed to such a person within that period, the time when the data controller does become, or ought to become, so aware, or

        (iii)   in any other case, the end of that period.

(3)   The information referred to in sub-paragraph (1) is as follows, namely–

    (a)   the identity of the data controller,

    (b)   if he has nominated a representative for the purposes of this Act, the identity of that representative,

    (c)   the purpose or purposes for which the data are intended to be processed, and

    (d)   any further information which is necessary, having regard to the specific circumstances in which the data are or are to be processed, to enable processing in respect of the data subject to be fair.

3   (1)   Paragraph 2(1)(b) does not apply where either of the primary conditions in sub-paragraph (2), together with such further conditions as may be prescribed by the [Secretary of State] by order, are met.

(2)   The primary conditions referred to in sub-paragraph (1) are–

    (a)   that the provision of that information would involve a disproportionate effort, or

    (b)   that the recording of the information to be contained in the data by, or the disclosure of the data by, the data controller is necessary for compliance with any legal obligation to which the data controller is subject, other than an obligation imposed by contract.

4   (1)   Personal data which contain a general identifier falling within a description prescribed by the [Secretary of State] by order are not to be treated as processed fairly and lawfully unless they are processed in compliance with any conditions so prescribed in relation to general identifiers of that description.

(2)   In sub-paragraph (1) 'a general identifier' means any identifier (such as, for example, a number or code used for identification purposes) which–

    (a)   relates to an individual, and

    (b)   forms part of a set of similar identifiers which is of general application.

The second principle

5   The purpose or purposes for which personal data are obtained may in particular be specified–

(a)   in a notice given for the purposes of paragraph 2 by the data controller to the data subject, or

(b)   in a notification given to the Commissioner under Part III of this Act.

6   In determining whether any disclosure of personal data is compatible with the purpose or purposes for which the data were obtained, regard is to be had to the purpose or purposes for which the personal data are intended to be processed by any person to whom they are disclosed.

The fourth principle

7   The fourth principle is not to be regarded as being contravened by reason of any inaccuracy in personal data which accurately record information obtained by the data controller from the data subject or a third party in a case where—

(a)   having regard to the purpose or purposes for which the data were obtained and further processed, the data controller has taken reasonable steps to ensure the accuracy of the data, and

(b)   if the data subject has notified the data controller of the data subject's view that the data are inaccurate, the data indicate that fact.

The sixth principle

8   A person is to be regarded as contravening the sixth principle if, but only if—

(a)   he contravenes section 7 by failing to supply information in accordance with that section,

(b)   he contravenes section 10 by failing to comply with a notice given under subsection (1) of that section to the extent that the notice is justified or by failing to give a notice under subsection (3) of that section,

(c)   he contravenes section 11 by failing to comply with a notice given under subsection (1) of that section,

(d)   he contravenes section 12 by failing to comply with a notice given under subsection (1) or (2)(b) of that section or by failing to give a notification under subsection (2)(a) of that section or a notice under subsection (3) of that section [or

(e)   he contravenes section 12A by failing to comply with a notice given under subsection (1) of that section to the extent that the notice is justified].

The seventh principle

9   Having regard to the state of technological development and the cost of implementing any measures, the measures must ensure a level of security appropriate to—

(a)   the harm that might result from such unauthorised or unlawful processing or accidental loss, destruction or damage as are mentioned in the seventh principle, and

(b)   the nature of the data to be protected.

10   The data controller must take reasonable steps to ensure the reliability of any employees of his who have access to the personal data.

11   Where processing of personal data is carried out by a data processor on behalf of a data controller, the data controller must in order to comply with the seventh principle—

(a)   choose a data processor providing sufficient guarantees in respect of the technical and organisational security measures governing the processing to be carried out, and

(b)   take reasonable steps to ensure compliance with those measures.

12   Where processing of personal data is carried out by a data processor on behalf of a data controller, the data controller is not to be regarded as complying with the seventh principle unless—

(a)   the processing is carried out under a contract—

(i)   which is made or evidenced in writing, and

(ii)   under which the data processor is to act only on instructions from the data controller, and

(b)   the contract requires the data processor to comply with obligations equivalent to those imposed on a data controller by the seventh principle.

The eighth principle

13   An adequate level of protection is one which is adequate in all the circumstances of the case, having regard in particular to—

(a)   the nature of the personal data,

(b)   the country or territory of origin of the information contained in the data,

(c)   the country or territory of final destination of that information,

(d)   the purposes for which and period during which the data are intended to be processed,

(e)   the law in force in the country or territory in question,

(f)   the international obligations of that country or territory,

(g) any relevant codes of conduct or other rules which are enforceable in that country or territory (whether generally or by arrangement in particular cases), and

(h) any security measures taken in respect of the data in that country or territory.

14   The eighth principle does not apply to a transfer falling within any paragraph of Schedule 4, except in such circumstances and to such extent as the [Secretary of State] may by order provide.

15—(1)   Where–

(a) in any proceedings under this Act any question arises as to whether the requirement of the eighth principle as to an adequate level of protection is met in relation to the transfer of any personal data to a country or territory outside the European Economic Area, and

(b) a Community finding has been made in relation to transfers of the kind in question,

that question is to be determined in accordance with that finding.

(2) In sub-paragraph (1) 'Community finding' means a finding of the European Commission, under the procedure provided for in Article 31(2) of the Data Protection Directive, that a country or territory outside the European Economic Area does, or does not, ensure an adequate level of protection within the meaning of Article 25(2) of the Directive.

SCHEDULE 2
Conditions Relevant for Purposes of the First Principle: Processing of any Personal Data

Section 4(3)

1   The data subject has given his consent to the processing.

2   The processing is necessary–

(a) for the performance of a contract to which the data subject is a party, or

(b) for the taking of steps at the request of the data subject with a view to entering into a contract.

3   The processing is necessary for compliance with any legal obligation to which the data controller is subject, other than an obligation imposed by contract.

4   The processing is necessary in order to protect the vital interests of the data subject.

5   The processing is necessary–

(a) for the administration of justice,

[(aa) for the exercise of any functions of either House of Parliament,]

(b) for the exercise of any functions conferred on any person by or under any enactment,

(c) for the exercise of any functions of the Crown, a Minister of the Crown or a government department, or

(d) for the exercise of any other functions of a public nature exercised in the public interest by any person.

6—(1)   The processing is necessary for the purposes of legitimate interests pursued by the data controller or by the third party or parties to whom the data are disclosed, except where the processing is unwarranted in any particular case by reason of prejudice to the rights and freedoms or legitimate interests of the data subject.

(2) The [Secretary of State] may by order specify particular circumstances in which this condition is, or is not, to be taken to be satisfied.

SCHEDULE 4
Cases where the Eighth Principle does not Apply

Section 4(3)

1   The data subject has given his consent to the transfer.

2   The transfer is necessary–

(a) for the performance of a contract between the data subject and the data controller, or

(b)   for the taking of steps at the request of the data subject with a view to his entering into a contract with the data controller.

3   The transfer is necessary–

(a)   for the conclusion of a contract between the data controller and a person other than the data subject which–

(i)   is entered into at the request of the data subject, or

(ii)   is in the interests of the data subject, or

(b)   for the performance of such a contract.

4—(1)   The transfer is necessary for reasons of substantial public interest.

(2)   The [Secretary of State] may by order specify–

(a)   circumstances in which a transfer is to be taken for the purposes of subparagraph (1) to be necessary for reasons of substantial public interest, and

(b)   circumstances in which a transfer which is not required by or under an enactment is not to be taken for the purpose of sub-paragraph (1) to be necessary for reasons of substantial public interest.

5   The transfer–

(a)   is necessary for the purpose of, or in connection with, any legal proceedings (including prospective legal proceedings),

(b)   is necessary for the purpose of obtaining legal advice, or

(c)   is otherwise necessary for the purposes of establishing, exercising or defending legal rights.

6   The transfer is necessary in order to protect the vital interests of the data subject.

7   The transfer is of part of the personal data on a public register and any conditions subject to which the register is open to inspection are complied with by any person to whom the data are or may be disclosed after the transfer.

8   The transfer is made on terms which are of a kind approved by the Commissioner as ensuring adequate safeguards for the rights and freedoms of data subjects.

9   The transfer has been authorised by the Commissioner as being made in such a manner as to ensure adequate safeguards for the rights and freedoms of data subjects.

Glossary

Applications Service Provider (ASP)

Applications Service Providers are suppliers which instead of licensing software in the traditional way (eg by issuing software on a CD and charging a licence fee), 'rent' software titles which are downloaded from the Internet as and when needed. Users commonly pay fees based on usage, which can be more economical than paying one off or annual licence fees. This type of software delivery is expected to be the next big thing, but may not take off in the UK until the bandwidth of equipment currently connecting many potential users to the Internet is much greater. (ASP also refers to Active Server Page which is a web page containing small programmes.)

Bandwidth

Measure of the amount of data/traffic transferred via a given communications circuit per second. Also often used as a measure of the maximum capacity of a circuit.

Bespoke Software

This is software specifically designed for a company or business. Websites often come under this category – especially as many businesses want one that differentiates them from the competition.

When someone is designing software for a business, a software development agreement should be entered into between the business and the software designer to set out the parties' rights and obligations.

Bluetooth

A microchip with built in radio transceiver which connects computers, mobile phones, mobile computers and other handheld devices within a ten to 100 metre range. Bluetooth technology is the result of collaboration between companies such as Ericsson, Intel, IBM and Microsoft and is expected to be built into hundreds of millions of electronic devices, doing away with the need for connecting cables.

Bookmark (or favourite)

Most browsers have the option of adding a URL to a favourites list or marking it with a 'Bookmark'. By doing this, you can store the linking information to any websites you plan to revisit.

Browser

A program that allows access to the World Wide Web. The most well known are Microsoft's Internet Explorer and Netscape's Navigator.

Business to Business, Business to Consumer (B2B, B2C)

The high growth in the levels of B2B commerce on the Internet has surprised many people who expected the greatest area of growth to be in B2C commerce.

Cache

Temporary storage area for data (whether in memory or on disk) used to speed up access and/or response times. On a personal computer a cache may be used to improve access times to data stored on disk, and when accessing the Internet a cache is often used to improve access times to website pages.

Chat Room

Area of a website which allows users to send and receive messages to each other in real time.

Connectivity Ratio

This is the ratio of modems (the piece of hardware needed to connect people to the server a website is stored on) to the number of people trying to connect to the server.

A low connectivity ratio may mean access to a website is denied because all the modems are being used. It is vital, therefore, that the connectivity ratios of companies offering to host a website are compared. Having an all-singing, all-dancing Internet service is not much good if people can't buy a ticket for the show.

Cookies

Cookies are small pieces of information that are placed on a user's computer by a website which identify and provide other information to that website when it is revisited. For example, a website may require user identification. To save the user having to enter this information manually every time the website is revisited, the information is automatically extracted from a cookie. However, cookies can also provide other information, such as which other websites the user has visited and how long was spent at them. In effect, the user could unwittingly be providing free market research.

Cyberlaw

These are the laws regulating the Internet. If you read scare stories in the tabloids you might think that the Internet does not actually have any laws. This is a common misconception. In reality, the Internet is over regulated.

Every country has its own laws for the Internet and the real problem is to say which apply. For example, a website in the UK may be accessible from the US but the information may pass through Japan – whose laws apply?

Cybersquatting

The name given to the practice of registering a domain name with a view to someone with an interest in the name paying for its transfer.

Data Protection

The *Data Protection Act 1998* sets down rules on how data which can identify living individuals (personal data) must be handled. This includes security, fair use, the data subject's rights of access and transfer to countries outside the European Economic Area. Failure to comply can lead to heavy fines and can be a criminal offence. If a company's website asks for customer information then it must ensure that it conforms with the Act.

Further information can be obtained from the website at www.dataprotection. gov.uk.

Domain Name

This is the electronic 'address' of the computer where information is stored. Using the structure (company name).com it allows people to understand an address better than if we used the numeric computer code that computers understand (called the 'IP Address').

All countries use a final two letter code to denote the country, eg 'uk' for the United Kingdom, 'ca' for Canada and so on. These are known as 'country-code Top Level Domains' (ccTLDs). There are also 'generic Top Level Domains' (gTLD), such as .com and .org. US companies generally use a gTLD instead of .us.

The registration of such names is operated on a first come first served basis, which is why most of the gTLD addresses registered are owned by US-based companies and individuals. Therefore, even if you do not plan to have a website immediately, the domain name that you would use should be registered as soon as possible to protect it from being used by anyone else.

Dongle

A device to ensure that a program being used is an original and not an unauthorised copy. It is usually small and attaches to a spare socket on a computer. When a program is running it will continuously check for the presence of the dongle. If it is not there, the program will cease to operate. As only one dongle is provided per licence, it can be an effective way to stop the illegal copying of a program.

Downtime

The time when a computer or server is 'down', meaning that is inaccessible. Companies should try and plan downtime so that computers are upgraded and maintenance carried out when demand for the service is low, such as overnight or at the weekend.

Dot Com

'.com' is a suffix used in a URL to refer to a commercial activities domain name. The term is also used to refer to Internet companies and start-ups.

E-cash (electronic cash)

Data representing money, which data can be transferred by means of a computer network and can be traded as a token exchangeable for real money.

E-commerce

Sale and supply of goods and services by electronic means over the Internet.

Economic and Monetary Union (EMU)

If you intend to sell goods and services on the Internet, EMU will have a great impact on the way you do business. Is the website capable of taking orders in euros? At a simple level, many computer keyboards do not even have a euro symbol key.

Electronic Data Interchange (EDI)

The transfer of business data between one company and another. Previously this was done through secure dedicated computer networks. These were expensive. Much more data is being transferred across the Internet, though this can be less secure.

Electronic Signature

Also known as a digital signature. In legal terms, this is not simply a scanned signature which is attached to a data file, but instead is electronic data which is incorporated into an electronic communication or other data which can be used to establish the authenticity of the communication or data, or the integrity of the communication or data or both.

Encryption

The translation of data into a form meaningless to an unauthorised user who does not have the necessary decoding hardware and software. The technology exists for virtually uncrackable encryption. Governments in particular are keen to make sure such technology is not used by criminals to avoid observation by the security services.

Escrow

This is where the source code to a program is kept by a third party independent of the supplier of the program and the licensee. On the occurrence of certain events, such as the liquidation of the supplier, the third party may release the source code to the licensee. It is a safety mechanism which seeks to enable the licensee to support the program in the future, notwithstanding any problems with the supplier. The main third party in the UK to provide such a service is The NCC Group (www.nccglobal.com) which also provides a number of standard form documents to govern the escrow procedure.

Extranet

This is an intranet (see Intranet) which also allows limited access by third parties external to the company running the intranet. Usually, Extranets are limited to carefully selected suppliers and customers which have adequate security systems in place and a close working relationship with the company running the intranet.

Firewall

This is either dedicated equipment (hardware firewall) or software (software firewall) which protects a company's internal network from being accessed through the Internet by unauthorised people. If any request for information arrives externally to an internal network, the firewall will validate the request and, if appropriate, pass it on. It avoids any direct connection to the outside world.

A firewall must be installed properly and monitored otherwise it may be worse than useless. You should always work on the principle that if there is a gap then a hacker will find it.

Flaming

Verbal dressing down often used in academic discussions on the Internet.

Framing

The practice of putting a border around a website that remains even after the user has moved to another website so that the new website is displayed, albeit in a reduced version within it. This means that the initial website's advertising remains on screen for a longer period.

There is a debate as to whether framing is legal. It is argued that frames can cause confusion in that it can become difficult to distinguish between the company in the frame and the company outside it. Legally, it is wiser to give the user the option of removing the frame as well as specifically stating that the information within the frame is not necessarily connected to the company outside it. In any event, frames can be a double-edged sword – would you want your company to frame a pornographic or defamatory website?

Freeware

Software which is distributed free of charge or for a nominal charge.

Gateway

Hardware or software that bridges the gap between two otherwise incompatible networks or applications so that data can be transferred among different computers.

Hacker

A person who, without authorisation, accesses a computer for either malicious fun, fraud or industrial espionage. Certain types of hacking can be liable to criminal prosecution under the *Computer Misuse Act 1990*.

Hardware

The physical components of a computer system, such as the screen, hard disk drive and keyboard. These are independent of the programmes. It is important to ensure, when acquiring a program, that the hardware has sufficient capability in order for it to run – and ideally the supplier of a program should state in contractual documentation that the program will be able to run on the hardware available. It is no good having a software supplier provide you with a fantastic piece of business software if it will not run on the new machine that has just been bought.

Home Page

Usually the first page of information accessed on a website containing details of and links to other pages of information on the website.

Hosting Agreement

An agreement whereby an ISP provides hardware and connectivity to the World Wide Web and sometimes software for a website to be run and accessed.

Hyper Text Mark-up Language (HTML)

A computer language used in website design. It allows the integration of text and graphics and the ability to link with other websites and pages.

Integrated Services Digital Network (ISDN)

A digital (as opposed to analogue) telecommunications system that is much faster than traditional telephone lines as there is no need for it to convert information into a form that can be transmitted and reconverted at the end of the line (see Modem). 'Home Highway' from BT uses ISDN technology. ISDN can be compared with ADSL (Asymetic Digital Subscribers Line) which provides high speed data communications over existing standard telephone lines.

Intellectual Property Rights

The name given to a group of legal rights including patent, copyright, database rights, trademark and design rights.

Internet

The global computer network connection of governments, businesses, universities and other users.

Internet Corporation for Assigned Names and Numbers (ICANN)

ICANN is the non-profit corporation that was formed to assume responsibility for the allocation of IP addresses, domain name system management and other related functions, which were previously performed under US government contract by IANA and other entities.

Internet Protocol (IP) Address

A universally recognised address made up of numbers and dots which identifies each sender and recipient of information passing over the Internet. Every computer connected to the Internet either has its own ('static') address or is assigned one automatically when it visits a website through an ISP.

Internet Service Provider (ISP)

A business that provides connection to the Internet and sometimes additional services to its subscribers. Well known examples include BT Internet, America Online (AOL) and Freeserve (now known as Wanadoo).

Intranet

Not a misspelling of Internet but an internal computer network. It allows staff to access information that an organisation may not wish an external audience to see. Businesses should ensure that when setting up an intranet it is secure and that if access is possible via the Internet then it is restricted (see Firewall).

Liquidated Damages

If a party to a contract has failed to fulfil its obligations under the contract, the other party may be able to claim damages. Broadly speaking, the damages awarded would be those necessary to put the claiming party in the position it would have been in if the other party had performed its contractual obligations correctly. Although damages are available under the general law, going to court can be expensive and time consuming. There are complex rules as to what can be claimed. Therefore, to avoid dispute, a Liquidated Damages clause is often inserted into contracts. This clause will set out the exact circumstances in which damage may be claimed and also sets out the amount of such damages, being calculated by the parties as a genuine pre-estimate of the loss.

For example, if a customer requires a computer system which controls its manufacturing process by a certain date, it knows that if it is not installed by that date it will suffer losses relating to lost production time, management time and so on. The amount of such loss is calculable at a daily rate and, therefore, rather than relying on a court to decide issues it is inserted into the contract.

If the supplier does not meet the deadline it knows it must pay the sums specified. Specialist advice should be obtained before such a clause is inserted. One danger is that the liquidated damages must not be a penalty for non-performance. If it is not a genuine pre-estimate of the loss, a court may find the clause unenforceable.

Local Area Network (LAN)

A group of computers located in a relatively limited area (like an office building) and connected by a communications link that allows them to interact with each other. Many LANs are connected to the Internet.

M-commerce

Mobile commerce is carried out on wireless devices such as WAP enabled mobile phones and PDAs.

Metatag

An invisible description buried in a website that states what the website is about. This allows the automated database search engines to place the website into the correct category in its database so that it can match websites to a user's query.

MicroPayments

Low value payments (typically a few pence or cents). Low value payments such as these are rare in the 'old' economy (unless cash is being used) due to the fact that the cost of collecting the payment is equal to or greater than the payment itself.

Modem (Modulator – demodulator)

Computer data cannot normally be sent directly down telephone lines. If a computer wants to send information to another computer the modem translates information from a digital form into noise which can be transmitted down a telephone line. Once it has travelled down the line, another modem at the other end retranslates the signal into a digital form that the receiving computer can use. Modems can be internal to a computer or external. The speed which a modem can translate and send information is usually expressed as 'bps', which stands for bits per second. A bit is the smallest unit of digital information. The higher the bps, the faster the modem.

MP3 (MPEG-1 Layer 3)

This is a standard for music file compression which reduces the size of files by discarding signals inaudible to the human ear.

Network Solutions Inc (NSI)

A register of.com domain names.

Object Code

An executable version of software created by compiling source code. A compiler converts source code which is not executable (ie cannot be run in that form on a computer) into object code which is executable (ie can be run in that form on a computer).

OFT

Office of Fair Trading. A UK government body that works to protect consumers.

Outsourcing

This is the contracting out of defined activities, such as the provision of IT services. This may involve the transfer of assets, staff and premises to the third party. The third party agrees to provide the services to agreed standards for an agreed period of time. The usual reason for outsourcing is to achieve cost reductions. Outsourcing deals tend to be complex and at a minimum should:

- entail thorough due diligence on the prospective supplier, including site visits;

- clearly set out the services required at the outset;

- appoint a project manager and have board support; and

- examine the worst case scenario of what happens if the third party does not perform to expectations.

Passing off

The legal term for the situation where one company pretends that its goods and services are that of another (see Framing).

Peer to Peer (P2P)

P2P technologies allow two computers connected to the Internet to communicate with each other directly (rather than both having to connect to a server). Examples of this technology include instant messaging and the more infamous file swapping systems, such as the first incarnation of Napster.

Personal Digital Assistants (PDA)

Small computing devices (including handheld PCs) which can be used on the move for running applications, such as calendars, address books and personal organisers. Some PDAs can connect to a modem, mobile phone or wireless LAN allowing them to be used for sending email and accessing the Internet.

Phising

'Phishing' is a general term for criminals' creation and use of emails and websites – designed to look like emails and websites of well known legitimate businesses, financial institutions and government agencies – in order to deceive Internet users into disclosing their bank and financial account information or other personal data, such as usernames and passwords. The 'phishers' then take that information and use it for criminal purposes, such as identity theft and fraud.

Public Key Infrastructure (PKI)

This enables users of a public network, such as the Internet, to exchange data and money securely through the use of keys. These are used to code or encrypt information, for example the contents of a document, using special software which scrambles the contents. The sender sends a message using the recipient's public key. Only the recipient can make sense of the message using their private key, which decrypts or unscrambles the message. This technology is also used to aid the production of electronic signatures.

Portal

A page on the Internet that people use to search the World Wide Web and often providing access to useful information, such as news, weather and travel (for example MSN). Also a company that provides these pages.

Programmes

These are instructions that tell a computer how it is to operate. Programmes can be divided into two main categories: applications software and system software.

Applications are the programmes that most people use, such as word processors, spread sheets and databases. System software, in contrast, is a more basic program which a user rarely sees. This allows the applications software to run on the hardware and translates the functions of the applications software into a form that the computer can understand.

Protocol

A standard or set of rules that two computers use to communicate with each other. Any product that uses a particular protocol should be able to communicate with any other product using the same protocol.

Search Engines

These are programmes accessible via the Internet which help users find information. Essentially, they are large directories which index information on the Internet which can be searched by typing in a key word or phrase relating to the topic you are searching for. Some of the most popular search engines are Yahoo, Google and Lycos.

If you have a website it is important that it is registered with such search engines otherwise people may have difficulty finding it if they do not know the exact address.

Secure Sockets Layer (SSL)

An industry standard protocol allowing secure transmission of data over the Internet. It is generally accepted as being a safe way of sending sensitive information, such as credit card details. SSL is built into browsers such as Microsoft's Internet Explorer and Netscape's Navigator.

Server

A computer that is used to store websites, data and software and which can be used and accessed by other computers.

SMS

Short Message Service or 'Text Messaging'. This is the system whereby messages are sent and received between mobile phones.

Software

The generic name of the instructions given to a computer telling it how it should operate (see Programmes).

Source Code

This is the expression of programmes in a written form that a human can understand. Access to the source code is important if a program is to be updated or amended. Without it, a program is virtually impossible to decipher, being merely a collection of numbers (see Escrow).

Spamming

The Internet version of junk mail. Usually used to advertise something, spamming is sending the same message to a large number of users who generally have not invited the mailshot.

Trusted Third Parties (TTPs)

Also called 'Certification Authorities'. They are being established on a self regulating basis although powers exist to regulate that they are government approved providers of information services. These include the holding of public keys for verification purposes and the issuing of digital certificates.

Uptime

Time when a website is available for end users to access.

Universal Resource Locator (URL)

This is an Internet address of a website, file storage site or Internet news site or any page which may be accessed using a browser or other software (see Domain Name).

Virtual Private Network (VPN)

A less expensive alternative to a private network running on private telecommunications lines. VPNs use the public telecommunications system and utilise encryption and decryption to keep information secure.

Virus

Software which is usually harmful (ie causes damage to data) and which replicates and distributes itself via floppy disks, over the Internet or through the word processor files which utilise macros.

Vortal

A portal for vertical B2B (see B2B) markets in industries, such as electronics, aviation or pharmaceuticals.

Web Hosting

Commercial storage and operation of websites on computer equipment (usually situated at purpose built data centres) by third party service providers. ISPs often provide web hosting services and usually have computer equipment which offers high speed links to the Internet and increased bandwidth.

Website

Collection of information (which can include text, graphics, sound, music and other materials) accessible via the Internet. Each website can be identified by and located using its domain name/URL.

Website Development Agreement

A contract between a business and a website developer regulating the creation of a website.

At minimum it should include:

- a specification;
- a method of testing and acceptance;
- website maintenance provisions;
- intellectual property rights ownership provisions; and
- price and payment details.

Wide Area Network (WAN)

A network that connects computers over long distances via telephone cables or satellite links.

Wireless Application Protocol (WAP)

WAP allows Internet information services to be accessed by mobile phones. Despite limitations imposed by screen size, businesses should ensure that the terms and conditions on which they are prepared to supply goods and services are properly brought to the attention of the WAP user.

Without Prejudice

Where negotiations or letters written during negotiations are stated to be 'without prejudice', then any proposals made and not accepted will not later be admissible in evidence at the request of the other party. But if they are accepted a complete contract is established.

World Wide Web (www)

A part of the Internet where information is accessible in a graphical form through a browser.

Further Reading

Aitken, S, *ICT Banana Skins, Real Time Club*, 2004

British Standards Institution, ISO 17799 (BS 7799) Part 1:2000 Information security management: Code of practice for information security management

British Standards Institution, BS 7799 Part 2:2002 Information security management: Specification with guidance for use

British Standards Institution, BS 15000 IT service management

Bundesamt für Sicherheit in der Informationstechnik, *IT Baseline Protection Manual*, 2001

Carr, Marvin J; Konda, Suresh L; Monarch, Ira; Ulrich, Carol F; Walker, Clay F, *Taxonomy-Based Risk Identification* CMU/SEI-93-TR-6, Software Engineering Institute, Carnegie Mellon University, 1993

CASU Risk Register Working Group, *Building and Populating the Risk Register*, UK Department of Health's Controls Assurance Unit, 2003

Couprie, Dale et al, *Soft Systems Methodology*, University of Calgary, Department of Computer Science, 1997

The *Data Protection Act 1998*, Stationery Office Limited ISBN 0 10 542998 8, http://www.hmso.gov.uk/acts/acts1998/19980029.htm

Dresner, D, *Desert Island Standards*, National Computing Centre Guideline 275, 2003

Dresner, D, *Managing Risk and Your Business*, IT adviser, 30 March/April National Computing Centre, 2004

European Committee for Standardization, CWA 13620, ESCROWGUIDE – Source Code Escrow – Guidelines for Acquirers, Developers, Escrow Agents and Quality Assessors, 1999

Federal Reserve Bank of San Francisco, *Economic Letter Number 2002–02*, 2002

Financial Services Authority, *The firm risk assessment framework*, 2003

Greer, D and Bustard D W, *SERUM – Software Engineering Risk: Understanding and Management*, The International Journal of Project and Risk Management, 1997

Harris, R, *Emerging Practices in Operational Risk Management*, Federal Reserve Bank of Chicago, 2002

Humphreys, Ted; De Soete, Dr Marijke; Mitchell, Prof Chris, *Securing e-business*, ISO Focus, January 2004

ISO 9001:2000 Quality management systems – Requirements, International Standards Organisation

ISO/IEC 12207:1995, Standard for Information Technology – Software Life Cycle Processes, International Standards Organisation

ISO/IEC 15288: Information Technology – Life Cycle Management – System Life Cycle Processes, International Standards Organisation

ISO/IEC 16085 Standard for Software Life Cycle Processes – Risk Management (was IEEE standard 1540), International Standards Organisation

ISO/IEC 18019 Guidelines for the design and preparation of user documentation for application software, 2004, International Standards Organisation

ISO/IEC 9126 Software engineering– Product quality, International Standards Organisation

ISO/IEC TR 15504 Information technology – Software process assessment, International Standards Organisation

Kontio, Jyrki, *The Riskit Method for Software Risk Management, version 1.00*, Institute for Advanced Computer Studies, Department of Computer Science, University of Maryland, 1998

Lopez, Jose A, *Overview of the Basel Committee's Second Working Paper on Securitization*, Economic Research Department, Federal Reserve Bank of San Francisco, 2003

Morton, W, *Managing Risk: A Practical Guide*, National Computing Centre Guideline 265, 2002

The National Computing Centre, *STARTS Purchasers Handbook*, 1989

The National Computing Centre, *Intellectual Property Rights – Protecting Your Key Assets*, 2002

Nicholls, Shelton, *Techniques for risk analysis*, Central Bank of Trinidad and Tobago, 2003

Office of Government Commerce (OGC), *Successful Delivery Toolkit*, Version 4.02 October 2003

Office of the e-Envoy e-GIF (the e-Government Interoperability Framework), version 6.0, 2004

Power, M, *The Invention of Operational Risk*, ESRC Centre for Analysis of Risk and Regulation, London School of Economics and Political Science, 2003

The Standish Group, *CHAOS: A recipe for success*, 1999

Vidgen, R; Wood-Harper, T; Wood, R (JRG), *A Soft Systems Approach to Information Systems Quality*, Scandinavian Journal of Information Systems, vol 5 (1993)

Index

Index